STUNG

The Incredible Obsession of Brian Molony

GARY STEPHEN ROSS

M&S

For P.J.

First published by Stoddart 1987
Mass market edition published by General 1988
McClelland & Stewart trade paperback edition published 2002

National Library of Canada Cataloguing in Publication Data

Ross, Gary, 1948-
Stung : the incredible obsession of Brian Molony / Gary Ross.

ISBN 0-7737-2118-5

1. Molony, Brian. 2. Embezzlement – Ontario – Toronto.
3. Compulsive gamblers – Ontario – Toronto – Biography.
I. Title.

HV6685.C32T67 2002 364.16'2 C2002-902210-X

We acknowledge the financial support of the Government of Canada through the Book Publishing Industry Development Program for our publishing activities. We further acknowledge the support of the Canada Council for the Arts and the Ontario Arts Council for our publishing program.

Typeset in Minion by M&S, Toronto
Printed and bound in Canada

This book is printed on acid-free paper that is
100% ancient forest friendly (100% post-consumer recycled).

McClelland & Stewart Ltd.
The Canadian Publishers
481 University Avenue
Toronto, Ontario
M5G 2E9
www.mcclelland.com

1 2 3 4 5 06 05 04 03 02

Contents

Acknowledgements

I'm indebted to the many people who shared their knowledge and their opinions of banking, and of the Bay and Richmond, Toronto, branch of the Canadian Imperial Bank of Commerce in particular; casinos, and Caesars in Atlantic City in particular; gambling, and Brian Molony's compulsive gambling in particular. Some contributions were invaluable, and I thank those who made them: in Toronto, Sherry Brydson, Barb Elson, Mark Osborne, Eddie Greenspan, Jeremy Brown, Craig Law, Ron Andrews, Bob Greig, and Bob Barbour; in Milton, Ontario, Sheila and Sieg Stadler; in Kingston, Ontario, Brian Wallace and Kathleen Lippins; in London, Ontario, Trish Hilton, Barney Rooney, Father John Harper, and Father Joseph Moss; in Buffalo, New York, Maud McCabe; in Baltimore, Maryland, Joanna Franklin and Vic Lehmkuhl; in Wilmington, Delaware, Gerry Fulcher; in Washington, D.C., Robert Custer; in Trenton, New Jersey, John Sheehy, Richard Handzo, and Tony Parillo; in Roseland, New Jersey, Thomas O'Brien; in Haddonfield, New Jersey, Steve Schrier; in Atlantic City, New Jersey, Walt Devlin, Don Russell, Roger Gros, and Dan Heneghan.

For help that ranged from the practical to the inspirational, I'm grateful to Sheilagh McEvenue, Wanda Wilkinson, Bruce Ramsay, Lucinda Vardey, Michael Levine, Peter Foster, and Sheila Willson. I thank Bill Hanna at Stoddart Publishing for his faith in this project, and Glen Ellis, my editor, for his careful attention to the manuscript.

This book is a work of non-fiction, accurate in its factual detail. Because several people asked that their anonymity be preserved, however, I have in some instances used pseudonyms.

"Tomorrow, tomorrow, it will all be over!"

– Dostoevsky

I

THE FIRST TIME

"Reckless with misery, I made a plunge."

– Stephen Leacock

Molony worked late at Bay and Richmond, locked the doors, and drove to the racetrack. He found Colizzi by the concession stand. Molony had a burger and a Coke while Colizzi told him about some crocodile boots he'd had made. "Nice crocodile has to die so you can have new cowboy boots," said Molony, looking up over his glasses. He finished dinner, wiped his bushy moustache, and borrowed Colizzi's program.

"Baby crocodiles," said Colizzi. "Nice and soft. Who you like in the first? Want to bet the double?"

Molony bet at the fifty-dollar window and laid three hundred more with Colizzi. His pick, a 6–1 shot, was four lengths in front when it broke stride. Ten races, one winner: he ended the night without enough money for gas. Colizzi loaned him a hundred.

Next morning Molony drove to Yorkdale Shopping Centre. Yorkdale was one of the few branches of the Canadian Imperial Bank of Commerce open Saturdays, and it was on the way to Woodbine. He wanted to cash a $400 cheque. When the teller asked for identification, he showed his Visa card. The number signified that he was a bank employee. "Oh, staff card," she said. Molony told her he was an assistant manager at Bay and Richmond and showed his business card. He filled in a countercheque rather than an encoded personal cheque, which gave him until Tuesday to cover it. Not kiting, really, just utilizing his skills at cash management.

Woodbine was no better than Mohawk had been. He didn't cash a ticket until the eighth, then won two in a row. His reserves were low and he bet less than he should have. After the last race he was down $3,000 to Colizzi. At least he had $2,500 in his pocket for the harness races. He called Brenda to say he wouldn't be able to see her after all, maybe tomorrow afternoon? She reminded him she was going bowling with her parents. Would he like to come with them? Molony said he'd think about it – could he let her know in the morning? In the car between tracks he fiddled the radio until he found the baseball scores. Up $1,000 on the afternoon games: he was only down $2,000 to Colizzi. Maybe the night games would bail him out.

Colizzi had left after the sixth race to pick up his son. Molony had booked three races with him on the evening card, and he bet them again that night at the windows. One decent win and he'd be back on his feet. But he had another bad night at Mohawk, and when he caught the late scores on the car radio, heading home at midnight, he wanted to scream. He'd lost every game but one. He had $120 and owed Colizzi and Beck almost $14,000.

He stopped at the cash machine, timing it perfectly. He got his limit before midnight; when the date ticked over – new week – he punched in his numbers again and got another $300. Sunday was usually his day. A week earlier he'd aced the NFL games, winning eleven of thirteen. Another big day would make up for the baseball. Things were tight, but they'd been tight before. Couple of weeks earlier he'd gone to Atlantic City owing Beck and Colizzi almost $6,000. He could scrape up only $3,000 cash. So he took the day trip to the new casino, Caesars, with a couple of card-game pals and tried his luck at craps. He didn't know how to play, but he was a quick study. For an hour he practically told the dice what to do. The dealers paid everybody and the table turned into a party. The others on the junket wore Velcro dice on their lapels. Molony, entranced, looked up to find a dozen guys from Toronto cheering him on. They told him he had to quit or miss the plane. On a $2,000 buy-in he cashed out $13,000. They'd been holding the bus for him. When he climbed aboard he got a round of applause. He was not only back on his feet, he'd found his lucky casino.

In Toronto, his streak had continued at the races. The bookies didn't like raising his limit when he was losing but were happy to bump it when they owed him. In his second good week he called Colizzi to say he wanted to double up. Colizzi said no problem, long as we settle every Monday. Molony went up to the dining-room before the first race and found Beck there, too, nervously chewing his program, spitting out little wads. Some nights he ate the whole thing.

"Here comes The Banker on the outside," said Beck, in the dramatic tones of an announcer. Molony had once bet a horse called Banker Fretz, and the announcer called the horse two or three times. Beck loved it.

"Sure you want to go double?" said Colizzi.

"Starting tonight," said Molony.

"Here comes The Banker, moving up between horses."

Colizzi made a pistol of thumb and forefinger and pretended to shoot Beck in the head.

That was the night Molony had started losing the photo finishes, betting the place horse to win, boxing the exactors and watching fifty tickets turn into confetti. Things kept sliding downhill. He lost all week, lost at both tracks on Saturday, hit rock bottom Sunday. He lost ten of thirteen NFL games, took a beating on baseball, and didn't cash a ticket at Woodbine. Should have gone bowling with Brenda and her parents after all – he would have lost to them, too, but at least it wouldn't have cost anything.

When he got home at two o'clock Monday morning and crossed his name off the list in the hall – in a family of nine children it was the only way to keep track – he owed $22,300. The house was silent. Everyone was sleeping. Twenty-two three. Not a number he dared think about. He'd get back on his feet during the week. He wasn't tired, but there was nothing else to do. He turned off the outside light, looked in the fridge, then went upstairs and climbed into bed with a pen and the early edition of Monday's paper.

Funny, actually, to think of himself as The Banker. If you'd suggested such a thing in his boarding-school days, he'd have been as surprised as boyhood friends were, a few years later, when they heard he was with the CIBC. One day Molony bumped into an old schoolmate who told him he was a fool. "Guy with your smarts? I can't believe you'd get into the banking system. It takes so long to get anywhere. It's so boring."

Molony's idea had been to try it for a short time after university. He had really wanted to be a financial writer. At the University of Western Ontario in London he took honours journalism. He paid as much attention to the trotters at Western Raceway as to his studies, but did well. He wrote a piece on the provincial health insurance plan and sold it to the local radio station. Having worked on his father's dairy farm in Milton, he knew cattle and sold a piece about an evolving breed to *The London Free Press*. In history class he did a particularly good paper on the American Revolution. One of the causes of the revolution, so the books said, was the onerous stamp tax imposed by the British. Molony decided to look at the economic argument, calculate the dollar relationship between colony and mother country. It turned out, in his analysis, that the British were heavily subsidizing the Americans. The taxes Britain was collecting were minor compared to what she was spending to support the colony. The stamp tax, though it may have had symbolic implications, was a mere pittance. Molony's prof told him it was a fine paper, excellently argued, a fresh way of looking at history.

The business press was in its infancy, and Molony saw a future for a good financial writer. When a notice went up one day at the placement centre that the CIBC was conducting interviews, he dropped around. He hitchhiked to Toronto for the aptitude test. The bank intended to place him in the officer-in-training program, but he scored so well he was moved up to the management-training program. At the end of the school year he had planned to sell teaching aids in Nova Scotia, as he'd done the previous summer, before joining the bank in the fall. But the bank wanted him to start in July. Why not? After slugging furniture and driving a truck part-time at the university, $10,000-plus seemed a decent salary, especially as he could live at home. Couple of years in the bank – direct experience – and he'd be better trained than most people writing about business. "I thank you," he replied in his letter of acceptance, "and look towards a rewarding career with the Canadian Imperial Bank of Commerce."

For the first six months he was posted to a small branch in west-end Toronto and given a general introduction to banking. He spent a few weeks as a teller before working in savings, current accounts, loan accounting, and foreign exchange. He then went on relief, floating among different branches, which gave him broad exposure and a chance to consolidate what he had learned.

He hadn't realized what a vast and formidable organization he had joined. The CIBC's 1,600 branches reached from Sooke, British Columbia, to Mount Pearl, Newfoundland, and could be found in virtually every city and town between. The Canadian Bank of Commerce was established in 1867, the year of Canada's Confederation, and acquired Gore Bank (1870), Bank of British Columbia (1901), Halifax Banking Company (1903), The Merchants Bank of PEI (1906), Western Bank of Canada (1909), The Eastern Townships Bank (1912), The Bank of Hamilton (1923), Sterling Bank of Canada (1924), and The Standard Bank of Canada (1928), before merging with Imperial Bank of Canada in 1961 to become the Canadian Imperial Bank of Commerce. Its 36,000 employees made it twenty times larger than the federal department of finance. With $34-billion in assets it was one of the country's mightiest corporations, four times the size of Bell Canada. It was the second biggest bank in Canada (behind the Royal), and bigger than all but four American banks (Citicorp, BankAmerica, Chase Manhattan, J. P. Morgan). Once you became part of it, you saw it was a world unto itself, governed by its own laws, defined by its own culture, sustained by its own myths.

Canada – a minor economic power – was home to internationally competitive banks because its banking system was more concentrated than those of other western countries. France had more than 50 banks, Switzerland more than 500, West Germany more than 5,000, the United States more than 15,000. Canada had only eleven chartered banks, and five of them controlled more than 90 per cent of the combined assets. These Big Five banks represented an extraordinary concentration of power. The CIBC's board of directors included some of Canada's corporate titans – Conrad Black, Jack Gallagher, George T. Richardson, Galen Weston, Douglas Bassett, Alf Powis – and its international lending gave it a presence from Argentina to Poland, Mexico to the Middle East, New York to Hong Kong.

The CIBC's historic and largely unchallenged role in Canadian economic affairs had important implications for the bureaucracy it engendered and the culture it evolved. Molony soon learned that you did things by the book. The Branch Management and Operations Manual, sixteen fat volumes, told you how to complete a money order and how to react to a bomb threat. The bank told you how to dress, how to behave, even how to sign your name – two initials plus surname. Until recently it had expected employees to ask permission to marry. If the regulations were tight and tedious, they were also comforting. Once familiar with BMO you could find the approved way of performing any duty.

Women in the bank were treated as a sub-species. They held the low-paying jobs; the higher you went the fewer women you encountered. It was 1975 before they were allowed to join the company pension plan. If a man and a woman were equally qualified, the job went to the man. The bank was also virulently anti-union, firing employees who got involved in an organizing drive and withholding scheduled wage increases at branches that became unionized. In one case, the Canadian Labour Relations Board found that the CIBC had interfered with its employees' right to organize and ordered the president to send a letter to all the branches, explaining that the CIBC had broken the law. If the bank tended to be steadfast, sexist, and conservative, the atmosphere was not discomfiting to someone from a large, strict, Irish-Catholic family.

The salaries, it turned out, weren't so hot compared to what other corporations paid, but there were company benefits. And a date's parents looked at you differently when they learned you were with the bank. You were established. You had prospects, and you would realize them in a prescribed manner. The country was divided up; your salary took into account the cost of living in your region. Each job was graded; each grade had a pay range. You climbed the corporate ladder from one grade to the next. If you were capable and hard-working, who knew how far you might go? The chairman and chief executive officer at the time, Russell Harrison, was an ultra-conservative fellow from smalltown Manitoba who had started as a teller in Winnipeg and three decades later reached the top rung. Like three other Big Five chairmen, he had never worked anywhere but at the bank he headed. The CIBC was an insular system that encouraged conformity, expected diligence, and rewarded loyalty. Molony felt quite at home.

The next stage of his training entailed a choice: head-office accounting or audit and inspection. He chose the latter and spent nine months working as an audit assistant in Toronto, Ottawa, Sault Ste. Marie, and Hamilton. He checked dormant accounts, counted Canada Savings Bonds, ensured that the standards of the bank were being upheld. This provided his first insight into how loans were rated, what made one authorized credit look solid and another shaky. It also gave him thorough familiarity with the bank's working systems.

A camaraderie developed among the people in audit and inspection, and over drinks the stories got tossed around. One fellow had been on the audit of a small branch out west when the accountant attracted the attention of the auditors. The accountant, in bank parlance, was an office manager who handled the non-credit aspects of branch operation – the updating of BMO regulation books, performance reviews of non-credit personnel, the balancing of the branch's books, safety deposit boxes, tellers' cash, and so forth. One of the audit officers noticed this accountant's habit, before opening the safe, of checking behind the wall calendar. The accountant had a poor memory and had written down the combination. The auditor had a field day with this breach of security, and the accountant's prospects were dimmed. When the branch was next audited, a year and a half later, the accountant, not surprisingly, was still there. The new audit team, having consulted notes from the previous audit, kept a close eye on him. Sure enough, before opening the safe, he checked behind the calendar. When the new auditor went and looked, he found, neatly lettered, "Not this year, you bastards!"

Someone told the story of an audit at another branch in western Canada. "The only security system was an alarm that rang in the hotel next door. Not exactly sophisticated, but maybe it was effective, right? We decided to test it, sounding the alarm and timing the interval until someone arrived. One of the hotel waiters showed up with a tray of draft beer."

Molony, by now, had collected a few stories of his own. At the Kensington Market branch in Toronto, the whole bank had a terrible reek. "I couldn't figure it out until somebody told me that the Portuguese kept their cash in freezers and refrigerators, with the fish and fowl, before depositing it." At another branch, where Molony was on relief as office manager, one of the tellers lost the Visa slips from the restaurant down the street. Normally, getting second copies was easy enough, but this restaurant was patronized by gays. "It took me a week to convince the owner I wasn't compiling a list for the RCMP."

Everyone laughed, filing away tales that would be embellished and recirculated. Quirky bankers would become eccentrics, characters would become legends. Establishing yourself in the CIBC meant more than learning the business. It meant absorbing the ethos, acquainting yourself with a huge cast of characters, acclimatizing to the culture. By the time Molony was appointed credit officer at Bay and Richmond, he had grown a moustache and put on twenty pounds. In bearing and appearance he was already a banker, more sombre and composed than some people twice his age. He'd forgotten all about business writing. In his early twenties, he looked forward to a long, secure, and comfortable career. One that left very little to chance.

One of Molony's daily responsibilities was to review overdrafts in the personal chequing accounts. On the Monday morning after his dismal weekend at the track, a girl from the PCA department dropped by his office with the printout – four pages of PCA overdrafts. She listed each, and Molony told her how to deal with it. Some bankers considered it a tedious task, but Molony thrived on decisions of any kind. Weigh the variables, choose a course of action, stick to it. He had the right mix of decisiveness and arrogance, and the persuasive skills to justify his decisions to others. Tellers sometimes came to him for direction on accounts that weren't even his responsibility.

"That's the third time in a month, send it back.

"Who is this person? Find out what he does for a living.

"Send this one back NSF, but first check and make sure he doesn't have term deposits with us. Excuse me a moment." His phone was ringing. "Molony here."

"It's after eleven. We're waiting."

"I have someone in the office right now. I'll look after it in a day or two."

"Wait a minute, Banker."

"I'm busy, speak to you later," said Molony, and hung up.

He finished the overdrafts, then met with a fellow seeking a business loan. Nine times out of ten Molony knew the moment a customer sat down whether he'd grant the loan. This fellow, a budding restaurateur who had never worked in a restaurant, was out of luck. Molony nodded politely for ten minutes before showing the man out. He was back at his desk when Beck and Colizzi sauntered in.

Colizzi, ill at ease, was wearing his crocodile boots. A pale blue V-neck sweater revealed the gold chain in the hair of his chest. Beck, a skinny man in running shoes, no socks, and worn jeans, had evidently just got out of bed. Molony was paralyzed with shock. This was not the racetrack, this was Bay Street.

"Good morning, Mr. Molony," said Beck, seating himself in one of the guest chairs. A high-strung fellow, he made an exaggerated show of ease. Colizzi took the other chair.

"What are you doing here?"

"Well, we were a little concerned when you didn't show up."

The door was open, you could see in. Molony thought of closing it, but that would draw attention: he never closed his door. The partitions didn't reach the ceiling, anyone could have been listening. He lowered his voice. "You can't be here," he said. "I told you, a day or two."

"I do apologize, Mr. Molony," said Beck. Talking the way he imagined people talked in banks, he sounded ludicrous. "My associate and I don't feel we can leave until we're in possession of the funds that are owing to us."

"Look, I'll . . . meet you."

"Half an hour?"

Molony nodded.

"With the money?"

"Get out of here," he said, and rose to see them out.

"With the money?"

"I said yes."

Molony walked them to the door. What would he say if anyone asked? Couple of bozos looking for a loan. I told them to try the branch across the street. But the noon rush had started – there were lineups for the tellers and foreign-exchange clerks – and no one seemed to have taken any notice.

What to do? If he didn't show up, they'd come back. If he showed up empty-handed his credibility would be shot and he'd never be able to collect from them – you didn't pay off, Banker, why should we pay when you win? Molony's mother loved dabbling in the stock market and did some trading through his "Brian Molony in Trust" account at Richardson Securities. With her blessing he had already borrowed as much as he could against her stocks. He could sell the stocks to raise the $22,300 and buy them back in a couple of weeks. Not enough time – it took five days to settle a brokerage account. Borrow from his parents? All he needed was a short-term loan, and it wasn't worth the grief of inventing an explanation. Besides, he had only half an hour before Beck and Colizzi would be back. Same problem with a personnel loan: not enough time. By calling up friends he might be able to piece the money together in a few hours. That, too, would mean stalling Beck and Colizzi. Maybe he should stall them, work out what the bank would call an extended payment plan. No, bad precedent. When he won they'd do the same thing, avoid paying off.

Molony took a call and, speaking on the phone, noticed a loan sheet on his desk. The answer was staring him in the face. He could set up a loan and hold the debit overnight. Except that he couldn't count on winning $22,300 in one night. He could make up a fictitious customer, give him a loan, turn the loan into a bank draft . . . No. How was he going to turn a bank draft payable to John Doe into $22,300 cash? Make the draft payable to Beck and Colizzi? Ask them to hold it for a couple of days, until he could raise the cash? At least that would be a way of buying time.

Or he could write them a loan, issue a draft, and repay the money when he won. If he did that – a purely hypothetical scenario – would he make the draft payable to Colizzi or Beck? Beck. More common name, and he wasn't certain how to spell Colizzi. If he did write them a loan and issue them a draft he would have kept his word – half an hour, with the money – without having set an unfortunate precedent. The loan would be small enough that all records would remain in the branch. When he repaid the money he could dig out the documentation and destroy it. Who'd be the wiser?

You, fool.

The bank had a name for it. Defalcation. Employee theft.

Would it be theft, really, if the money were promptly repaid, with interest? Or would it simply be the most convenient way of getting from one week to the next?

Defalcation.

Would it be theft if the money were used to exit one set of circumstances and enter another? Or would it be more of a loan, the sort of thing customers came to him for? He was a customer as well as an employee. In effect, he'd be giving himself a loan. A bridge loan.

He crossed to the foreign-exchange department, where bank drafts were prepared, and told the girl he needed a draft, payable to N. Beck, for $22,300. The girl asked how it would be paid for.

"A loan," said Molony. A bridge loan. Why was his back drenched with sweat?

He went to the discount department and told the girl they were putting through a loan for $22,300. She would open a loan account on the computer, assigning it a number. Molony scribbled the name and the sum on a piece of paper. "Here's the base information. I'll give you details later today."

Before long the girl from foreign exchange brought him the draft. He looked at his watch: his half hour was up. He tore off the branch copy of the draft – it would eventually go to the teller – and slipped the other copies into his pocket. He had solved a short-term problem. He had done something else, too, but before the thought could take shape he hurried out of the branch. The something else was intangible, like the state lines you crossed on the drive to Florida. A sign announced that you'd left Michigan and entered Ohio, but everything looked exactly the same – blue sky, tilled fields, blackbirds rising from a power line. Nothing had changed, except you were no longer in Michigan.

Molony hurried down to Temperance Street. The blue TransAm pulled up. Colizzi opened the door and broke his seat forward.

"Get in."

"Here comes The Banker on the outside," said Beck, revving the engine.

Molony climbed in back, trying not to think of the Louisville Slugger under the front seat, trying not to let the something else take shape. They drove in silence, fighting traffic, until Beck found a spot. He killed the engine and glanced at Molony in the mirror. He was sour and unshaven, with sleep in the corners of his eyes.

"OK, right," said Beck, in his nervous, hectoring voice, "somebody don't got, they don't got. That's all there is to it."

Beck and Colizzi both had criminal records; Colizzi's included convictions for drug possession, bookmaking, and assault. Evidently they had talked it over. Violence versus a repayment schedule. They'd decided on a repayment schedule. They had figured Molony wouldn't bring the money. Beck once owed another bookie and swore all his cash had gone up in a bank fire. The kind of thing a not-very-bright child would say. Molony had given his word and they'd assumed he'd go back on it. He was insulted.

"Maybe we can work something out," said Colizzi.

"Right," said Beck.

Fine. He would rip up the draft, destroy the documentation, pretend it never happened. At the track he'd bet with discipline, passing on the races he didn't like, betting the limit on horses he did. Maybe he could get his limit raised again. Now wasn't the time, he'd mention it at the track . . .

"What have you got in mind?"

"Like, something each week," said Beck.

Colizzi turned in his seat. "Course, you can't play till you're paid off."

As a boy, Molony had delivered papers, shovelled snow, and done babysitting to make money for the track, and when he ran through his own money he had stolen from his mother's purse. In the past few months he had not only liquidated his own stocks and borrowed against his mother's, he had exhausted his savings, cashed his retirement savings plan, and taken out a personal loan. Can't play till you're paid off? How would he be able to pay off if he didn't play? What was he supposed to do – go to the track and watch?

"I told you I'd have it." He handed over the negotiable copy of the draft, keeping the customer's copy. "Didn't I tell you? What are tonight's lines?"

"The hell is this?" said Colizzi.

"A bank draft. What are the lines?"

"Me see that," said Beck. "What's this supposed to be?"

"You said you wanted it today. We don't keep that kind of cash on hand. What are the lines?"

"I got to give this creep half."

"Cash it," said Molony. "Give him half."

Beck turned in his seat. He waited until Molony met his eye. "OK, Banker, I'll cash it. We'll go over to your branch right now and I'll cash it."

"I just told you, we don't keep that kind of cash on hand."

"Big branch like that?"

"Ever read the fine print? Banks keep as little on hand as possible. We need a day's notice."

"What do I do with this?"

"Deposit it in your own bank. Give him cash, write him a cheque, I don't care. Am I supposed to do your banking for you?"

"I don't like this," Colizzi said to Beck.

"You will when you cash it," said Molony. He settled back in his seat. "What are the lines?"

Beck glanced at Molony in the mirror. He glanced at Colizzi, who shrugged. He inspected the draft again, then tucked it in his pocket. "Too early for the lines," he said, and started the car.

One year at Christmas, on the way down to Florida, Molony and his brother almost had an accident. Michael was learning the standard gearshift – he stopped the Datsun by stalling it – and Brian did most of the driving. In Georgia they pulled off for food and gas. Re-entering the freeway, trying to shift gears, Michael lost control and veered toward the median. Traffic was heavy and fast-moving, and Brian had to lunge and grab the wheel. They joked, but then Brian began shuddering so violently they had to pull off the road.

Back at the bank, speaking on the phone, Molony couldn't hold the receiver still. He spread his fingers beneath his desk; they trembled as if he had palsy. He controlled both halves of the entry, debit and credit, but the tellers liked to have everything by three o'clock and when he turned over the debit-loan voucher and the branch copy of the draft he'd be fully committed. The loan would show up on the next day's printout. Once it appeared on the books it would need a writeup. What was he going to put on the loan sheet?

What if he'd been seen with Beck and Colizzi? What if someone asked, "Who were those characters in your office this morning?" What if Bay and Richmond were asked for confirmation when Beck tried to cash the draft? What if the audit were sprung unexpectedly in the next few days? What if Mr. Osborne questioned the loan?

That would have been most mortifying of all – thank heavens Osborne was on holiday. If there was one reason Molony had risen so quickly, it was Alex Osborne. That's how you got ahead in the bank, by attracting the attention of a superior; Osborne himself had been Des Hazelton's boy, climbing the ladder in Hazelton's footsteps. Molony considered himself fortunate to be working for Osborne.

When Molony got posted to Bay and Richmond, Roy Bridge had been manager – "Father Roy" they called him, nice enough fellow. Bridge was from the old school, the kind of manager who had no contact with junior staff, dealing only with his assistant managers. When Bridge was promoted, in early 1979, he showed Alex Osborne through the branch, introducing the staff. "This is Brian Molony," he told Osborne, "an excellent credit officer and one of our best workers." Molony couldn't believe his ears. Coming from a manager who had never said so much as "boo" to him, this was a ringing endorsement.

Alex Osborne was slightly portly, with a Chaplinesque moustache and a rigorous eye for detail. Because of his demanding standards and tough facade not everyone liked him, but he was responsible, decisive, and astute. His smarts were those of a man who had worked his way out of humble beginnings. The Osipovicz family had emigrated to Canada from the Ukraine after the war with nothing but the clothes on their backs, and Alexander had grown up intending to become a doctor. In high school, however, he got rheumatic fever and nearly died. Hospital bills used up the money for his medical education, and he had to go to work. He took a job as a teller and quickly proved himself a most capable banker.

Osborne had been promoted to Bay and Richmond from Credit Room, where he had been superintendent. In other words, he'd been in charge of authorizing loans that exceeded the discretionary limits of the various branches. A loan within the branch limit could be granted on the manager's signature; any larger loan, to a maximum of $3-million, needed authorization from Credit Room. Once Osborne took over the branch, nobody in Credit Room – his former underlings – had the nerve to overrule him. Any credit application that left Bay and Richmond bearing his signature was almost automatically approved.

Osborne's son, Mark, was a fine hockey player, a lanky, dark-haired boy who left home at seventeen to play Junior A in Niagara Falls. Alex Osborne travelled all over the province to watch him. He thought nothing of driving through a snowstorm to London or Kitchener, Belleville or Kingston, Hamilton or St. Catharines, covering hundreds of miles and returning home in the middle of the night. In the off-season he got his son jobs with bank customers, Dufferin Steel and Teperman Wreckers, so Mark could build up his muscles. Mark sometimes dropped into the branch, and Osborne made a point of introducing him to Molony.

One day Molony's phone rang. Osborne said, "Reality is a temporary illusion brought on by the absence of alcohol," and hung up. The manager, joking with a credit officer. Molony joked in return, though always respecting the professional relationship. One winter morning he noticed a tall, thin fellow waiting for a teller. Something about the man seemed odd, and Molony kept an eye on him. When the fellow reached the wicket, the teller's eyes opened wide. She began taking money from her drawer. Molony hit the alarm. Before the police arrived, however, the man started for the Richmond Street doors. Molony intercepted him. "Excuse me, sir," he said politely, not sure what to say next.

"Out of the way or I'll blow your fucking head off."

Molony chastised himself for not having followed the robber out of the branch. The security people could have reprimanded him for having involved himself at all. It was right there in the holdup procedures, specific instruction on how to act. What you were absolutely not supposed to do was interfere with a robbery in progress. Loss of funds was nothing compared to the possible consequences of violence. Imagine the damages that might be awarded to a customer wounded in an incident precipitated by a bank employee.

Molony and the teller went to police headquarters to look at mugshots. The teller, shaken, was given the rest of the day off. Back at the branch, Molony said to Osborne, "Could I have the day off, too, Mr. Osborne? All that emotional upheaval."

"Get the hell back to work."

The joke was that Molony never took a day off. He prided himself on his spotless record. He wouldn't miss work no matter what – trips, illness, all-night card games. One morning, though, a few weeks later, he felt so unwell with flu he couldn't get out of bed. He waited till the last moment, hoping he'd feel better, before dialing the branch. For some reason Osborne himself answered the phone.

"Mr. Osborne, Brian Molony."

Silence. Osborne could be chilling on the phone.

"I'm calling to say I won't be in today. I don't feel all that well."

Silence.

"OK?"

"All right," said Osborne, and hung up.

Molony tried to sleep, but Osborne's reaction haunted him. And he did have work on his desk. He made his way unsteadily to the bathroom. After a shower he felt better, put on his suit and drove to the branch. At his desk, trying to concentrate, he realized Osborne was behind him.

"Miraculous," said Molony.

Osborne chuckled as he walked away, and the others had one more indication of the interest the new manager was taking in Tom Johnson's credit officer. In a way, Molony was a young Alex Osborne – the dry humour, the glasses, the moustache, the propensity for putting on weight – and Molony encouraged the comparison by modelling himself after the older man. Osborne did not like fools. He did not like explaining twice. He did not like the assistant manager who took sandwiches downstairs and read Tolkien over lunch. He did not like layabouts or whiners or anyone slow on the uptake. Molony quickly grasped new concepts, worked hard, and was himself intolerant of laziness and incompetence. Osborne was deft at handling people – customers who'd been refused a loan left his office smiling – and Molony had a similar knack. One morning, when a particularly obnoxious customer had the securities girl on the verge of tears, Molony said something that got them both smiling. Osborne noted such things. Molony was not only learning the mechanics of credit, he was learning the more subtle nuances of dealing with people's money.

He wasn't learning it from his own superior. Tom Johnson treated Molony the way many assistant managers treated their credit officers – as a serf – and it was clear to everyone that the two didn't always see eye to eye. Johnson was a sour, sarcastic, pipe-smoking Englishman. He brought a strict, by-the-book mentality to his work, walking proof of the need for discretion. One day he told Molony to bounce a cheque, not realizing or perhaps not caring it was a restaurant's cheque to the liquor licence board. Bounce it and the restaurant would have had to pay cash for its booze. Bounce it and you might have been putting the place out of business. Molony got the impression Johnson didn't fully appreciate the consequences of his actions. He instructed Molony to bounce another cheque and, when the customer called to complain, said, "Did we talk about that?" After the girls had done the paperwork, Molony had to tell them, "Sorry, we've changed our mind." We. Molony told another customer, "We'll have a decision for you by eleven o'clock," and Johnson put off making the decision until noon.

Molony was careful not to join in the whining about Johnson. It would have been all over the branch in no time – "Brian thinks he's a jerk, too." For political reasons he had to stand up for his assistant manager. "You don't appreciate the pressure he's under," Molony would say, when the gang went for drinks after work on Friday. If pressed – "Admit it, you don't like him either" – he changed the subject. It was enough that, at Christmas, he got bottles of liquor from customers. Would have been nice to get recognition from Johnson, but that was the nature of the beast. Eventually he'd have a credit officer who would no doubt think the same of him.

One day he got recognition from an unexpected source. A customer in the business of freight-forwarding was looking for a sizeable loan. Johnson wanted to make the loan at prime, but Credit Room rarely approved loans at prime. Molony did an analysis of the customer's borrowing options. They could get money from their Swiss parent company at a good rate, in which case the CIBC would get no business. They could borrow at a good rate from a merchant banker in the U.S., in which case the CIBC would get no business. Or the CIBC could loan them money at prime, obtaining their business and, more important, showing them the bank would do everything to accommodate them. That attitude might have long-term benefits. Besides, the loan was fully secured. The credit went out under Johnson's signature, but Osborne brought it to Molony's desk and said, "You did this, didn't you." Not often did Osborne approve a credit without making changes. This one went out just as Molony had written it.

Osborne was also impressed by Molony's performance on the Visa campaign. The bank was promoting Visa cards. Osborne was politically astute, always eager to show off his branch in a good light. Knowing the results would be circulated internally, he offered staff members ten dollars for every approved Visa application they brought in. Molony took blank applications and a sack of silver dollars to the variety store, across from St. Michael's College, where he had booked his bets in Grade 9. For every completed application, the owner was to give the applicant a silver dollar and keep one himself. It didn't matter if the applicant already held a Visa card, so long as the card was with another bank. Molony did the same thing at his barber shop.

Most employees brought in a single application now and then. Molony held onto his completed applications. On the final day Osborne threw in a lottery ticket with the ten dollars. Other staff members produced three or four applications. Molony walked in with forty-five. That earned him $450 in Simpsons gift certificates and forty-five lottery tickets. Osborne called a meeting to announce that the branch had exceeded budget. "And," he told the sixty employees, "it's thanks to Brian Molony. Why don't you come up here, Brian, and explain how you did it." Everyone applauded. Molony, though embarrassed, appreciated being singled out. He knew Osborne wanted to see how he handled himself.

One of Molony's Visa applications was rejected because the applicant was under eighteen. Tom Johnson, instead of offering congratulations, made some remark about Molony's having padded his total. Molony realized he not only had no respect for Johnson's work, he disliked the man. There was something about his pipe, his corrosive humour, his bitter defensiveness. One of Molony's card games was in back of a hairstyling place, and the owner talked Molony and a couple of other players into getting perms, a fad at the time. When Molony walked into the branch there was a collective gasp. Alex Osborne stuck his head out to see what was going on. Molony liked his perm – you didn't have to pay attention to it – but the reaction made him sensitive. Johnson, at exactly the wrong moment, took the pipe from his teeth long enough to say, smugly, "Get our hair done, did we?" Molony divided the English into two types, the kind you liked and the kind you didn't.

As it happened, Osborne felt the same way about Johnson. The two men had worked together at Credit Room. Johnson had preceded him to Bay and Richmond. When Osborne took the branch over, the buzz was that Johnson wouldn't last. The two men had minor run-ins, but the incident that sealed Johnson's fate grew out of a dispute with a customer. The customer – an accountant who represented an investment syndicate – had borrowed heavily to buy and lease airplanes. Since the assets weren't fixed, it was a rather unusual account. Besides Johnson himself, only his credit officer – Molony – really understood it. Johnson and the customer argued. The customer went to Alex Osborne demanding that someone else handle the business or he'd take it elsewhere. Osborne turned it over to the senior assistant, Ralph Robinson. "Fine, I understand," said Johnson. "Sometimes there are personality clashes. The man's an ass." Molony thought the remark inappropriate. There's no such thing as an ass with a $6-million line of credit.

Ralph Robinson was a likeable chap who commuted from his pig farm near Orangeville, northwest of Toronto, and aspired to one day manage his local branch. He got on well with customers and staff alike, roasting a pig each year for the branch picnic. He knew little about the aircraft leasing account and told Osborne he wanted Molony to stay on it. Ordinarily this wasn't done – Molony was Johnson's credit officer – but Osborne agreed. "Fine with me," said Johnson, "but only if my work gets done first."

The day soon came when Molony found himself in a delicate spot. Robinson had asked him to prepare a report for Credit Room on the leasing account, and Johnson had piled work on his desk as well. Johnson stopped at Molony's desk and asked what he was working on.

"A report that has to be downtown today."

"But you haven't finished my work."

"This has priority. I'll get to yours this afternoon."

Johnson hit the roof. His own credit officer telling him what had priority! He stomped off to Robinson's office. After an exchange behind closed doors, he took the matter to Osborne. Molony was asked to join them.

"Now," said Osborne, "what's the trouble?"

"Mr. Osborne, this can't continue. I find the arrangement unacceptable. The understanding was that my work would be done first. Molony is my credit officer. Robinson has his own credit officer. That credit officer should work on that credit."

"Tom," said Osborne, "don't be a child. We take a team approach at this branch. If you don't feel you can be a member of the team, perhaps we'd better find someone who can."

The writing was on the wall. Molony had unwittingly challenged Johnson's authority and Alex Osborne had backed him, showing up an assistant manager in front of his own credit officer.

It wasn't long before Johnson was transferred to another branch.

Which left an opening at Bay and Richmond for an assistant manager. Molony fantasized about the appointment, knowing he didn't have much chance. For one thing, promotions were almost invariably accompanied by transfers. One day the staff views you as a credit officer, a glorified gofer. The next they're supposed to view you in a supervisory role? The bank also liked to keep you moving so you didn't deal too long with the same customers: friendship might impede professional judgement or lead to a breach in security. The promotion would also have meant a tremendous leap in responsibility. Ordinarily a credit officer at a major branch would move to Credit Room, then perhaps manage a small retail branch, then do another stint at Credit Room, and then, perhaps, be appointed assistant manager at a major branch. If Molony did get the appointment it would represent a six- or seven-year shortcut in his career. The senior assistant said to him, "Alex thinks you'd make a good assistant, but don't get your hopes up. No way it will happen."

One morning while Molony was on holiday his mother called him to the phone. The eldest of his eight sisters and brothers, Annemarie, was visiting from Ireland, and Molony had taken the week off. He was in the shower and his mother had to knock. It was the week before his twenty-fifth birthday.

"Alex Osborne here."

"Sir."

"You might find it's in your best interest to come down to the branch."

"Be there in half an hour."

When he got to Bay and Richmond, Osborne was with a customer. The senior assistant came over to shake his hand. "Congratulations, Brian." Molony gave him a quizzical look. The senior assistant said, "I'd better let Osborne tell you."

When the customer emerged, Molony went in. Osborne's oak desk was always tidy; he did one thing at a time. Bank appointments were announced by letter sent in care of the manager. The only thing on Osborne's desk was something on CIBC letterhead. Without a word, he handed it to Molony. "Dear Mr. Molony, We have pleasure in advising you that you have been appointed an Assistant Manager at Bay & Richmond, Toronto, Ontario branch at a commencing salary of $20,700 per annum . . ." Molony was so thrilled he could barely finish the letter, which was signed by Des Hazelton, vice-president, regional general manager, and Osborne's mentor.

"Sir, I appreciate it. I'm sure you had something to do with this."

Indeed, the job was a plum and Personnel had insisted there were a hundred people more suited. To say nothing of the possible consequences at the branch. One of Osborne's assistant managers had put in three years at Credit Room – how would he react if an inexperienced underling were made his equal? But Osborne had gone out on a limb. He'd insisted on Molony and used his pull with Hazelton to get his way. He extended his hand.

"You've worked hard, Brian, you deserve it. I have no doubt whatsoever that you'll make an excellent assistant manager."

"Thank you, Mr. Osborne. It's a decision you won't regret."

Molony tucked the sports section and the Mohawk program in his jacket pocket and went to the men's room. He'd given the $22,300 bank draft to Beck and Colizzi. What's done is done. The important thing was to replace the money as quickly as possible. Locked in a cubicle, he went through the night's card, filling the margins with tiny calculations. Twenty minutes later he'd handicapped ten harness races. He checked the major-league schedule. He'd had success betting streaks, and five or six teams were on a roll. One big night and he'd have the money back.

A big night was all he needed, but he needed it so badly that the something else – the unnoticed border between Michigan and Ohio – became suddenly clear. Yesterday he had gambled because he loved it. Tonight he'd be gambling because he had to.

Over lunch he stayed at his desk, half expecting a call from the branch where Beck tried to cash the draft. Each time his phone rang he braced himself. Nothing happened until three o'clock, when Beck finally phoned. He seemed no more nervous than usual.

"Ready?"

"Go ahead," said Molony.

Beck rattled off the betting lines for all the major-league games. Molony scribbled them on an envelope. He'd intended to bet only streaking teams, but why not bet every game?

"Give me the favourite, dog, dog, favourite, favourite, dog, dog, favourite, dog, favourite."

"All right. You got the Red Sox, Yankees, Jays, Orioles, Brewers, Dodgers, Cubs, Braves, Expos, and Cards. What are we talking here?"

"The maximum," said Molony. "All for the maximum."

"By the way, Banker, they did it."

"Of course," said Molony, reaching for his pen. He began filling in the loan sheet. Name: Nick Beck. Occupation: Businessman. "Told you it was as good as cash."

"Don't put my name on anything again. Hear me?"

Purpose of loan: Investment. Repayment schedule: To be arranged, subject to periodic review.

"I won't have to," said Molony. "I'm going to win."

2
LAS VEGAS

"Artistic creation is the adventure chosen by the best in man. Gambling is the art of the wounded and haunted and faithless."

– Robert Kalich, *The Handicapper*

The day Alex Osborne returned from holiday and attacked the work that had accumulated on his desk, he marched into Molony's office and said, "Who's this?" In the backlog he had come on the application for a loan to Nick Beck. Because it fell within the branch limit, the loan needed no approval other than Osborne's. Molony had hoped he'd sign it routinely. Not Osborne.

"New customer," said Molony.

Virtually everyone who knew him thought of Molony as rigorously honest. Yet how easily the lies came when they were needed. In eighth grade, Molony used to tell his parents he was going to babysit and instead, with money from his papers, he took the subway and bus to Greenwood, the dingy, hundred-year-old racetrack in the east end of Toronto. It had an air of squalid destitution and it thrilled him – the anticipation of people clicking through the turnstiles, the exquisite suspense while PHOTO was up, the whoops and yells of the winners. A freezing wind blew in off Lake Ontario, and the ride home seemed to take forever, but the excitement affected him as nothing else did. He longed to be part of it. Too young to bet, he tugged the sleeves of people in line. "Sir, buy a ticket for me, please? Number five to win."

An old woman asked him, "Why you like the five?"

"He ran fourth the last two times out," Brian replied, pushing his glasses up his nose. "Both times he started from the eight hole and had the lead at the three-quarters, then tired. New driver today, better post. At seven to one it's worth a shot."

One evening he had just left the house when Mrs. O'Reilly up the street phoned to ask if he could babysit. "Why, he's on the way over there now," said Mrs. Molony. Around eleven, as he was coming up the walk, his brother Joey tipped him off – "They know you weren't babysitting." Dr. Molony, who overcame a serious hearing impairment to become an ear, nose, and throat specialist, was affiliated with six different hospitals, taught at the University of Toronto, and maintained offices in Toronto and Mississauga. His schedule left him precious few hours at home. His knowledge of his children was mostly secondhand, but he was in charge of discipline. He sat his fourth child down at the kitchen table. "You weren't at Mrs. O'Reilly's, were you?" "No," Brian admitted with a hangdog look. "Where were you?" "At a movie." "Which movie?" "*The Magnificent Seven*." "Where was it playing?" "At the Carlton." "Why didn't you tell your mother that's where you were going?" "I didn't think she'd let me go," Brian replied, gaining confidence, the story seeming to invent itself . . .

"New customer," he told Alex Osborne. "Investment loan. Fully secured."

"He may be involved in that stock fraud."

Some months earlier the newspapers had been full of a swindle in which a stock promoter and the founder of a merchandising company had conspired to buy and shell shares to mislead the public into believing there was great market interest in the stock.

One of the principals was named Teck, or Peck, or Beck. Osborne didn't miss a trick.

"Couldn't be the same guy," said Molony. "This fellow's only thirty or so."

"It might be his father." This was Osborne's way of saying he had no intention of approving the loan until Molony had established that there was no link with the criminal case.

"I'll get back to you," said Molony, and found himself in the rather awkward position of having to ask a neurotic bookmaker what his father did for a living. In the bank you learn to get answers to delicate questions. That afternoon, while betting the baseball games, Molony was able to learn that Beck's father was a truck driver. He informed Osborne, who, to Molony's inestimable relief, authorized the loan.

Relief was short-lived. When Monday came around again Molony was back in the hole. Trying to recover the $22,300, he had lost another $16,500 to Beck and Colizzi. This was turning into a bad dream. What now? Since Alex Osborne had already approved the Beck loan account, it could be debited further. More crucial than how much he owed the bank was his standing with Beck and Colizzi. Refuse his action – as they'd threatened the day they walked into his office – and they'd remove his means of escape. What choice did he have but to use the fraudulent account again?

The second loan caused him almost as much anguish as the first, though for a different reason. This time he forged Beck's signature and cashed the draft right there at the branch. His manner suggested that Beck was waiting, that he was doing the customer a courtesy. If the teller had happened to pass his empty office, he might have had some explaining to do. Terror gnawed at him, but it was no worse than after the first fraud. So long as Beck's loan was within the branch limit . . .

A week after the second advance Molony had to bump the loan yet again. Another horrible week. The bad dream was becoming a nightmare. What could he do but continue until he hit the streak that would bail him out? The trick now was to control the panicky sensation that threatened, at times, to immobilize him. Stay on his feet, keep moving, persevere until his fortunes changed. He was in Ohio now, Michigan was unmistakably behind him, and he had to do whatever would get him back across the border. Only a big win would solve his problem; only money could make a big win possible. This time he tacked on $27,000 U.S.

Molony began putting in longer hours than ever at the branch, generating new loans, insatiably busy. Activity was the only defence against reflection. He saw less of his friends, spent more time among the familiar, anonymous faces at the racetrack. Not only did the track represent salvation, it was the one place he was able to put out of mind – if only for 120 seconds at a time – the secret buried in the bank's books and the pit of his stomach. He saw Brenda only if they had made specific plans. He couldn't bear to be idle, watch television, chat about banalities. To put himself anywhere that did not demand full concentration was to risk being reminded of the unbearable.

The unbearable idea was not that his career would be ruined – you make your own bed – but that his family would be hideously shamed, his friends appalled, his colleagues outraged, and his manager dragged down with him. Alex Osborne had been assigning him more responsibility, steering accounts his way and introducing him to higher-ups. To betray Osborne: that was the prospect that filled him with urgency and determination.

Osborne had brought another assistant manager to Bay and Richmond, and people at the branch thought of Rick King as Osborne's protege. An unspoken rivalry developed between the two assistant managers. As Osborne took keener interest in Molony, he grew disenchanted with King. Bay and Richmond was King's first stint as an assistant manager. His post was newly created, his credit officer was new, and his accounts were a mishmash of loans other managers didn't want. He had a difficult post, in short, and Osborne expected him to whip it into shape. When he failed to meet Osborne's expectations he began to feel the force of Osborne's discontent. One Friday, at the meeting of assistant managers, Osborne asked him to stay behind. Behind closed doors he said something that made King storm out in a rage. Osborne was trying to light a fire under King, but the strategy backfired. A couple of weeks later the two men nearly came to blows. Their relations were irreparably damaged, and King was transferred out of the branch.

If downtown's resistance to Molony's promotion had given Osborne any doubts, they were soon dispelled. Brian Molony was his kind of banker. While other assistants read up on the theory of credit, Molony combed through the bad loans – four drawers full of dusty, yellowed files – looking for signals that had gone unnoticed. Each morning in *The Globe and Mail* he studied the Osgoode Hall proceedings, in case a branch customer turned up in a legal action. The activity at his post was increasing dramatically with no deterioration in service. On the contrary, customers seemed uniformly impressed by his handling of their business. If a loan account showed no activity for a couple of months, Molony called the customer. If he found a large balance in one of his accounts, he suggested putting the money in a term deposit. He handled several hundred accounts and kept on top of them all.

Only once did the bank receive a complaint about Molony, and Osborne stood firm behind him. Reviewing overdrafts in the personal chequing accounts, Molony had to deal with a woman who had bounced a $300 cheque to a finance company. Molony told the girl to take the money from the woman's Visa. But the customer hadn't made a payment in months: Visa wouldn't accept further charges. Molony told the girl to tell the customer to come in and make a deposit. The customer demanded to speak to Molony, who told her the bank was unable to honour her $300 cheque.

"I can't get down there this afternoon. I have a baby. There's no one to look after her."

"Tomorrow morning, then," said Molony. "If we don't have your deposit by noon, we'll have to return your cheque."

The woman said she'd be there. When, at three the next afternoon, she still hadn't appeared, Molony phoned again.

"I couldn't make it this morning," the woman said, "and I can't get there this afternoon."

"I'm sorry, we can't honour your cheque."

A couple of days later the branch got a call from Customer Relations. The woman had lodged a complaint, claiming Molony had ordered her to come in immediately, leaving the baby untended. Osborne had to reply in writing to Customer Relations. He'd been out of the branch at the time, and asked Molony for an explanation. Molony wrote a memo to the effect that he had deliberately used the overdraft as an excuse to separate the woman from her baby, seeking to harm its development. He had wanted to provide the baby with future grounds for a lawsuit against the bank, since the bank's lawyers seemed in need of fresh challenges.

Osborne laughed aloud.

Brenda and her father both enjoyed the races, and one night Molony invited them to Greenwood. He was on a roll. Two good weeks had left him just short of the $70,000 he had borrowed. A decent night would give him the $70,000, plus interest. Brenda and her father didn't know it, but the evening was meant to be a celebration.

Before each race they made their picks. Molony hurried off to buy the tickets. Beck, a frenzied gambler himself, was waiting at one end of the grandstand. Colizzi, cool and deliberate, was waiting at the other. Mark Epstein, another bookmaker, was waiting downstairs. Over the evening Brian and Brenda each won $10.40 on their shared tickets. Her father grinned with delight; he had won more than thirty dollars. But Molony had dropped $8,000 to Beck, Colizzi, and Epstein, and the late scores on the car radio nauseated him. Depression nearly overwhelmed him. To have got so tantalizingly near . . .

The following week he again came close to recovering what he owed; then a losing streak ate his winnings and sank him even further in debt. A month after debiting the Beck account by $27,000 U.S. he had to take another $10,000 to settle up at his Monday meeting.

The bad luck was unrelenting. A week later he put another $20,000 in Beck's name and gave it to the bookies. Disconsolate, he walked back to Bay and Richmond wondering how long he could hold up. He had to do something – anything – to relieve the burden or he'd collapse beneath its unremitting weight. He phoned Brenda at her branch. Sorry, he said, but he wouldn't be able to see her that night after all. Could they maybe go out next Wednesday instead?

God, Brian could be infuriating! Brenda sometimes wondered why she'd ever got involved with him. They'd met while he worked on the audit at her branch. Someone had warned him, "You'll be fine, as long as you don't get Mr. Major." The first morning, a bald, paunchy fellow said, "I'm Major. You're with me." He was a crusty man who wore a rubber thimble to turn pages and told people who swore to keep a civil tongue in their heads. When a girl walked by trailing an odour of perfume, Major, a bachelor, shook his head: "Those damn womanly smells." He asked for a file and was told it was in the manager's office. "Of course," said Major, "we wouldn't want to disturb him." An hour later he asked for another file, got the same answer, and said, "I don't care where it is! I want it and I want it now!" He was a character, all right, but he was also a fund of knowledge. Molony liked him.

One of the girls asked if they wanted coffee. Major, without looking up, snapped, "Can't you see I'm working?" Molony smiled at the girl and pulled a face. Brenda had long dark hair, lovely brown eyes, and an air of quiet competence. She returned his smile, and Mr. Major became the basis of an understanding between them.

The auditors were in the branch for a week, and Brenda couldn't help admiring the way the young audit assistant handled Major. So many men in the bank took everything so seriously. There was something different about Brian. Sure, he said the right things and wore the same dark suit and had a bushy moustache that made it hard to tell what he was feeling. But he took it all with a grain of salt and smiled in a sympathetic way. I'll show you how to deal with Mr. Major, he seemed to say, and peppered the older man with questions. Major realized this wasn't just another incompetent putting in his obligatory nine months on the audit and they got along like a house on fire.

Thursday afternoons the auditors went for a drink at the Nag's Head, and Brian asked Brenda to join them. They gossiped about the bank and joked about Mr. Major. When the audit ended he made a point of thanking her for her help. They didn't stay in touch, but a year later a girl from Brenda's branch got transferred to Bay and Richmond, where Molony had been posted. Brenda dropped by to see her friend and there was Brian. She was wearing a godawful red thing on her head and he couldn't resist a playful jab.

"Very nice hat. Most attractive."

"Thank you," she said, as if the compliment had been genuine.

"Get much sun under there?"

"Why do you think it's called a sun hat?"

Brenda's girlfriend invited them over to play euchre. Brian and Brenda were partners, and thanks to his skill they won every game. He had an easygoing manner but he put away the rum-and-Coke. She worried that he was overdoing it. "I never get sick on booze," he assured her. When he stepped outside for a breath of air, she followed to see if he was okay. With his glasses off, on hands and knees, he looked as helpless as a little boy with the flu.

"Are you all right?"

"You must be pretty impressed."

"Would you like a glass of water?" said Brenda. "Anything I can do?"

They started meeting for lunch or a drink after work. Brian kept things to himself but he was a good listener, sympathetic and helpful. He asked her to the races and she thought it a great idea. At Mohawk his uneasiness disappeared. There were no awkward silences to fill – something happened every thirty minutes. Brenda couldn't decide which horse to bet and suggested going together on the one he chose. Bad luck, he told her. Close your eyes and bet the one your pen lands on. He had his own system, made all sorts of incomprehensible calculations and went to the windows by himself. She never knew how much he was betting or whether he won or lost.

They began seeing more of each other. She did most of the talking. She told him about her work, her family, the guy she'd been going with. He was understanding and supportive. If she asked for advice he offered it, otherwise he listened. Not that he wasn't entertaining. He had a dry wit and was great fun to be around. It's just that he never said much about himself. He thought you should leave work at the office and deal with your own problems. And she'd never met anybody with quite the same attitude toward money. He never bought anything because he liked it; he only bought what he definitely needed. He left tips so miserly she snuck back to leave more. One day he caught her. "Fifty cents is plenty," he said, upset. "She didn't have to slaughter the chicken. All she did was bring it to our table."

Brenda got the idea he was seeing other women but didn't pry. They were just friends, after all, that was his business. On weekends he saw Beth, who lived a couple of hours from Toronto. They had started going out just before he finished university. The first time she was a virgin; the next night she had a small library of how-to books by her bed. She was so eager to make love to him that sometimes she started in the car. What could be better? Driving to Mohawk for the evening card, carrying on to Kitchener, spending the night with Beth, leaving in time to catch the next day's races. During the week he could always phone Daphne. She had her own apartment and he had only to say he was coming over. Trouble is, he'd say nine o'clock, figuring to catch a couple of races. He'd stay for another, then another, until there were none left. At midnight he'd have to invent some cock-and-bull story.

Brenda stood up to him in a way the others didn't. They became close friends and, once she and her boyfriend split for good, lovers as well. She was the pitcher on the bank's softball team and one afternoon Molony went out to watch. He wasn't good at watching. Before long he suggested Sue ought to lead off because of her speed, Carol should hit cleanup because of her power, the centrefielder and rightfielder ought to switch positions, and they should shift the defence when the other team's heavy hitters were up. A couple of weeks later he was the coach.

Not easy, seeing three women, none of whom knew about the others, while working long hours and holding down what amounted to a second job, the blood avocation of racetracks and ball games. But he dreaded idleness, and the complications sorted themselves out. One night in bed Beth asked him, "When are you going to marry me?" He thought she was joking. When he saw she was serious he explained he couldn't even think about marriage until he'd established his career. It seemed to her his career was already established. That was the end of that. As he got more deeply involved with Brenda he lost interest in Daphne as well. Or, rather, as he made more excuses and called less frequently, she lost interest in him.

Brenda lived with her parents. She'd moved out once, taken a place in a raunchy neighbourhood and ended up returning home. Her parents were happy she did. Her father worked for a manufacturing company and her mother worked part-time at the bank. They felt a daughter ought to live at home until she married. She was free to come and go, of course, but she felt obliged to return at a decent hour. When Brian was picking her up she went down to the lobby to wait. When they were together, they always seemed to be running out of time.

Molony's parents were staunchly Catholic; they attended Mass daily and placed their faith at the centre of their lives. The idea of their son living in sin was unthinkable. To find privacy, Brian and Brenda had to use a friend's place or shell out thirty or forty dollars for a room. She hated feeling sleazy, he hated spending money. One afternoon, at a hotel, he said, "Wouldn't it be great if you had your own place?" She had to admit it would be. Her mother would be upset, and it might be a financial strain, but she was twenty-four and had worked at the bank almost five years. She'd saved money, contributed to a retirement savings plan; she knew how to budget. Brian could help with the rent. After all, what was stopping him from getting a place? He had it so easy at home he'd hate to lose a good thing.

She heard about a one-bedroom near High Park, twenty-third floor, balcony, nice view, not a bad size, with underground parking. The rent was $395. Encouraged by Brian she took it, but once she'd moved in she began to feel cheated. He hardly ever spent time there. Had he not implied they'd spend more time together? Had she misunderstood? He'd leave her with a clear expectation and then, when she wound up disappointed, he'd shrug – "Did I say that?" And he hadn't exactly said it, of course, it was she who'd been at fault, making unwarranted assumptions.

She'd had the apartment two months now and he rarely spent more than a few hours. If she was lucky he might stay Saturday night. He seemed more preoccupied than ever. She wondered if something was bothering him but he wasn't someone you could come out and ask. He had a way of deflecting questions, talking his way right past an answer. She'd bought a queen-sized bed and a sofa, a diningroom table and chairs, but the place still felt barren. She'd looked forward to decorating it, choosing curtains and lamps, placemats and wine glasses, imagining they'd do it together. He showed no interest. Not that he expected her to do it; he didn't notice, didn't care. During the day he was consumed by work. Evenings they had to be doing something – seeing people or going somewhere – otherwise he went to the track. He couldn't bear just being with her. He studied the race results, watched the ball games, spoke to someone on the phone: "Give me two on the one, and wheel the double."

Why wouldn't he include her? She liked sports, too, knew all the players on the Blue Jays and was delighted when her father gave her a subscription to the sports network for her birthday. Brian was in another league. Sometimes, in bed, she wanted to be held. "Can't we just cuddle for a minute?" But he didn't like cuddling and a minute was all she got before he padded out to the livingroom and flicked back and forth through the channels. He didn't like dancing, either, you couldn't have got him onto the floor with a shotgun. Literally. You got the idea he'd choose being shot. Once he said he wasn't going to do something, that was it. He was a man of his word. In many ways it was a wonderful quality. In many ways he was a wonderful guy – he was close to his family, as she was, and fun to be around, and well-mannered, highly principled, hard-working, achievement-oriented. He never lost his temper, always acted the perfect gentleman. On her birthday and on holidays he sent flowers and a card. Sometimes she sat in her half-empty apartment and listed his attributes, making the list go on as long as she could. But she always ended up wishing he'd give more of himself, wondering if she was making a terrible mistake.

Here it was Hallowe'en. She'd got the impression they'd go out – hadn't he given her that impression? Go down Yonge Street maybe, see the outrageous people, she didn't care so long as they did it together. She'd got herself into a great mood, joking with the girls at her branch, imagining the evening. And then he'd phoned and said he couldn't see her, embarrassing her, making her feel presumptuous for having assumed they'd get together. He didn't explain – Brian never explained – just said something had come up.

How humiliating! She hung up the phone and put on a brave face. She couldn't tell the other girls at the branch what had happened, not after saying what fun she was going to have with Brian. No, she'd pretend they were going out just the same.

Molony had made his own plans. He was back in the hole with Beck and Colizzi and feeling the iron weight of his deception. He slept poorly; his stomach had begun acting up; he had to do something.

He'd been to Las Vegas once before, putting up $1,500 front money in return for chips at the Stardust. The trip had sounded great – everything paid for – but turned into disaster. Not only did he lose $1,500 at blackjack, he lost $500 on the plane. It had been three years and he still recalled his despondency. But he needed a win in the worst way and Las Vegas held more promise than the racetrack.

First he needed working capital. Nick Beck was already over his supposed limit – no way Molony could tack on another advance. Besides, he wasn't going to recoup $100,000 with a $20,000 win. He needed a new source of funds and recalled, some months earlier, having established a line of credit for Sun Crown Trading, a group of Italian businessmen intending to start an import-export operation. After setting up the credit, however, they had run into partnership problems and never bothered to take out a loan. The documentation and security, approved by Alex Osborne, were already in place.

Just before Hallowe'en, Molony had opened a loan account in Sun Crown's name. He told the clerk in the discount department, "Sun Crown needs fifty thousand U.S." She asked if it was to be credited to the current account. No, said Molony, they needed cash. The loan was the bank's credit, the cash its debit. Just so long as everything balanced. On the loan card he indicated that all correspondence was to be referred to the manager of post 2 – himself.

Molony was unaware that any U.S. cash parcel of $50,000 or more had to have downtown approval. The tellers' supervisor phoned Main Branch Treasury for the cash. She told Molony she had placed the order but that Main Branch Administration would be calling to get the manager's approval.

God, no! He had to head off the call to Alex Osborne. He phoned Main Branch Administration himself.

"I don't understand what's going on. I've got a customer here who needs fifty thousand U.S. You're telling me I can't get it without approval? This is Bay and Richmond."

"Those guys at Treasury, Jesus. All we do is phone the manager anyway. We've told them, if it's a big branch, they don't have to worry about approval."

"Would you mind phoning them and looking after the paperwork? If you do need the manager's approval I'll have Alex Osborne call down." A bluff: if approval were required, Molony would cancel the order.

"Don't worry about it. I'll get on it right away."

Twice a week Brinks delivered cash and securities to Bay and Richmond. Molony envisioned a dozen things that could go wrong before the delivery. Nothing he could do but hope no further mention was made of the order. The wait was excruciating. He feared every phone call. Finally, on Friday afternoon, the tellers' supervisor rang him.

"Brian, your cash is here."

In ninth grade, at St. Michael's College School, Brian Molony was asked what he wanted to be when he grew up. In his awkward, left-handed script he printed: "1. Priest 2. Accountant 3. Store owner." Partly it was emulation – the Woodcrofts next door, with two priests in the family, were held in high esteem. Partly it was a wish to please his parents – he had never made them happier than the day he brought home his prize, a crucifix, as top student in first grade at Our Lady of Perpetual Help. Partly it was a deeply personal response to the majesty of the church. For two years he had attended St. Michael's Choir School, where religious, voice, and musical instruction were part of the curriculum. He loved to sing at Massey Hall and at weddings and funerals, clad in red and black robes, just as he loved to throw hockey cards against the wall at recess. He considered himself privileged the year he served Mass at St. Michael's Cathedral.

Yet even as he committed his aspirations to paper, they were changing. He couldn't have said why. The process of disillusionment was a series of unpleasantries and letdowns rather than a conscious renunciation. The nun in eighth grade who tried to force him to switch his pen to his right hand. The monseigneur who, the day Brian arrived with a cut lip, told him to wash himself. Brian started downstairs. "Clean yourself here," said the monseigneur, indicating the tap for holy water. How could he use holy water? "Go ahead, son, water's water." The day the other altar boy failed to show up and he had to give the Latin responses by himself. The congregation at St. Michael's Cathedral was huge, and each time the priest uttered his amplified celebration and then fell silent, waiting for Brian to fill the monumental stillness with the response, everyone seemed to be sitting in judgement. With two you could fake it; when you were alone, it was obvious you didn't know the Latin. Afterwards the monseigneur said, "You don't have the responses down too well, do you?" He didn't seem to care, though, and Brian was ceasing to care. The church, once a mysterious sanctuary, became a neutral presence, neither alluring nor repellent, like the smell of cooking fish when he got home from school on Fridays.

Having skipped a grade, Brian found himself one of the youngest in his ninth-grade class at St. Mike's. The other boys were reaching puberty; he was immature, and getting acne. He won money in the lunch-hour card games, though, and usually won the hockey bets. His mother became concerned by the comments of his teachers: "Careless work habits." "Improvement needed." "Would like to see you on Parents Night." The boy who had loved going to Mass was sneaking out to Harvey's instead, eating french fries until it was time to go home. The boy who had stood atop his class got 44 in Mathematics, 51 in Geography, 46 in French. The boy who had read *The Lives of the Saints* each night in bed, eager to understand suffering and sacrifice, now studied the standard-bred entries.

At the store where kids from St. Mike's went to smoke and hang out, Brian was one of the few boys the owner didn't have to keep an eye on. Others pocketed gum, or candy, or drank three bottles of soda and paid for two. Brian nibbled chips, listened to race results, ate an ice-cream bar, bet the baseball game on the radio. When he left he said, "I owe you one-sixty," and paid it. Yet one night at a neighbour's he stole two hundred dollars, having run out of cash for the racetrack. His father strapped him and sent him off to repeat Grade 10 at boarding school.

Dr. Molony wished to discipline his son and remove him from the bad crowd he had evidently fallen in with; but he also wanted to give Brian the advantages he himself had enjoyed at private schools in Ireland and England. Regina Mundi had been established as a seminary; when it failed to attract sufficient numbers of aspiring priests it was turned into a boarding school. From a distance it resembled a modern, minimum-security prison, set off by itself on 138 flat acres outside London, a prosperous city of 250,000 a couple of hours west of Toronto. Many of the teachers were priests; the fostering of Christian values was central to the program. The atmosphere was intended, as the school's brochure said, "to nurture a boy's academic, social, physical, and spiritual growth."

Soon after Brian arrived at Regina Mundi he met Doug Fox, a boy his own age from Sarnia. Brian's acne flared terribly at times, making him self-conscious and a focus for the meanness of pubescent boys. They called him Lurch, after a ghoulish character on a TV show. Possessed of his father's verbal gifts, Brian became adept at cloaking his insecurity in wit. Doug, handsome and likeable, had embarked on adolescence with the same easy confidence he brought to the tennis court. He sympathized with Brian. They began spending time together, and before long they were friends.

Doug was social and outgoing; Brian was quiet and reserved. Doug started a rock band; Brian liked the Carpenters. Doug was a natural athlete; Brian was a dedicated plodder. Doug's dark good looks made the girls giggle and whisper; Brian's acne was the first thing they noticed. Doug asked to change roommates so that Brian could move in with him. Doug kept his side of the room spotless; Brian scattered clothes, newspapers, and junk-food wrappers all over.

Despite the surface differences, though, they had a good deal in common. Doug, too, had aspired as a boy to becoming a priest. He was bright, but Brian was brighter, and they were highly competitive. Doug studied diligently while Brian goofed around or went to the track. At the last minute Brian borrowed Doug's notes, crammed, and aced the exam. They were always trying to outdo each other. Brian bet that Doug couldn't drink a bottle of Listerine in three minutes. Doug chugged it, feigning enjoyment, ending with a dramatic belch. "Pay up, Molony."

Doug knew about Brian's fascination with the racetrack. He knew what happened to the $1,200 Brian earned one summer working fourteen-hour days on his father's dairy farm. He knew why Brian went back to the farm and worked over the Christmas and Easter holidays. He knew Brian had a bookie in Toronto.

Gambling just happened to be what Brian loved most, even if his parents disapproved. One night at dinner with Brian's family Doug started to say something about the track, where he and Brian had spent the afternoon. Brian shot him a look that shut him up in mid-sentence. Later, Brian explained he'd written a bad cheque to the priest who ran the tuck shop at school. When he wrote a second cheque to cover it and that one bounced, too, Dr. Molony had had to make good the money. Best, said Brian, not to raise the subject of gambling at the house.

The boys at Regina Mundi often socialized with the girls at Mount St. Joseph's, the Catholic girls' school a few miles away. Doug started going out with a local girl, Trish Hilton. Usually they invited Brian along. Sometimes he went to the basketball game or the dance; more often they dropped him off at Western Raceway and, five hours later, picked him up. Brian's idea of a perfect Saturday was to go to the track, have dinner by himself at Swiss Chalet, then see a movie. If he got cleaned out at the races, he ate a chocolate bar for dinner and watched TV. Doug, thinking Brian would have liked to date but was just too shy, tried to set him up with Trish's friends. Great guy once you get to know him, Doug assured her, and Trish agreed. So did her parents, who came to see him as a model young man. Complicated, though, with a layer of cocky arrogance beneath his shy reserve, and a foundation of thoughtfulness beneath that. His glasses hid an air of fierce concentration. A bright, intense, decent kid, the sort who remembers to send a thank-you note after spending the weekend as a house guest.

Doug introduced him to his cousin, and Brian and Linda started going out. She liked the races, too, and they went as often as possible. Brian's Irish ancestors had been involved in breeding for generations and his knowledge was extensive. He enjoyed passing on what he knew. Linda disliked the betting side of it, but she didn't object to spending dates at the track. Then, out of the blue, she gave him a magazine article about Gamblers Anonymous. Brian pretended he wasn't surprised and offended. He found a lesson in the incident – he shouldn't have revealed so much of himself – and vowed not to make the same mistake again.

Brian went on to the University of Western Ontario. He dated a girl named Nicole, but she was attracted to Doug. Soon she and Doug were dating heavily. When they moved in together, Brian ended up spending most of his time at their place on Elias Street. It was only a couple of blocks from the track. He had been staying with an alcoholic couple – he didn't want to waste gambling money on rent, and they charged him only seven dollars a week for a room. In third-year university Doug and Nicole announced their engagement. Doug's brother was best man, Brian master of ceremonies. After graduation Doug went back to Sarnia and Brian joined the bank in Toronto. Sometimes Brian drove down for a visit, sometimes Doug came to Toronto. Brian took him to lunch at Hy's, quietly pointing out the politicians and corporate heavyweights at nearby tables. Brian still handled their joint stock portfolio; they told each other how much they were making and talked about their investments. They remained best friends, but their lives were pulling them apart. When Brian phoned long distance one night to see if Doug could get away for a couple of days, Doug was enthusiastic. He was ready for a little R and R, and he hadn't seen Brian in months. Las Vegas? With someone who loved gambling the way Brian did? You couldn't ask for a better combination.

Molony hit a bad streak the moment he walked into the Marina. He shot craps through the desert night. At dawn he went around to the other casinos at the top of the Strip. Toward noon he had a run at the Tropicana but had to cash out to meet Doug's plane.

Red-eyed, sweat-stained, and unshaven, he went to the airport in the same clothes he'd worn down.

"Sir, good to see you."

"Shouldn't have got all dressed up to meet me."

"Did you get the right plane? If it's a fashion show you're after, you should have gone to Paris."

They had a lot of catching up to do. The friendship now had gaps that needed filling. Doug was doing well in the family hotel business, making good money and building his own house. He and Nicole had a little girl. Over dinner Brian brought him up to date on all the Molonys. Everyone was doing well. Sieg and Sheila were still running the farm in Milton. Maud – the housekeeper who had come from Ireland with Mrs. Molony – was looking after the monseigneur at a parish in Cheektowaga, New York. His parents were both fine, Brian said, or so they seemed. He didn't see as much of them as he should have.

After a few drinks, Brian told Doug about something that had happened that morning. The way the casinos were laid out, it was a three-dollar fare from one to the next. Brian hated wasting money. He was hurrying along in the blistering heat when, outside the Dunes, he saw an elegant Oriental woman. Each time a man walked by, she approached him. She couldn't have been a hooker. She was middle-aged and dressed in a silk blouse, black slacks, and black leather pumps. She wore a pearl necklace and delicate gold chains. Brian, intrigued, timed it so that he was within earshot when she intercepted a stooped man in a peaked cap. "Blowjob, ten dollar. You want good blowjob, mister?" Brian could hardly believe it. Something about the woman – her naked desperation – had upset him terribly. She had run out of money and was debasing herself to get back in action. Weird, he told Doug, shaking his head. It made no sense. What she'd been doing was so at odds with who she was.

That night they went to the Wayne Newton show. Afterwards, in the hotel room, Doug was putting away his things when he happened on a pile of deposit slips. They added up to more than $30,000. Doug was stunned, a bit scared. Stocks, pari-mutuel tickets, corner-store bookies were one thing. This was serious bucks. He took the slips into the bathroom and made Brian shut off the shower.

"Holy shit, Brian, have you lost all this money?"

Brian said he'd had wins, too, he was down a couple of thousand. Any luck and he'd be even in an hour. Doug wanted to know where he'd got so much money. Brian said a customer had loaned it to him. Doug wanted to know why he was playing for such high stakes. Brian said he was trying out a new system – a conservative system, low risk, but it required big bets. He was heading out now for an hour. Did Doug want to go with him? Doug looked at his watch and said no thanks. It was 3 a.m. and he needed his beauty sleep.

In the morning Doug awoke to find Brian's bed had not been disturbed. Still at it, probably – Doug had never known anyone so fond of gambling. He showered and shaved and, when there was still no sign of Brian, began to feel anxious. What if he did owe money? What if his system had screwed up? Doug had heard stories about what happened to people who didn't pay off. What if Brian had run into trouble? Doug went downstairs to pick up the newspaper, and Brian walked into the lobby. Doug told him he'd started to worry – hadn't Brian said he was going out for an hour? Brian shrugged and said he'd lost track of the time, you know what it's like in these places.

Doug had breakfast while Brian took out his pen and scribbled on the sports page. Despite not having slept he was cheerful, and before long Doug was back in good spirits. They went around to all the casinos on the Strip. Doug had a drink while Brian tried his luck. He lost at one place after another. Finally, at the Aladdin, he got on a roll. He started playing with five-dollar chips, won, and moved up to twenty-fives. Before long he was playing with hundred-dollar blacks, four or five on the layout at a time. As he raked in chips he gave half to Doug, who stuffed them in his pockets.

"If I ask for them back," said Brian, "don't give them to me."

Suddenly Brian was playing with five-hundred-dollar chips and Doug had $40,000 in his pockets. Doug was half thrilled, half petrified. In his jeans he had almost twice what he'd earned the previous year. It was a hefty down payment on a house, yet Brian treated it as if it were Monopoly money.

Brian started losing – you could feel the tide turn. Doug nudged him. Brian didn't notice. Doug kicked his shin. Brian was oblivious. Doug kicked him again, hard.

"Let's get out of here."

"Not yet."

"Come on, Brian, fun's over."

"Hold on," said Molony, his attention fixed on the layout.

"You're going downhill. We're leaving."

Molony was now losing as quickly as he'd been winning. He was almost out of his own chips. "Give me some money."

"You can pay off what you owe. Let's take a break."

"If you want to go, go. Give me the money."

"Molony, look at me. What is this bullshit?"

Others were glancing their way. The floorman fixed Doug with a reptilian glare. Doug glared right back. He didn't care, he wanted Brian out of there.

"You just told me not to give it to you."

"It's my money."

"Remember what you told me? Soon as you lose three in a row, walk away. You've lost five in a row. Come on. We're going."

"Give me my fucking money."

Everyone was watching. He and Brian were holding up the game. Doug had no choice. He handed over the money and stormed out. Across the street he rented a car. Fuming, he drove down the Strip, then into the desert. The look on Brian's face. Doug had always been able to pull him back. If he put his foot down, Brian listened. This was different. Brian may as well have said, "Screw you. I value the chips more than I value your friendship."

Doug drove aimlessly, cooling out, then went looking for Brian. He found him at the sports book next to their hotel, a dismal place that smelled of desperation and disinfectant. Brian was dispirited. He'd lost most of the money at the crap table and put the rest on the ball games. Doug didn't like football but he took the molded seat next to Brian's, half afraid to leave him. While the parade of losers shuffled in and out, discarding old slips and buying new ones, Brian and Doug watched game after game on the elevated screens, eight straight hours of NFL football. Of the ten games Brian had bet, he lost nine. Doug couldn't believe it. To be in debt, win back what you owe, and lose the whole works again? How could anyone with Brian's smarts be so dumb?

On the plane home Doug said he had something important to say. They were best friends, right? "If you've got money problems, I don't think gambling's going to solve them. Why not borrow and pay off what you owe? Your parents will give you a loan. I'll loan you what I can. We just took out a mortgage, and Nicole's expecting again, but I could scrape up a few thousand. What do you say?"

Brian almost blurted, "I owe a hell of a lot more than you think, and I owe it where they don't know I've borrowed it." It would have been such a relief to tell someone.

"I appreciate your concern, Doug. I'll look after it myself."

Doug shrugged. What can you do? Let the guy know he's your best buddy, tell him you think he's got a problem, try to get him talking. Offer to help, that's about it. Doug ordered a drink, put on his earphones, and looked out the window. They'd still talk at Christmas and on their birthdays. Brian would drive down to Sarnia now and then. When Doug came to Toronto they'd go for lunch. He would never go gambling with Brian again, though, never even raise the subject – it was up to Brian now. They'd carry on as if it hadn't happened, but the friendship would never be quite the same.

When they landed in Toronto, Brian took Doug aside and said, "Listen, I've got something to tell you. Something important. I'm . . . I'm sorry you didn't have a more enjoyable holiday. Glad you came."

When Brian asked to borrow twenty bucks, Doug assumed it was cab fare home. It was something to put on the Monday night triactor.

"When I was growing up, our family lived a couple of blocks from Brian's family," recalled Andy Williams, now a chartered accountant and general manager of an outdoor furniture manufacturing company. "Brian and I both went to Our Lady of Perpetual Help for grade school, and we went to the same boarding school. The Molonys were a fine family, highly regarded in the community, in the Catholic community, and I'm sure also in the medical community. My brother went out with Brian's sister, and I knew most of Brian's brothers. Dr. Molony was our family doctor for various throat ailments. Mrs. Molony was very kind, very loving. Always supportive of her family. A really fine woman. Brian was a bright boy and I'm sure they were very proud of him.

"Dr. Molony was into horse racing, but I don't think he was much of a gambler. He was in it more for the sport, the breeding. You come along as the son and you get caught up in it. My father was into it and I have the gambling bug myself – haven't missed a Queen's Plate in twenty years. Brian and I used to take the newspaper and go through the next day's races. Brian would pick a horse and I'd pick a horse. We'd play for a quarter or fifty cents a race. He was very good at it and I wasn't, so of course he wanted to do it all the time. He was an expert handicapper at an early age. I remember him bent over his *Racing Form*, studying it at length. He was a serious gambler, in the sense that he went about it carefully and took pride in the results.

"We also played a lot of cards at a young age. Mostly poker. I think that's where Brian got the nickname 'Weasel.' He was shrewd in everything he did, and he was also lucky. He was brighter than the rest of us and he took it more seriously. We were doing it for the fun and excitement, but he was doing it for the challenge and the victory. He hated to lose. It seemed to mean more to him than to the rest of us.

"I was kind of incorrigible at that age and my marks weren't very good. My father heard about Regina Mundi from Brian's father, and my parents sent me down there a year after Brian's parents sent him. Back then there were only about a hundred and twenty-five kids at the school, so basically you knew everybody. Brian's best friend was Doug, no question. They were inseparable. Anywhere Doug went, Brian went. I mean almost to an insufferable level. Doug was outgoing, more of a lady killer and a jock, but they had the same sense of humour. Brian had his father's sense of humour, very dry, and he and Doug found the same things funny. You have to be on a certain wavelength to appreciate certain people, and they seemed to be on the same wavelength.

"At Regina Mundi I remember Brian telling me about going to the track with a girl he was seeing and Doug's girlfriend. The girls couldn't decide which horse to bet on. Brian said, 'Close your eyes, see which one your pen lands on.' The pen slipped across two horses, so he said, 'OK, we have to bet the exactor. Those two horses.' Damned things finished one-two and paid a hundred and fifty dollars. How's that for luck?

"Brian always had the ability to con, no question. He must have conned me a zillion times. Never in a mean way, but he'd take any edge he could get. He knew how to get what he wanted. If you were up against him you got the feeling you were going to lose, he was going to do whatever it took to win. And you knew that in his quiet, unassuming way, he had the balls to do it.

"You certainly never would have thought of him as doing anything illegal. He was a very moral and honest person, but at the same time he had a streak you could almost call ruthless. Maybe that's too strong a word. I'll give you an example. At Regina Mundi one year I won the golf tournament. Brian was editor of the newspaper, and he presented me with the prize. It was thirty dollars, I think. At the time I owed him twenty because I'd been short of cash or whatever. So I go up to the podium in front of everybody and Brian presents me with the envelope. Most guys would have cracked a joke, you know, 'Congratulations, glad to see you won enough money to pay me what you owe me.' Not Brian. He'd already taken the twenty. I got a net figure in the envelope."

"Eli, it's Brian. I wonder if I could ask a favour."

Molony had met Eli Koharski at a poker game shortly after starting at the bank. Koharski's marriage had collapsed; he filled the void with cards and dice and pari-mutuel tickets. The camaraderie of gamblers developed into friendship. They often went to the races together, shot craps in hotel rooms, watched sports. Sometimes Eli and a pal of his played euchre with Brian and Brenda. Brenda thought they were playing for dimes – each dime was a hundred dollars. Unlike some denizens of the track, Koharski was utterly reliable. An immigrant's son, he had risen from a janitorial position to vice-president and part owner of an importing company. Molony admired his self-made career. He had given Koharski a bank loan to consolidate his debts, and Koharski had offered Molony the use of his townhouse before Brenda got her apartment. They viewed each other with warmth and respect, though they hadn't spent much time together since Molony stopped attending the poker games.

"I'm taking cash out of my account," said Molony, "but I don't want to do it through my own branch. I sold some stock and I don't want people here to know my affairs. I thought I'd arrange it through your branch, if you wouldn't mind picking up an envelope for me."

Molony had set up a loan account and a current account in Koharski's name and given him a $19,500 advance. The money had been debited from the loan account and credited to the savings account. Koharski had $19,500 in the bank he knew nothing about.

"No problem," said Koharski. "I have to go today anyway. Do I have to sign anything?"

"It's all looked after," said Molony. "I know you're busy. Appreciate the favour. I'll call you back with the name of the woman you should ask for."

Molony called the Dufferin and Ranee branch of the CIBC and said a valued customer was making a withdrawal from Bay and Richmond but would pick up the cash there. Molony supplied the account number and asked that the money be readied for pickup.

That evening Molony dropped by Koharski's place. Koharski

invited him in, but Molony was late for a rendezvous at Yorkdale Shopping Centre. Nick Beck insisted on meeting in busy, open places, and Molony had suggested the CIBC branch in the plaza.

Beck had grown up in the area. It was where he'd done his first boosting, slipping through basement windows and unlocking back doors for the older guys. It was where he'd been revered by the other kids for telling the teachers to fuck themselves, where he'd bought grass in half pounds and moved it in half ounces, where he'd cruised around in his black Mustang and challenged anybody to anything. "Wanna bet?" he'd say, pulling out a wad of twenties and fifties. Sixteen years old. The others moved on, but Nicky never left. Once the area had been a neighbourhood – low-cost housing, hardware stores that smelled of sweeping compound, corner marts where you got smokes and, if you knew the magic word, a bottle of rye on Sunday. Now it was a commercial wasteland – Burger King and Radio Shack and Yorkdale Mercury. But these were still his streets. He and his wife had an apartment not far from Yorkdale, and her dress shop – his office – was a few blocks away.

Beck was usually punctual, but Molony couldn't find him. The TransAm was nowhere in sight. Molony got out and walked back and forth in front of the branch. Idleness was deadly: it brought the loans to mind. There were now three bad accounts, three sums to pay down. Three ways to be found out. Where was Beck? Had he got the time screwed up? Could something have happened to him? Something that might involve Molony? Paranoid guy, Beck. What if his paranoia wasn't paranoia after all?

"Here comes The Banker, saving ground on the inside."

He'd been into the cocaine. He stood there, not two feet away, unshaven and wild-eyed, radiating nervous energy. He might have materialized out of thin air.

"You scared hell out of me."

"What you got for me, Banker?"

Molony passed him the envelope. "You going tonight?"

"I have to see that creep."

"I'll give you a ride," said Molony. "If you'd been on time we might have even made the first race."

"Your car's a mess. Take my car."

"Mine's right here."

"Junk that piece of shit, Banker. I'll sell you the TR6. Hardly any mileage on it. Beautiful little car."

"Great car," Molony agreed, spirits soaring. His miserable anxiety had vanished – twenty minutes to post time. "But tell me, Nicky, and I want you to be perfectly honest. A red convertible? Do you really think it's me?"

3

LUCK BE A LADY

"Risk! Risk anything! Care no more for the opinions of others, for those voices. Do the hardest thing on earth for you. Act for yourself."

– Katherine Mansfield

As a young girl, Sherry Brydson lived with her mother, aunt, and cousins at her grandfather's house in Port Credit, Ontario. It was a wonderful place, with nanny's quarters, servants' quarters, and a gardener's cottage. When Sherry was six, her grandfather moved to Scotland, but he returned to the house each summer, spending as much time with his family as his busy schedule allowed. Sherry visited him in Scotland; every summer he took her and her mother on a trip. One year they drove to Rome, where they met her uncle Ken and his new wife; another they went to the World's Fair in Brussels.

At the University of Toronto, Sherry studied political science and economics, served as news editor on the student paper, and immersed herself in radical politics. She considered the world in terms proposed by Chairman Mao: "What is the central contradiction?" She worked summers as a journalist for Canadian Press. On graduation she was hired by CP, but soon moved to London with her boyfriend, an editor on *The Globe and Mail.*

Brydson's grandfather had moved down from Scotland, and she

saw him often. He was no longer just Roy Thomson, a barber's son from Toronto who had launched his business career selling radios. He was Lord Thomson of Fleet, having been made a baron in 1964 by Queen Elizabeth. During Sherry's lifetime he had built an empire of holdings – newspapers (including *The Times* of London), television and radio stations, insurance companies, travel agencies, merchandising chains, computer data services, book and magazine publishing companies, trucking outfits, North Sea oil – that girdled the globe. Nearing eighty, he peered out through impossibly thick glasses and hopped on planes to wherever impulse took him. "Let's go see Sally Aw," he'd say, and next thing you'd be in Hong Kong. He had lived his three score and ten and considered this part of life a bonus. If he fell down dead in the middle of Burma, so be it.

Often he took one of his grandchildren with him, to Florence or Karachi, Beirut or Madrid. He disapproved of Sherry's politics, her habit of wearing slacks, and her "arrangement" with her beau, and he voiced his displeasure strenuously. At least, she told herself, their relationship was not based on indifference. They frequently argued but liked each other, and Sherry saw a good deal of the world in his company. When she wasn't travelling with him, she and her boyfriend got around, spending five months in Paris learning French, travelling overland to Katmandu. In England they did freelance work for CBC Radio. Eventually Paul returned to Toronto and Sherry went off to Australia.

In Sydney she got a job on one of the newspapers in Rupert Murdoch's chain, News Limited. A year later, at a convention in Hong Kong, she got an offer to work in Bangkok. She had visited Thailand with her grandfather and been seduced by the diversity, beauty, and complexity of the country. Might there be two openings, one for her boyfriend? There were. The only hitch was that her employer would be Allied Newspapers, which her grandfather owned. She did not feel it would be proper to live common law. She phoned Paul in Toronto and said, "Let's get married and go to Bangkok."

They spent three years working on *The Bangkok Post* and exploring the country. Sherry edited a coffee-table book on the handicrafts of Thai hill tribes. She studied Thai cooking. She learned photography. The life appealed on many levels, but she and Paul began to fear losing touch with their backgrounds, becoming as disaffected and rootless as the dipsomaniacs in the diplomatic corps. In 1977, with mixed feelings, they returned to Toronto. Paul resumed his editing job at *The Globe and Mail*, and Sherry pondered her future.

At the family cottage on Georgian Bay, she scratched her leg on a thorn, developed an infection, and was treated with penicillin. The drug triggered an allergic reaction. Pancreatic complications undermined her body's immune system. Her food allergies, which had been mild, became devastating – she could not have sugar, beer, wine, cheese, bread, anything brewed with mould or fermented with yeast – and she was grievously ill for almost a year.

As she was getting back on her feet, eager for new challenges, she learned she was to receive a substantial disbursement from the trust Roy Thomson had established for his grandchildren. Brydson had always been comfortable – if she wanted to take six months off, she could apply to the trustees for money – but she had worked for a living and did not have expensive tastes. Her grandfather had been confusingly ambivalent about where she fit in, one day proposing a toast to her at a huge formal dinner, the next expecting her to do his laundry. He urged her to attend the Harvard School of Business; he asked why she hadn't had children. For all his attempts to overcome his Victorian attitudes, he believed she really should have found a nice chap from Upper Canada College and made babies – boy babies. Her exposure to wealth didn't mean she had been encouraged to learn its management. Nor did she know anything about Canadian banks, having lived ten years abroad. The cash portion of the disbursement amounted to $4-million. The day she received the cheque, she couldn't have told you how a trust company differed from a merchant bank. She had no idea what to do with all this money.

John Tory would have been a good person to ask. One of Canada's eminent corporate lawyers, Tory had been Roy Thomson's personal advisor and estate planner. He administered the trust that disbursed the funds, having left the Toronto firm he headed with his twin brother – Tory, Tory, DesLauriers and Binnington – to oversee the Thomson empire. After Roy Thomson's death in 1976 the second Lord Thomson, Sherry's uncle Ken, decided to restructure the family holdings and move headquarters from Britain to Canada. Tory helped engineer the International Thomson takeovers of The Hudson's Bay Company (Thomson acquired a 75 per cent interest for $641-million) and FP Publications (it purchased the newspaper chain, which included *The Globe and Mail*, for $165-million). Because Tory represented the grandchildren collectively in the trust, he would have had a conflict of interest if he represented any one of them. He told Sherry she'd best get her own advisors.

That was fine with her. She wanted to keep her affairs separate from those of the family, lest bankers view her as a pipeline to Thomson money. Step one was to sever ties with the Royal Bank – Canada's largest – since family members sat on its board of directors. She hired a legal advisor, Stuart Butts, who steered her to the Bay and Richmond branch of the CIBC and introduced her to his assistant manager. Tom Johnson opened an account for her. Brian Molony inherited the account when he succeeded Johnson.

Brydson divided her money, placing half with an investment counsellor and half with the bank. She got into the stock market, developing a particular interest in oil and gas. She and her partner, Barb Elson, set up a Thai importing company, Eastern Accents, and began looking for a Victorian space in which to establish a Thai restaurant.

One potential site was a decrepit, unoccupied, four-storey building on Elm Street, a stone's throw from the raunchy Yonge Street Strip. The Elmwood Hotel had been home to many things in its ninety-year history, including the first YWCA in Canada, a halfway house for women discharged from mental institutions, an antique store, an optical factory, and a downtown youth centre. Its owners had tried to get permission to tear it down; it was so derelict that its occupancy permit covered only the ground floor and the basement. The building came with a ten-page list of outstanding work orders.

Brydson needed 8,000 square feet for the restaurant. If she bought the building, what would they do with the other 34,000 square feet? They had earlier done a feasibility study for a women's club, and the plans could easily be adapted to the Elmwood. They would put a spa on one floor, a French restaurant on another. Possibilities were endless. Encouraged by Barb Elson, Brydson became enchanted by the idea of The Elmwood Club. She purchased the building for $640,000, believing it would take $3.5-million to transform it.

Brydson planned to sell the club to its members, so The Elmwood was incorporated as an autonomous company that could be hived off. The Thai restaurant, Bangkok Garden, was incorporated separately. Soon she had a welter of companies: Toronto Health and Beauty Centres (the spa on the second floor of the building), Eastern Accents Trading (the importing operation),

Feung Fah Holdings (the real estate company, which owned the building and other Toronto properties), Feung West (which owned properties in Calgary and Canmore, Alberta), Willowbank (an oil-and-gas exploration company she created), Springbank (an oil-and-gas company she bought into and wound up owning), and Brydson Management (the operating company). The funding arm, which provided capital for each company, was called Westerkirk, after the Scottish town her maternal ancestors – the Thomsons – had come from.

Brydson's father, it turned out, knew Brian Molony's father. Glen Brydson had been an NHL hockey player, mostly with the Chicago Black Hawks, before putting together a stable of thoroughbreds. Dr. Molony was a familiar and well-liked figure at the morning workouts, and the two men became friendly. When Glen Brydson developed cancer in a lymph gland in his throat, Terry Molony did the surgery. Though delicate and uncertain, the operation was a success. Sherry told her father that Brian Molony was her banker. Glen Brydson said, "Terry Molony saved my life. If you're with his son, you're in capable hands."

Sherry Brydson didn't know what bankers were supposed to be like, but she was rather fond of Molony. Unlike many bankers, he had a sense of humour and enjoyed exercising his wit. She ribbed him about his ill-fitting suits and godawful ties. She was surprised he didn't smoke: burn-holes in his lapels would have fit his rumpled image. In a way they couldn't have been more different. She was a feminist, he a male chauvinist. Her tastes were cosmopolitan, his parochial. She was a graduate of the Cordon Bleu cooking school in France, a former food editor in Australia, and a budding restaurateur. He ate nothing but fast food and Coca-Cola. Over lunch they traded barbs, Molony making a face at each plate of Asian delicacies ("I'm a meat-and-potatoes man, myself"),

Brydson refusing to let him off the hook ("You flatter yourself, Brian"). She got him to try satay by assuring him it was fast food in Thailand.

When Brydson decided to invest in a cosmetics company, she went to Molony to negotiate her first loan. The company was badly managed but the product was good. There was talk of marketing the cosmetics through the spa at the women's club. Brydson set a limit on what she was prepared to lose: $50,000. Maybe it was a gamble, but she wanted to be an entrepreneur and entrepreneurs took risks. She needed to learn how to deal with the bank, how to manage people, how to handle an ailing enterprise. Wasn't that how Roy Thomson had made his fortune, by resuscitating businesses on the verge of bankruptcy? Maybe the talent was in her genes. If it wasn't, well, she would have got the equivalent of an MBA.

Her relations with Molony grew increasingly cordial. Because her stock certificates went directly from her broker to the bank, she alerted him each time she bought or sold shares. She traded actively; they spoke often. Molony was keenly interested in the market and happy to exchange street talk. When she did a loan proposal for the cosmetics company he was encouraging and helpful, recommending the loan. Alex Osborne recommended against it. The two men discussed it and Molony's enthusiasm carried the day – or so it seemed to Brydson. In fact, she kept term deposits as well as stock certificates at the branch, assets she planned to liquidate to pay for construction of the Elmwood. This abundant security and her personal guarantee meant the bank was not at risk.

Still, Molony's work delighted both his customer and his boss. Osborne was impressed that he had obtained Brydson's personal guarantee, and Brydson was impressed that he had got her the loan.

In December, Molony found himself in desperate need of cash. He and Brenda and another couple were leaving for Florida on Boxing Day, and he was determined to settle his loans first. The idea of being away for two weeks – turning over his post to Steve Richardson, his credit officer – nearly made him retch with anxiety.

He had debited the Koharski account a second time, taking another $35,000, and did not want to risk tacking on more. Shortly before Christmas he opened a new account in Sherry Brydson's name. This seemed natural enough: Brydson had been looking at deals in Oklahoma, and there was talk of merging her oil-and-gas companies with a U.S. exploration firm. For tax reasons, many corporate borrowers have two or three loan accounts – investment loan; operating loan; term loan. In this case it would seem the existing Westerkirk account was for Canadian dollars, the new Sherry Brydson account U.S. dollars. Like most corporate customers, she had presigned a number of promissory notes and lodged them with the bank, to be used as loan advances were required. The signed notes did not specify Westerkirk Holdings. If she had opened a second account – others at the branch assumed she had instructed Molony to do so – the notes could conceivably apply to it as well.

Molony created the documentation for a loan of $48,000 U.S., keeping it below $50,000 because of the trouble he'd had with the Sun Crown U.S.-cash parcel. The girl in the foreign-exchange department asked if the funds were to be credited to a branch account. No, he said, the customer wanted cash. He went to the head teller to order it.

The head teller reported the request to the branch accountant, who asked Molony about it. Caught off guard, he said Sherry Brydson needed cash to pay Christmas bonuses to her staff. Instantly he saw his error. Why, when Brydson's employees were in

Toronto, would she need American currency? The branch accountant didn't think to ask.

Brinks brought the cash in its Friday delivery. The money was on hand, his story satisfied everyone, the documentation was done. But Molony had said Brydson would pick it up. How could he obtain it? Suppose Brydson happened to call or drop by. Had he made the fatal blunder? Was there some other way to raise money? He could say Brydson had changed her mind, didn't need cash after all. No, that might arouse suspicion. Too rattled to think, he procrastinated. At closing time the teller asked him, "Is this lady coming or not?"

"She said she'd be here," said Molony. Brydson was viewed by some of the female staff as flighty – it figured she'd be late. "I'll phone her."

At ten after six the girl asked again.

"I just got a call from her," said Molony. "She'll be another half hour. Why don't you girls go ahead."

"You want me to give you the cash?"

"I'll sign for it," said Molony.

Half an hour later, pockets bulging, he locked the branch and headed for the races. Do-or-die weekend. Beck stood at $68,800 plus $27,000 U.S., Sun Crown at $50,000 U.S., Koharski at $54,500. And now there was Brydson's $48,000 U.S. Passing through the turnstiles at the track, hurrying up to where Beck and Colizzi were waiting, Molony felt a tremendous surge of emotion. For three months he'd been living a nightmare, but it was undeniably thrilling. Here comes the Banker along the rail, should be quite a finish . . .

At the races he lost $7,000.

After midnight he shot craps with a dozen other men in a Yonge Street hotel room and won $12,000.

Saturday morning he flew to Las Vegas, went to the casino nearest the airport, and played baccarat. He gambled through the afternoon, breaking only to bet basketball, hurrying from casino to casino, pausing to see who'd won the games, trying his luck at craps, heading up to the Tropicana beneath a canopy of stars, emerging into dazzling sunshine, the Barbary to bet the Sunday games, the Dunes to try his luck there, Caesars to play baccarat, the Barbary to check the scores, dice at the Flamingo, baccarat at the Marina, catching a hot streak that fizzled just in time for him to catch his flight home.

Dazed and dishevelled, his back sore from leaning over the crap table, eyes irritated by the cigarette smoke and processed air, knuckles burned from the baize, he looked like someone coming off a bender. He hadn't slept in thirty-six hours. In the cab to McCarran Airport he counted his money.

He had forty dollars less than the $48,000 he'd started with.

Brenda loved Christmas, and this year promised to be special. Brian's family was in Florida – his parents took a place in Fort Lauderdale – so he stayed Christmas Eve at the apartment. In the morning they exchanged gifts. He gave her a jewellery box, she gave him shirts and a sweater. They went off to see her family. Her father still worked for the manufacturing company, her mother part-time at the CIBC, but they had both developed serious health problems. Brenda spent as much time with them as she could. They had come to like Brian; Brenda's father made a point of inviting him to his monthly poker game, which Molony attended out of politeness. One of the other players was a police sergeant. The betting limit was twenty-five cents.

After breakfast they drove out to visit Sieg and Sheila at Dr. Molony's farm. Dr. Molony had bought the place when it was in the middle of nowhere. The land was scrub, the farmhouse a mess, but over fifteen years he'd built it into a self-sustaining dairy operation, thanks largely to Sieg Stadler. Sieg was a barrel-chested German who had emigrated after the war and viewed Canada as a land of boundless opportunity. All the Molonys were fond of him, but Mrs. Molony had a special affection. She was grateful that, by running the farm so ably, he took pressure off Dr. Molony, and she shared his interest in the market. Each time they got together they discussed their investments. Dr. Molony gave his wife a monthly allowance to run the household. Whatever she was able to save, she sunk into stocks. Sieg, too, studied the market, and whenever he had a little extra he put on his suit and went to see his broker. They both preferred highly speculative ventures, searching for the ten-cent bargain that would one day be worth five dollars.

All the Molony boys worked with Sieg, and the farm had become a rich repository of lessons and memories. Brian had spent five summers milking and haying and ploughing. One day, early the first summer, Sieg asked him to clean out a big tub of debris. Brian was afraid of what might be slithering around at the bottom and asked why he was getting all the dirty jobs. Sieg told him, "I'll never ask you to do anything I haven't done myself." Brian adopted the principle and applied it to his work at the bank.

After Brian's last summer on the farm, the barn was struck by lightning and burned to the ground. All the family gathered to help out and commiserate. It was shattering to see the charred corpses of cattle huddled together in the ruins, one of the most affecting experiences of Brian's life. Sieg, of course, was devastated. All his work had been wiped out. Rebuilding the dairy operation would have required a huge infusion of capital. There was talk of selling the place. Eventually they decided to turn it into a beef farm, and the hard work began all over again.

Sieg's honest labour, diligence, and loyalty were a formative example; in some ways Brian felt closer to him than to his own family. When Brian joined the CIBC, Sieg – with Brian's help – wrote one of the references the bank required of new employees ("I realize that six 'outstanding' marks may seem somewhat 'fishy.' However, anyone who starts work at six in the morning after finishing at midnight . . ."). When Sieg wanted a bank loan to play the stock market, he went to Brian for it.

Over Christmas drinks and Sheila's chocolate chip cookies, Sieg recalled some of Brian's misadventures. The Molonys all tended to be mechanically inept, but Brian was legendary. "He was all thumbs," Sieg told Brenda. "Any piece of equipment he was using automatically broke down. And then he'd be completely stuck. When Brian was around you couldn't take anything for granted. Things that are just commonsense were a mystery to him. But he was a bright boy, and nobody worked harder."

Sieg told Brenda about the time Brian had been carting hay from a farm several miles up the road. On a steep grade, trying to gear down, Brian depressed the clutch. The wagon, loaded with five tons of hay, took off. Sieg, ahead on the tractor, was about to cross the creek at the bottom of the hill when he saw the wagon bearing down on him, out of control. The bridge was barely wide enough for one vehicle. It seemed certain they'd crash. Sieg braced himself, but Brian managed to cut in front of him, missing the tractor by inches and careering wildly across the bridge. The wagon came to a stop on the far side; Brian climbed down like a shell-shocked survivor of a bombing. Miraculously, he hadn't even lost the load of hay. Everyone howled at the memory. It was Brian in a nutshell: saved from his ineptitude by his lifelong good luck.

Brenda couldn't understand why, when it seemed they were going to crash, Brian wouldn't have jumped off the wagon. Sieg shook his head. "Most people would have," he said, "but Brian wasn't the kind of boy who'd take the easy way out of something he'd got himself into. He'd see it through to the bitter end."

Brenda found it a wonderful luxury to spend so much time in Brian's company. She only wished he could be as happy as she felt. Back at the apartment, waiting for the late sports report, she fixed him a rum-and-Coke and tried to get him to open up. He assured her nothing was the matter. "What are you thinking about?" "Work," he said. "Business I should have tidied up." He was casting about for a way to back out of the Florida trip. Brenda was in such good spirits, though, that he couldn't bring himself to ruin her holiday.

On Boxing Day they picked up Ian and Jackie Stewart and set off in the Buick that Brian had bought off his father's lease. The customs officer in Detroit was amused that he was taking figure skates to Fort Lauderdale. His family exchanged gifts in Florida; the skates were for his sister. They drove straight through, taking turns at the wheel. Ian and Jackie felt the drive would have been more pleasant if the Buick's cruise control hadn't been broken, but there was no point even raising the idea of getting it fixed. Brian wouldn't spend the money. He'd driven the old Datsun for six months with no brakes.

They stayed in a one-bedroom condominium. The year before another couple had gone with them, and they'd spent the holiday tripping over one another. Four people was more comfortable than six, and they got along well together. The girls went shopping or hit the beach, the guys tossed a football or watched sports on TV. Brian organized an outing to Pompano. Each race they split a two-dollar ticket four ways. At poolside Brian never wanted to get the drinks; at the track, though, he always volunteered to go to the windows.

In the evenings they brought take-out food back to the condo. Everyone else was tired from the sun, so Brian went off by himself. He didn't say where he was going but Brenda had a good idea. There were other racetracks in the area, as well as greyhound races and a jai alai fronton. Brian was Brian. He didn't like doing nothing, got restless as a child. "Cabin fever," he called it. He and Brenda had bought some stock together, and each morning he went out early for the newspaper. Ian saw him at a payphone one day and asked who he'd called. "My broker," said Brian, who was always phoning his broker – from the bank, from McDonald's, from the pub they went to on Friday afternoons. In fact he was calling his credit officer. "Just thought I'd check in, Steve. Anything new?" Richardson wondered how Molony could enjoy his holiday when he thought constantly about work. Molony wondered what he'd do if Richardson said, "The auditors are in." Fly to Las Vegas, maybe, for one last shot. Perhaps if he made full restitution the bank wouldn't prosecute.

Brenda read his anxiety as that of a workaholic. Funny the way he resembled his father – even on vacation Dr. Molony was up for six o'clock Mass. When Brian suggested cutting the trip short, Brenda said, "Don't be crazy, we drove all the way down here to have a good time. Can't you just relax?" He thought of inventing an emergency that demanded his immediate return. It was a commonplace in the bank, though, to beware the employee who didn't like to be out of the branch. He had no choice but to sweat out the full two weeks.

On their last day in Florida they went to Pompano, sat through ten races, then drove twenty-four hours straight, hitting Windsor, Ontario, in time for the races there. "Let's stop," said Brian. "After the palm trees and blue skies, it'll be fun to see them running in the snow." The others were exhausted from the trip and eager to get home, but once Brian had made up his mind that was that. They watched every race, shivering and turning blue beneath their suntans.

Late Sunday, back in Toronto, Brian dropped off the others and then let himself into the branch. His "in" basket was overflowing. He found nothing alarming until he came on a memo from Osborne: "re Brydson: see me about her loans." Construction had begun on the Elmwood Club. No doubt Brydson had been in for more money, and Osborne had noticed she was near the branch limit.

The last thing Molony wanted was to have Alex Osborne looking into the Brydson loans. Osborne had been giving him more and more responsibility, including a multimillion-dollar construction loan. Osborne knew construction inside out, and Molony had picked his brains. How big are the lots? What will they sell for? How will the financials work? When will we get our money back? You mean the developer incorporates a separate company for each project so that one lawsuit won't destroy the whole works? Are personal guarantees available? What's the cost of servicing? What letters of credit will be needed? How much will be paid out when each lot is sold? Do they usually put the streets down the first year and pave them the second? Osborne gave him an instant education.

"But why all the questions? It's fully secured."

Next time somebody came in about a construction loan, said Molony, he wanted to know what to look for.

"Quite right," said Osborne. "Good work."

Nothing to do but wait till morning. The bank hockey team played Sunday nights, and Molony drove to the rink. He was not the most gifted athlete, but he was intense and aggressive. The hockey was non-contact, so he could only skate up and down like a madman. At midnight, when the ice time expired, he drove the icy streets, ate a hamburger, and studied Monday's entries. Then there was nothing left to do but go home to the empty house and lie awake.

In the morning he drove to the branch early and plunged into work. His panic subsided. So long as he was fully occupied he could keep anxiety at bay. When Osborne arrived he went and knocked on the door.

"Welcome back," said Osborne. "How was your Christmas? Good vacation?"

"I get sort of restless sitting around, but the weather was good. You wanted to see me about Brydson."

"They seem to have aggressive expansion plans. Maybe we should find out what their needs are going to be and advise Regional Credit Office. Let's arrange an authorized line of credit."

"I'll speak to her," said Molony. "I see Mark got two goals the other night. He's doing well."

"I was at that game," said Osborne, beaming. "He was the best player on the ice. If he keeps it up, we'll be watching an NHL player next year."

A couple of weeks into the New Year, Molony used the Sherry Brydson loan account for the second time. He debited her U.S.-dollar account by $45,000 and told the foreign-exchange girl the customer needed a bank draft payable to the Marina. On a bank draft the word "Marina" had a pleasantly nautical ring.

Molony flew to Las Vegas Saturday morning, took a cab to the Marina, and deposited the draft at the casino cage. Rather than cashing it, the cage held it and issued him chips. This ensured he'd remain at the Marina. He played continuously, breaking only to urinate. By Sunday afternoon he had taken $45,000 in markers. He settled the debt by signing over the draft.

Before flying home, Molony spoke with one of the pit bosses, a gangly fellow whose narrow face and pinched expression suggested intestinal distress. The Super Bowl was a week away, and Molony said he'd be coming down to bet the game. He'd have another draft and wanted to be sure the Marina would cash it for him. The Marina did not have a sports book; he'd be taking the proceeds elsewhere to bet the game. Would there be any problem, he wondered, cashing a $50,000 draft? The pit boss spoke to a superior and told Molony, "No problem. See you next week."

The following Saturday, Molony returned to Las Vegas. Again he had debited the Sherry Brydson account and brought a draft payable to the Marina. When he presented it at the casino cage, the clerk said she couldn't honour it. Molony spoke to the manager. Because the draft was drawn on the CIBC in San Francisco, he said, they had to cash it there. Molony explained that he'd made arrangements the previous weekend. Sorry, said the cage manager, I have my instructions.

The instructions had come from the casino manager, a corpulent man whom Molony found in the coffee shop, with two showgirls, eating ice cream. Molony explained that he'd come on the understanding the draft would be cashed.

"Bill said there'd be no problem."

"Bill gave you the wrong information."

"Why would you let me fly down here before telling me?"

"We phoned your travel agent. Didn't she call you?"

"Unfortunately not."

The casino manager shrugged and licked his spoon.

"I don't see why you'd tell me yes one week and no the next."

The casino manager looked Molony in the eye. "You're a banker."

"No I'm not," said Molony, feeling the blood rush to his face. "My brother is."

The casino manager smiled. "We'll take the draft to San Francisco on Monday. If they cash it, fine."

"The Super Bowl's tomorrow."

"Tell me about it," said the manager, and returned his attention to the ice cream.

The first time Molony tasted beer, having snuck into a pub with underage friends, he downed twenty-two draft. On the subway home he got sick, and he spent the night stumbling to the bathroom. That was it for beer – he vowed never to drink it again. When the manager said, "Tell me about it," that was it for the Marina – he'd never set foot in the place again. That was it for his travel agent – he'd get himself another one. Molony was livid at himself. "I'm not, my brother is." How dumb can you get? He shouldn't have tipped them off a week beforehand. He should have deposited the draft, started gambling at the Marina, cashing chips here and there, freeing up Super Bowl money that way. He should have realized they'd be less accommodating when they weren't getting his action. But why had they checked him out? Was it the bank draft, or was it Colizzi?

Colizzi had flown down a few days earlier and had had trouble finding a room. He'd gone to the Marina and used Molony's name. Molony was a big enough player that they accommodated his pal. Perhaps, though, Colizzi had done something stupid. Or perhaps they simply hadn't liked the looks of him and decided to investigate his friend.

Molony found Colizzi's room and banged on the door. Colizzi was in boxer shorts, drinking Courvoisier with two black girls who looked about twenty.

"Girls, this is Brian. This is Mary, this is Stephanie."

"Other way around," one of the girls giggled.

"Other way around is right," said Colizzi. "You ever had a doubleheader? Hey, what's the matter? Come on in, you want a drink?" He turned off the TV. "Listen, girls, we'll call it a day. Party's over." He pulled on his trousers and threw money on the unmade bed. "Get out of here. I mean it. Move!"

The girls tucked the money in their purses.

"Cheer up. What's the matter with my buddy?"

"Last week they tell me I'll have no problem cashing a draft. You show up, you're my friend, all of a sudden they won't cash it?"

"I couldn't get a room. I knew you gave them action. I didn't mean to screw nothing up."

"You start using my name and look what happens."

"That's too bad," said Colizzi. "That's terrible. Sit down. Can I pour you a drink?"

"No."

"Tell you what, I'll let you double up with me. We'll go for ten instead of the five. Make you feel better? You like the Eagles, right?"

"Meanwhile, I need something while I'm here."

Colizzi counted out four thousand.

Molony took the money to the Tropicana and made it last until seven the next morning. Colizzi was on an early flight back. Molony caught the same plane. He hated coming home broke, changing in Los Angeles or Chicago, killing time. He had an exceptional memory for his gambling experiences and found it acutely depressing to spend five hours on the plane, replaying the losing bets in his mind, wallowing in self-pity and self-contempt. To compound matters, winter was disrupting the east. The plane was unable to put down in Toronto and landed instead at Buffalo. More waiting.

Somebody organized a pool on when they'd get home. Somebody else offered even money they'd bus it. Colizzi had a deck of cards, and while they sat on the tarmac he and Molony played blackjack. By the time the plane took off, two hours later, Molony had lost $7,000.

"This is turning into a wonderful weekend."

"You got a break," said Colizzi. "Buffalo, should be U.S. dollars. I'll let you off with Canadian. Meanwhile, I never should have let you talk me into doubling up on the game. Am I crazy? The Eagles are too good."

Molony watched the Super Bowl with Brenda. She wanted to know who he was cheering for, so she could cheer. The Raiders' offensive line gave Jim Plunkett time to throw, and he hit for two touchdowns in the first quarter. At the half it was 14–3. In the third quarter he hit again. The Eagles were never in the game; the final was 27–10. For a moment, watching the revelry in the Raiders' dressing room, Molony almost wept. Why did it always happen this way? The ones he really needed were the ones he lost. Players were pouring champagne over the announcer's head. Everyone was laughing and shouting. Molony switched off the set. Why me, God? How much do I have to endure? I got myself into it, fair enough. Why can't I get myself out?

"How about dinner?" said Brenda. "Want to go to La Bruschetta?"

"You can't get out of there for under thirty dollars," said Molony. "What's wrong with Swiss Chalet?"

If no interest were paid for more than ninety days on a loan made by any branch of the Canadian Imperial Bank of Commerce, the loan had to be reported as irregular to downtown. At Bay and Richmond, the Nick Beck loan account was about to become reportable. Molony had imagined retiring the Beck loans with his Super Bowl and casino winnings; instead he had to use the Brydson account again. He took one of her presigned demand notes and filled in a figure that would allow him to pay down the reportable loans and leave him something extra to work with: $200,000. But how could he obtain use of the money? He couldn't simply issue a bank draft, forge Brydson's signature, and cash it, as he'd done with the Beck and Koharski accounts. A specimen of her signature was right there on the promissory note; besides, the branch wouldn't have that much U.S. cash on hand.

Ever since university Molony had maintained an account at Richardson Securities, a brokerage firm on Adelaide Street, a few blocks from Bay and Richmond. Stocks were no good – it would take too long to buy them, sell them, and get the money – but brokers also dealt in government of Canada bearer bonds. In the U.S. bonds were computerized, but in Canada the purchaser still had the option of taking physical possession. What if he had a CIBC bank draft issued in favour of Richardson's? What if he purchased bearer bonds, sold them to the securities department of his own bank, and credited the proceeds to the reportable loan accounts?

Molony told the foreign-exchange girl Sherry Brydson needed a $200,000 draft payable to Richardson Securities. The bank draft was the clerk's debit, the promissory note her credit. So long as everything balanced. He hurried out to lunch. For his weekly reckoning with Colizzi he had dipped into the Koharski account. While they waited for a table at Hy's, he slipped Colizzi an envelope containing $18,000.

"Worked out all right for you," said Colizzi, tucking his scarf into the sleeve of his cashmere coat. He pocketed the cash and signalled the maitre d'. "Bet down there, you'd have lost the whole fifty. I saved you money. I'll even pick up lunch."

The transaction at Richardson's went smoothly, and Molony

was able to pay down the reportable loans. But the incident at the Marina haunted him. They'd looked into his background and found out where he worked. What if they alerted the bank, or the police? Casinos weren't known for integrity, but what if? The more transactions, the more people and institutions involved, the more ways to be tripped up. His life had become an exquisite torture. He hadn't slept properly in months. This must have been part of a painful apprenticeship. He would win enough to repay the loans only if he had paid his dues. Each fraud was the last. When he had to borrow more it could only have been that the dues were insufficient. It would take an extraordinary streak to save him; he had to suffer extraordinarily to earn the streak. There was no way of knowing when it would come. There was no turning back. Like a man borne out to sea on the outgoing tide, he could only point to shore, keep the faith, and paddle like mad.

Meanwhile he was growing paranoid. He saw sharks everywhere. One morning he spotted an unfamiliar face in the branch and convinced himself the man was from head-office security. Turned out he was a computer guy, but dread became part of Molony's emotional reflex. Each morning when he rounded Simpsons and hurried down Bay Street his stomach seized. He couldn't help peering through the glass, looking for strangers. Any memo, any phone call, the most innocent inquiry . . .

"I don't know if I should tell you this," Ian Stewart, a credit officer, said one afternoon, "but there's some interesting stuff going on in the branch."

"It's a big branch," said Molony.

Stewart viewed Molony as an older brother, though he was actually two years Molony's senior. "Listen, this is for your ears only. I don't know if we should tell Mr. Osborne. There's some undercover work being done in the branch."

"How do you know?" Molony said evenly.

"Well, I bumped into an old friend of mine by the elevators. He tried to avoid me. I couldn't figure it out. I asked him what he was doing here and he said not to tell anyone."

"What was his big secret?"

"The guy's an undercover RCMP officer. They're in that room upstairs, behind the supply room."

"The one that used to be the loans office? It's locked."

"They're in there, running a wiretap."

"Why would they use that room for a wiretap?"

"You have to be within a certain distance of the phone you're tapping. I wonder if we should tell Mr. Osborne."

Scared witless, Molony tried to think what he'd let slip on the phone. Nothing about the loans that he could recall. But what if they were monitoring his calls with the bookies?

"What do you think?" said Stewart.

"I think Mr. Osborne would appreciate having that information."

After that Molony took care to deal with Colizzi in person, meeting in the basement of Simpsons or betting the ball games at the racetrack. Beck didn't like the phone to begin with. If they didn't meet at the track, Molony dropped by the dress shop. Even there Beck was jumpy, scrutinizing each car that drove by, worried about surveillance. They stepped into the storage area, amid racks of dresses, to do business.

Just as Molony's anxiety about the RCMP was easing, Sherry Brydson called to say she wanted to see him. She was forever wanting to update him about the club, changes in plans, exploration activity in Alberta. Like Brenda, she used the word "relationship" in a way that made him cringe. She wanted a better relationship with the bank: wanted to meet more people, keep them abreast of things, get more feedback. Molony wanted to keep her as quiet as possible. Because she hired women she was viewed by the bank as a radical feminist – in the upper echelons, a radical feminist was any woman not serving coffee – and because of her eclectic interests she was seen as wingy.

The bank invited important customers to lunch on the fifty-sixth floor of Commerce Court. At one such lunch Brydson got talking about Thailand. One of the senior bankers asked if Thailand had a serious drug problem. Brydson replied that the major problem was the smuggling of heroin through Bangkok, where much of the downtown real estate seemed to have been financed by money from the opium and heroin trades. As for Thai people, she said, they often used drugs in cooking. She told the story of asking her Thai maid to prepare a curry. Because of her allergies Brydson couldn't eat airline food. She ate the curry on the plane, fell asleep in New Delhi, and didn't wake up until the plane landed in Toronto. When she returned to Bangkok the cook asked, knowingly, if Brydson had had a good flight. The cook had laced the curry with marijuana. Shows you how widespread drugs are in Thailand, said Brydson, laughing at the memory. Jungle curry, the Thais call it.

In the private diningroom of the CIBC, throats were cleared, crystal glasses raised, linen napkins touched to lips. The story became part of bank lore. The context gradually faded away, the curry turned into hash brownies, and Sherry Brydson came to be seen not merely as an amateur who was burning Thomson money while trying to put together some sort of farfetched girls' club, but also as a superannuated hippie who consumed cannabis in order to sleep on the plane. Senior bankers did not consume cannabis. They did not sprinkle their conversation with references to karma, astrology, and vitamin B6 therapy. They were not "into" anything. They did not use the phrase "touchy-feely," and they did not, speaking of a multimillion-dollar project, shrug and say, "Whatever happens, happens." Brydson's charm was lost on the executive floor at Commerce Court. The more senior people she was exposed to, the more chance she'd spook someone important.

"I wondered if I could drop by in half an hour."

"What would you like to talk about?" said Molony.

"I think you know."

Had she learned of the discrepancy? Was she coming to confront him? Molony could only let her play her hand. Swallowing anxiety, he ushered her into his office. She chatted about some fittings she was having shipped from Bangkok. She told a funny story about her trip to Calgary. She talked about the frustrations of dealing with contractors. The meeting, it seemed, was just an excuse to get out of her office. She wanted someone to talk to and, like most women, she found Molony a good listener.

Several girls at the bank confided in him, knowing their secrets would go no further. One woman had told him about her marital troubles. Molony listened sympathetically and asked what she was going to do. "I don't know," she said, meeting his eye. "Maybe what I need is an affair." He pretended not to have twigged. "I don't think that would solve anything. I think it might complicate your problems."

Another girl in the branch had come to him for advice. She was a fetching young teller whom a customer had asked for a date. When she turned him down, explaining she was engaged, he offered her a thousand dollars to go to dinner. She was in her teens, earned $11,000 or $12,000. A thousand dollars must have seemed a fortune. She wondered if it would be all right to accept. "Anybody who offers you a thousand dollars is after more than dinner," Molony told her. "I think it would be unwise." She later told him she had broken up with her fiancé. "Be careful," he counselled.

"You're vulnerable. Watch what happens on the rebound." Next thing she was in tears. She'd dated one of the other assistant managers. She felt lonely and hurt, he seemed to care, he invited her in, she'd had too much to drink . . . oh, it was awful, now he didn't have the time of day for her. Molony sympathized and consoled her. He couldn't help wondering if a girl who'd been offered a thousand dollars for a date would go out with him for nothing.

We're going to bet the one the pencil lands on? Isn't it exciting! How can you sit there like it's nothing? Where do you take the ticket? Why does that horse have bandages on its legs? How much money do the drivers earn? What do these symbols mean on the program? You're kidding! You have an interest in horses yourself? How old are you, Brian? You seem older. You sure know a lot for someone who's only twenty-five.

On the way home she told him what fun she'd had, a wonderful evening. Molony got the idea she wouldn't refuse his advances. He wasn't tempted – sex had never been a big deal – and he'd already won his bet with himself. She'd gone out with him for nothing. Besides, he was now living with Brenda – sort of. He had moved out of his parents' home and changed travel agents, again, when the agent sent his Las Vegas tickets to the house. That had taken some fast talking. Better to leave than to risk more screwups. His mother had a sixth sense about these things. She once followed him to St. Mike's and found him in the variety store, betting baseball. She cried in despair and told Dr. Molony, who strapped his son. Molony had to control very carefully who knew what. His life had become unending subterfuge. His parents thought he roomed with Eli. Koharski called Brenda to say Brian's parents were trying to reach him. He's not with me, she said, their wires must have got crossed. Hadn't Brian said he was going out to dinner with them? Or was it Eli who'd said he thought Brian was seeing his parents?

Was she the one who'd got confused? Had he said it, or had she just assumed . . .

Sherry Brydson chattered on. She told Molony how the club was shaping up, and they traded gossip about stocks. He let slip that he'd bought shares in a company she had mentioned. She had told him about the stock so that he'd expect the certificate from Wood Gundy; she certainly wasn't recommending it. It floored her that a banker would involve himself in a customer's affairs, but then Brian was not the typical banker.

Molony nodded and smiled. He couldn't bring himself to meet her eye. The fictitious Sherry Brydson account now showed almost $300,000 in loans she knew nothing about and he had no way of repaying. On her way out she stopped abruptly, as if she'd forgotten something. Molony froze.

"Thank you, Brian."

"Are you being sarcastic?"

Men. Bankers.

"I just wanted you to know that I appreciate everything you've done for me."

A week later, more deeply in the hole than ever to Beck, Epstein, and Colizzi, Molony booked a Saturday-morning flight to Philadelphia, as close as he could get to Atlantic City by commercial airline. Needing U.S. currency, he ordered a cash parcel from the head teller, debiting the Koharski account. He needed more than the $48,000 he could get through the branch. God, he was almost half a million dollars in debt to the bank. His only chance was to put together a substantial chunk to work with.

He had a certified cheque made out to Deak Perera, a currency dealer on King Street. At lunch he picked up his plane ticket, then went to Deak's, stood in line, and told the girl he wanted to cash the cheque. She asked for identification. Though the cheque was certified, she said, "I'll have to confirm this." Molony panicked: if a security guard hadn't been inside the door he might have fled. Thank heavens the money was drawn on his own account. Still, he didn't want anyone at the branch to know of his dealings and the sum was enough to attract attention. He could think of no way to stop the girl from phoning. She made the call while Molony, trying to appear nonchalant, felt the sweat trickle down his ribs. The girl returned and cheerfully counted out $10,000 U.S.

Molony tucked the cash in his pocket and got out. Back at the branch he spoke to the woman who'd taken the call. He mentioned he'd needed U.S. cash for his brother and apologized for the trouble. "No trouble," said the woman, busy with something else. "They were just making sure the certification was good." He had scraped through, but not without grief. That was it for Deak Perera.

Just south of Richmond on Bay Street was another currency dealer, Friedberg & Co. A few days later Molony had another certified cheque drawn on his account and took it to Friedberg's. The clerk cashed it without hesitation. That was more like it. Molony tucked the money away, returned to his office, and added it to the cash in his credenza. That afternoon, Brinks made its Friday delivery. The head teller informed him his cash had arrived. He went downstairs and signed for it.

Friday afternoons were wonderful. He'd survived another week. He had two days' grace. He'd put together a sizeable piece of working capital and had a marvellous feeling the apprenticeship was over. He called Brenda to say sorry, something urgent had come up and he wouldn't be able to see her on the weekend. How about going to the new Neil Simon play on Monday night instead? Strange, he was in a worse fix than ever but had never felt more exhilarated. An hour to post time, and that was just the start. In his pocket were plane tickets and almost $100,000 U.S. In the morning he was on his way to the casino. Not just any casino – his lucky one. The one that, after the most excruciating five months of his life, would finally lay his problems to rest.

4

ATLANTIC CITY

"Cities are for needs and wants, divine Father, that cannot be met in isolation. Have we expected from them too much and put in too little?"
– The Christophers

Molony climbed aboard the shuttle van at Philadelphia Airport. Through his fatigue he felt a pleasing buzz of anticipation. It was a splendid Saturday, the kind of winter morning that promised spring. He had not slept. Colizzi and Beck ran a dice game, and after the harness races he'd gone to the Westbury. People didn't show up until midnight; Molony couldn't bear to wait, so he played blackjack with Colizzi and lost ten thousand dollars. Shooting craps he won more than twenty thousand. By then it was five in the morning. After a burger, a shower, and the flight from Toronto, he felt confident and eager to get started. Why wasn't the van moving? The driver had been instructed to make the run with a full load. It was almost nine o'clock – they'd barely make the ten o'clock opening as it was. Molony suggested to the others that they all kick in to pay for the empty seats.

"Folks sure be eager to lose your hard-earned pay," said the driver, setting off through the warehouses and refineries of southwest Philadelphia. They crossed the Delaware River and before long were speeding past pine forests and fertile farmland. Billboards advertised casino shows and slot payoffs and parking deals. The expressway was surprisingly busy; stretch limos glided silently past, and buses belched diesel fumes as they roared by. Molony, suddenly drowsy, pictured himself in the casino, starting with craps, then moving to baccarat . . .

He opened his eyes to see huge red letters on a concrete overpass: WELCOME TO ATLANTIC CITY. Though he had dozed only half an hour he felt fully refreshed. He patted the bundles of cash in his pockets. Off to the left, cars were parked in long rows and shuttle buses were picking up casino employees. Beyond the salt marsh rose the city's skyline, a jagged mix of demolition and construction. The expressway ended abruptly; the van continued along the one-way streets of Atlantic City.

Molony had grown up amid the leafy spaces and sober affluence of Moore Park in Toronto. Inglewood Drive was a particularly charming street. The family home was a three-storey, five-bedroom, red brick house fronted by a grey stone wall and backing on a deep ravine. One of the papers ran a photo of Molony's oldest brother presenting Gina Lollabrigida with flowers when she took up residence in the palatial house on the corner. The children's upbringing had been privileged but not extravagant. Even a surgeon's income had to be carefully budgeted when there were nine children to clothe and feed and send off to Catholic schools; besides, Dr. Molony's beliefs led him to practise thrift and charity. He spent little on himself, invested shrewdly, and donated substantial sums to Catholic agencies.

Having been raised in this environment, and having never travelled, Brian Molony had gained his knowledge of destitution largely from television. Parts of Atlantic City reminded him of news footage of Beirut, people carrying on against a backdrop of house-to-house combat. Piles of debris alternated with burned-out buildings. A rusted car lay upside down on a vacant lot, rudimentary as something washed up on the beach. Black children played ball in the tiny courtyard of a grim, two-storey tenement dotted with graffiti and smashed windows and For Sale signs: "This prime property . . ."

Hard to believe the place had once flourished as a holiday and convention town, "the Queen of Resorts." It had been transformed from a fishing village by the advent of train travel. A link was opened between Atlantic City and Philadelphia in 1880, and before long the place had running water, paved streets, and arc lamps, drawing vacationers from Washington and Pittsburgh, Baltimore and New York. By the turn of the century it had become a popular, schlocky resort, with a gigantic, three-tiered carousel, dance halls, vaudeville shows, Steel Pier, forty-foot-wide boardwalk, the Moorish Palace, the London Ghost Show, the Haunted Swing, and Guvernator's Mammoth Pavilion.

Just as one century's advance in mass transportation made the place, the next century's unmade it. Inexpensive air travel marked the start of Atlantic City's decline. Resort destinations once inaccessible to the middle class were now only a couple of hours and a few hundred dollars away. The big old hotels suffered impossible vacancy rates and fell into disrepair. By the early 1960s tourism had slowed to a trickle, and Atlantic City found itself afflicted with the problems that beset most cities in the northeastern United States. In its heyday Atlantic City had been a twelve-week town, generating so much business between Memorial Day and Labour Day that many residents earned enough to see them through the year. Now the summer unemployment rate exceeded 20 per cent. There was no economic diversity to fall back on. The population dwindled, from a peak of about 60,000, and fewer homeowners were left to pick up the tax bill. Property values fell while property taxes rose;

more people departed; those who remained were mostly those who couldn't afford to leave, the elderly and the unskilled. Atlantic City clung to its enduring distinctions – home of the Miss America Pageant, site of the longest wooden boardwalk in the world, inspiration for the game of Monopoly – but it had become as bereft as the derelicts Molony studied, with pity and fascination, through the window of the shuttle van.

Many northeastern states felt the effects of America's growing attraction to the Sunbelt. In New Jersey, one proposed solution to the economic problems was casino gambling. The idea wasn't new. Atlantic City had long had a carnival atmosphere, with "Skillo" games on the Boardwalk and more lucrative action tucked out of sight. On August 31, 1899, *The Atlantic Review* included a report of gambling on races, faro, and roulette at a mansion in Margate. By the 1950s the question of legalized gambling was being debated, and in 1974 made it to a referendum. New Jerseyians were asked whether they were in favour of making casino gambling legal throughout their state. More than 60 per cent were opposed. Two years later, on a second referendum, they were asked if they favoured legalized gambling only in Atlantic City. This time 56 per cent said yes, and the city's residents celebrated what the proponents of casino gambling promised would be an urban renaissance. Jobs would be created, money would pour in, and Atlantic City would be restored to its former glory.

Molony watched a hooker in white leather shorts and a white fur coat emerge from a 7-Eleven. A sign in the storefront next door said: "Card reading, $1." Old Will's Liquors and Wines. Connie's Arcade. First Jersey National Bank. Live nude show, private booths. Praise the Lord Parking. New Jersey State Lottery. Three men sat on the stoop of a boarded-up restaurant, passing a bottle. The van turned a corner, and huge red-on-gold mock-Roman letters spelled the word "Caesars."

"Welcome to our fair city," said the driver. "Police got better things to do than go looking for you. Want to stretch your legs, best keep to the Boardwalk. And don't get greedy now. The minute you're up a million dollars, quit."

At the same table where, six months earlier, he had won $12,000 learning craps, Molony lost his entire stake – nearly $100,000 – in an hour. Cursing himself, disconsolate, he watched basketball in one of the bars, killing the hours until it was time to fly home. He called Brenda to say hi, then phoned Colizzi. Mario was out, said his father, but they reached him with the beeper and Colizzi had Molony paged at the casino. Molony said he wanted his limit raised, wanted to double up on all the horse and sports bets he'd made. His timing could not have been worse – he had one of the most miserable weekends of his handicapping life. When Monday came around he owed Colizzi $30,000.

Having paid down the Koharski loan with money from the Brydson account, Molony was able to debit Koharski again. He put through a $30,000 loan advance. The branch didn't have that much cash on hand, however, so he had to issue an interbranch settlement form allowing him to pick up the money at Commerce Court. He hurried across the street to Simpsons. Colizzi was waiting in the basement.

"Come on, we've got to go downtown for it."

"What are you talking about?"

"We don't have cash at the branch."

In biting cold, Molony, without a coat, led the way to the gleaming, fifty-eight-storey headquarters of the CIBC. Colizzi, with his cashmere overcoat and flabby, unshaven jaw, looked like a character in a gangster film. Molony didn't want to be seen with him but Colizzi couldn't pick up the cash by himself. The 343 form was an internal bank document that would not normally be handed over to a customer. The two men pushed through revolving doors into the mammoth foyer and presented themselves at the counter.

"Brian Molony, Bay and Richmond. I called earlier. This is Mr. Colizzi. Rush order for some cash." He handed over the 343 form and his business card. "Could you look after him, please?"

Molony thanked the girl, shook hands with Colizzi, and hurried back to the branch. He hadn't been at his desk five minutes when Alex Osborne appeared.

"Who's Mario Colizzi?"

Molony feared he'd lose control of his bowels. He hadn't even written up the loan yet. How could Osborne have known about it?

"New customer."

"Downtown's on the line. This Colizzi is trying to get some cash."

"I'll handle it if you like. What line?"

"Line two," said Osborne, and walked out.

Molony stared at the flashing button. He drew a calming breath and punched it. "Molony here."

"It's Commerce Court. We've got a gentleman trying to pick up some cash on an interbranch settlement?"

"Right." A gentleman.

"The spelling of his name doesn't match the spelling on his driver's licence."

"Our fault," said Molony. "I'll authorize that."

Colizzi was furious. That night at the racetrack he ranted. What did Molony take him for? They'd kept him waiting half an hour, grilled him, made him feel like a criminal. No more bullshit, picking it up at the bank. Molony assured him it wouldn't happen again. Damn right it won't, said Colizzi, dampening his distress with Courvoisier. Want to play, settle up like anybody else. Now who do you like in the first?

Directly across the street from the Bay and Richmond branch of the CIBC, not fifty yards away, was the City Hall branch. Rumours sometimes circulated that the two branches would be merged. Not long after Molony had begun defrauding the bank there were new rumblings from downtown about "rationalization of the branch system." Word had it that Russell Harrison himself had walked up Bay Street, looked from one corner to the other, and said, "What the hell." In early 1981 it was confirmed that the branches would be amalgamated. Speculation began about staffing – some people would be transferred, others asked to take different positions – and about who would manage the combined branch.

The manager at City Hall, Harry Buckle, had enjoyed a steady, unspectacular career in the bank. With his white hair, glasses, and fresh-shaved, pink cheeks, he was the perfect grandfatherly manager. He had grown up on the prairies; his father had been Saskatchewan's agriculture minister in the 1930s. Buckle attended the University of Saskatchewan and then joined the federal bureau of statistics. A year cured him of his desire to be a civil servant. He did postgraduate work in commerce at the University of Toronto and then joined the bank. His climb up the ladder was orderly and typical – he started in the branches, joined the audit staff, went back out to the branches, worked in the credit department, went back out to the branches, moved to San Francisco as an assistant vice-president, came back to the credit department, then managed the Westdale branch in Hamilton and the main branch in Halifax before moving to Toronto to manage City Hall branch.

The smart money was on Alex Osborne to head up the enlarged Bay and Richmond, which overnight would become one of the biggest and most profitable of the CIBC's 1,600 branches. Osborne's career had been exemplary; he confided to friends that he would one day like to be president of the bank. He was a bit rough around the edges for the top ranks – too quick to tell people what he really thought of them – but his skills and diligence were unquestioned. He would relish the challenge of overseeing the merger and turning the combined branch into a thriving concern. Here was another feather for his cap.

Harry Buckle, on the other hand, thought the merger ill-advised. He had audited City Hall in the 1950s and, when he returned a quarter-century later, found some of the same women at the branch. It would be a terrible disruption in their lives, to say nothing of his own. Buckle was from the old school. Though the Imperial Bank had merged with the Bank of Commerce two decades earlier, he still thought of himself as an Imperial man. He had never learned computers. He had a reliable senior assistant in John Galbraith, good rapport with his customers, and an array of handsome accounts, from Windfields Farm to Peoples Jewellers. An avid golfer, he was invited each year to Alan Eagleson's tournament and got to play with Marcel Dionne, the hockey star, whose investment account Eagleson maintained at the branch. Buckle had a home in Burlington, around the lake, to which he planned to retire. He was comfortably ensconced in what he'd thought would be his last posting.

When word came that Buckle had been appointed to head up the merged branch and Osborne transferred to Lawrence and Keele – an important branch in a terrible mess – the employees at Bay and Richmond were shocked and disappointed. Osborne had instilled pride, and it manifested itself in mild contempt for the employees across the street. They didn't know the meaning of work. The assistant managers had so little on their plates they chatted for half an hour at a stretch. Harry Buckle sometimes nodded off at his desk after lunch at the National Club.

No one was more disappointed than Molony. He was losing his mentor and his status as favourite son. He helped organize the goodbye roast for Osborne, and gave a speech no one else could have got away with, taking liberties with Osborne's life story (Osborne was sensitive about his immigrant background) and lacing his remarks with innuendo ("and then he met his lovely wife Nora – 'No' for short"). Harry Buckle dropped by to pay his respects, then slipped out. He preferred to socialize outside bank circles. Besides, this party had nothing to do with him. Sixty people were saying farewell to a boss whom – whether they all liked him or not – they obviously admired and respected.

The merger went smoothly, as mergers go. Still, there was mass confusion. People worked long hours of overtime and came in on Saturdays. Nobody was quite sure where things were. Incoming cheques, for example – it might be days before they could be located. There was friction among staff members. They may all have been under the same roof, but they thought of themselves as City Hall people or Bay and Richmond people. Harry Buckle found it a nightmare. He had to rely heavily on his assistants. John Galbraith had come over as senior assistant, but most of the others were Bay and Richmond people. Buckle didn't have the proper controls, and he had to acquaint himself with a new set of accounts. The combined total – 1,500 or so – meant he was lucky to review them once in a blue moon. Rumour had it the branch would be audited after the merger, so the new manager would start with a clean slate. The audit had to be postponed while things got sorted out. Quarters were cramped and chaotic. The atmosphere was one of frenzied work amid near confusion. For Buckle the move had been a promotion, but if he'd known what he was in for he would have told downtown what they could do with their appointment.

It didn't take Molony long to make up his mind about Harry Buckle. He was no Alex Osborne. Still, Molony was not unhappy to have a less rigorous boss. The merger meant a review of security and inspection of existing accounts; if he survived the transition, though, he stood a better chance of recouping his losses under Buckle than he would have under Osborne. Buckle wasn't the type to throw a writeup on your desk and say, "Who's this?" He was more likely to pull out snapshots of his curling buddies, or the fish he'd landed on his holiday.

Buckle at first was equally cool on Molony. He didn't really understand why Osborne thought so highly of him. Molony was bright, certainly, with a good command of the language. He attended all the functions and coached the girls' softball team. Everyone liked him: you didn't hear a bad word from staff or customers. He arrived early and stayed late.

But he didn't have the experience. John Galbraith, by contrast, had worked in Blyth, Ontario, for a year, then Dublin, Ontario, then Bloor and Church in Toronto, three years in the Bahamas, a year at University and Dundas, three years as a credit officer at Commerce Court, two years as assistant manager at Yonge and Eglinton, a year at Bay and Gerrard, and two years as assistant manager at Dundas and Victoria before moving to City Hall as Buckle's senior assistant. Molony had joined Bay and Richmond as a credit officer; two years later he was an assistant manager. He applied himself, no question, but he had his finger in so many damn pies and took so many calls and saw so many people he was always late with his work. Documentation was on its way, this or that was "to follow," the report would be in tomorrow.

"Brian, if you're behind," Buckle said one day, "maybe we should assign some of your accounts to someone else."

Molony didn't object, just squinted through his glasses, considering. "If you don't mind," he said, "I'd prefer to keep them myself."

Molony had begun flying to Philadelphia and taking the shuttle van to Atlantic City two or three times a month. On an early trip he asked a credit executive if Caesars would reimburse his plane ticket. That was done in Las Vegas, he was told, but not in Atlantic City. "We have a very strict Casino Control Commission here in New Jersey." Before long his action had become substantial enough that the casino not only paid for his flights but also comped his "RFB" – room, food, and beverage bills – while he was at Caesars.

One Saturday morning Molony drove out to Pearson International Airport in Toronto with more than $120,000 U.S. cash in his pockets. Passing through customs was always a trial. Anything over $5,000 had to be declared. He worried that his bag might be searched but figured they'd need a good reason to search him bodily, so he always carried the money in his pockets. Usually the questions were routine, and usually the customs officer was a man. This time he handed his ticket to the one female officer on duty. A stocky, broad-cheeked, grey-haired woman, she studied him intently and wanted to know everything – citizenship, occupation, destination, how long he'd be away, whether he'd booked a hotel, how much money he had, how often he travelled to the U.S., whether he'd be conducting business. He said he was going to the Meadowlands – a racetrack in New Jersey – to look at a standardbred investment. She spoke to one of the other guards. He glanced at Molony and said something that made the woman smile. For an awful moment Molony was sure he'd be searched. But when the woman returned she merely looked for his name in a big black book, then waved him through.

That was it for women customs officers.

Molony was at the drinking fountain, trying to pull himself together, when he felt a tap on his shoulder. A branch customer in the mortgage business, Michael Wynston, said hello and introduced his wife. They were obviously headed somewhere sunny. The Philadelphia flight continued on to Florida. They could have been on the same plane.

"So, Brian, where you headed?"

"Philadelphia," said Molony. "Visiting my aunt. She's getting on in years and hasn't been well lately. My parents couldn't get away, so I'm going as the family representative."

Wynston was so impressed he told his business partner, who also knew Molony from the bank. "Isn't that a fine young man? I tell you, that boy's got moral fibre. Who else would do that? Would you take the weekend to go see your sick aunt in Philadelphia?"

As Molony's trips to Atlantic City grew more frequent, so did his lunch-hour visits to Richardson Securities. He found it useful to purchase bearer bonds, paying for them with a bank draft and immediately selling them back to the bank. At Richardson's he was assumed to be acting for a group of investors – his account was in the name "Brian Molony in Trust." At Bay and Richmond he was assumed to be acting on the instructions of a customer who wished to apply the proceeds from the sale of the bonds against an outstanding loan. In this way he was able to take funds from one fictitious account and use them to pay down another. The brokerage firm provided him with an efficient way of juggling money.

Before long all the fraudulent accounts were overloaded. He'd tacked so much onto the Brydson U.S.-dollar loan he didn't dare add more – indeed, he had to reduce it before it attracted attention.

If he was going to win enough to retire the bad loans he needed a new source of funds and more flexibility. The problem became acute after a wretched weekend in Atlantic City and a losing streak at the track. He was stone broke; he owed Epstein, Beck, Colizzi, and a fourth man; he had no idea where the money might come from.

Leo Sherman? Not Leo Sherman. No.

Unable to find a solution, he invented one. He created the documentation for a loan to a nonexistent gentleman named Roger Oskaner and began placing orders for cash parcels on Oskaner's behalf. Oskaner also paid for the bank drafts with which Molony purchased U.S. cash from Friedberg's – casino money. When the Oskaner loan got too high, Molony bought bearer bonds from Richardson Securities, paid for by Brydson, and used the proceeds to get Oskaner back down to his supposed limit.

Molony's broker at Richardson's was a middle-aged, bespectacled history buff named Jim Surgey. Ever since Molony first opened an account, Surgey had been impressed by him. Some clients weren't the sort of people you'd go out of your way to have a meal with, but Brian was an exemplary fellow embarked on what promised to be a fine career. A bright, pleasant, responsible young man.

Surgey was delighted when Brian resumed his activity at Richardson's. If he seemed to be dealing in substantial sums, well, he was acting for a group of investors – they wanted to do this, they'd decided to do that. Evidently they wanted short-term security that offered the chance of appreciation and was available for immediate delivery. Lots of investors did. Government bonds were liquid and secure. Brian was the bearer. If he was unusually young to be shouldering such financial responsibility, well, his knowledge of the bond market was certainly sound. He studied balance sheets and knew how to read them. Presumably he had access to the

CIBC's research facilities. At the bank he must have been highly regarded – he would never have been promoted at his age had he not been quality material. Surgey had been in the Navy at eighteen, and you saw lots of people in their twenties in positions of power.

When Molony began turning over hundreds of thousands of dollars a week, Surgey did ask, in avuncular fashion, "Sure you're not getting in over your head?" A friendly expression of concern – it would never even cross your mind . . . You deal with a good many clients over the years and learn it's better, if there's any question, to have nothing to do with them. You don't want to send a fat commission walking out the door, but it's not worth getting into anything that might be shady. There are lots of brokers out there. If a client gives you a funny feeling, let him find another one.

Brian was not that sort. Not pushy, or flashy, or full of promises. Not a promoter. On the contrary, he was quiet, sensible, and informed. Nor was he a cold fish like some bankers. He had a sound mind and a sharp wit. He came from a good family. Surgey knew people at St. Michael's who thought the world of Dr. Molony – fine surgeon, involved in charitable work, past president of the Otolaryngological Society, and so forth. Brian's documentation was always in order. And he was meticulous in meeting his obligations, not one of those people who say, "I'll have the cheque tomorrow," then don't show.

One afternoon Surgey had to track him down in Owen Sound, north of Toronto, where Molony was attending the opening of a plaza the bank had helped finance. A stock he had shorted had jumped in value: Surgey informed him he had to cover his position immediately. Next morning, when Surgey dropped by the branch, Molony had a draft for $60,000, just as he'd promised. No, there was nothing about him to create even a scintilla of doubt.

He wasn't merely a client who aroused no suspicion, he was as active, well-financed, and conscientious an investor as any broker could hope for.

One Saturday afternoon, Molony was signing a marker in the dice pit at Caesars in Atlantic City when a fresh-faced man in his early thirties introduced himself. He had curly brown hair, glasses, and manicured nails, and wore a flannel suit, striped shirt, and silk tie.

"Brian, Michael Neustadter. Anything we can do for you, please let me know."

Molony kept a low profile in the casino, revealing nothing about himself, but his cash deposits and repeated losses were buying attention. Michael Neustadter was director of casino credit at Caesars, an important position he had come by through paternalism. His family was well known in Atlantic City. His father, Milton Neustadter, had once been an owner of Steel Pier and was one of the principals in Jemm Co., the company that built the Howard Johnson's on the Boardwalk in the late 1960s. When Michael graduated from Temple University in business administration, he took over management of the motor hotel.

In the 1970s Jemm was enthusiastic in support of casino gambling, contributing financially to the cause. The first company to file application to operate a casino in Atlantic City was Resorts International. Resorts opened its doors on Memorial Day in 1978. It was overrun. Gamblers crushed around the blackjack tables, five deep, betting on other players' hands. Some people wet their pants rather than relinquish their seats. It was clear there was a fortune to be made, and other companies scrambled to get in on the action. Playboy Enterprises intended to build a casino near Convention Hall; Bally, the world's biggest maker of slot machines, had leased the Marlborough-Blenheim Hotel; Penthouse planned to build on the site of the old Mayflower Hotel. Gaming interests were investing enormous sums to get in on the booty.

Jemm cut a sweetheart deal with Caesars World, the company that owned Caesars Palace in Las Vegas and Caesars Tahoe in Stateline, Nevada, as well as honeymoon resorts in the Poconos. Caesars leased the Boardwalk property and, instead of building from scratch, used the existing, 425-room motor hotel as the basis of a complex that included a 527-room hotel, eight bars and restaurants, and 48,630-square-foot casino. In addition to substantial rent, Jemm received 19.3 per cent of net profits. Milton Neustadter and Sonny Goldberg, the operating investors in Jemm, got offices and titles and handsome salaries for performing duties that were, in the words of Milton Neustadter, "practically whatever we want them to be." Their sons, Michael Neustadter and Roy Goldberg (brothers-in-law, Neustadter having married Goldberg's sister), were also hired by Caesars. Michael was given a five-year contract. He began as general manager of the hotel, but soon moved over to the casino side and ended up in charge of casino credit. Roy Goldberg ended up in charge of casino marketing. Jemm thus had fingers on the two critical pulse points of the new casino.

Most key casino employees at Caesars had come east from Nevada. They had spent years working their way up in the industry. In Michael Neustadter they had a boss who had never dealt blackjack and wouldn't have recognized marked cards if they'd been spray-painted. Neustadter worked hard; he was good at his job; he was liked by the dealers because he took the trouble to tell them about the high rollers. But his family had money enough that he didn't need to work at all. He'd sailed in on his old man's coattails, hadn't paid his dues. Many of his colleagues resented him, which made him all the more determined to show them he was capable.

As director of casino credit, Neustadter was responsible for ensuring that Caesars issued credit in compliance with the New Jersey Casino Control Commission regulations. That job description demands interpretation, since the credit extended by a casino is unlike the credit extended by any other business. In the conventional arrangement, you receive goods or services in return for your promise to pay over time. If the product happens to be money, as in a bank loan, you are ordinarily asked for collateral. Such credit is regulated by government, which limits the interest that can be charged and includes provisions for default. The provider of credit assumes the burden of risk. The provider, after all, stands to profit from the relationship. Sears doesn't want to have to repossess its bedroom suite; it wants your money. Sears must be astute in its judgement of your ability and willingness to repay or it will suffer. It has an implicit obligation to ensure you don't obtain credit beyond your capacity to repay; you, in turn, have an implicit obligation not to apply for credit beyond your means. The provider of credit ordinarily goes to some lengths to make sure you're not overly indebting yourself – Sears looks carefully at your credit history, net worth, and debt-service ratio. As anyone knows who's been turned down by a bank, obtaining credit is not always a simple matter. Credit, any banker will tell you, is a privilege and not a right.

At a casino, however, you can easily establish a "credit line." When you apply for credit, the casino checks where you bank and where you work. It pays much less attention to those factors other creditors scrutinize so closely – your net worth, outstanding debts, and so forth. If you already have credit at any other casino, it will show up at Central Credit Bureau in Las Vegas, which feeds information to all the casinos in Nevada and New Jersey. You'll routinely be granted the same credit line at the new casino. (Try that at Sears, or your bank.) Michael Campanara, a New Jersey security guard who earned $16,000 a year, had no trouble getting credit totalling $115,000 at several Atlantic City casinos.

The casino needn't put you through a stringent investigation because the marker you sign when you're given chips is not a loan agreement but a postdated cheque. It includes your assurance that you have funds in the account to cover the cheque. In return for "credit," you're providing not a promissory note but a negotiable instrument. For this instrument you get no real consideration in the legal sense. The casino won't even cash your cheque, only give you chips for it. The chips have value only in that particular casino. If you take more than $500 in chips and try to cash them, you'll be asked if you have outstanding markers. If you have, and you say you don't, you've committed fraud under New Jersey law.

The burden of risk in this credit relationship falls not on the provider, but on you the consumer. For the casino, providing credit entails no real risk. The "credit" is really only a prepaid opportunity to gamble. Sure, you might win some of the casino's money. But it's in the business of extending credit because the games are constructed to make sure that, in the long run, you lose. When a Rolls-Royce dealer sells you a $100,000 Silver Cloud on credit, he's risking a valuable car. When a casino provides you with $100,000 in credit, it's risking a seat at the blackjack table.

The casino is also risking bad debt, of course, but gamblers tend to be conscientious. Partly it's the myth of the guys with flattened noses and cauliflower ears. Many Toronto gamblers know the story of the carpet king who stiffed one of the Las Vegas casinos after a disastrous session at craps. Before long the carpet king receives a visit from two well-dressed gentlemen. One of them opens a briefcase, withdraws an electronic sensor, and sweeps the room. The other, satisfied the place is not bugged, says, "At eight-fifteen each weekday morning your thirteen-year-old daughter leaves your house by the side door. She walks down Palmcrest Court to Sheppard, and waits for the 164 bus . . ." Soon afterwards the carpet king holds a warehouse liquidation sale, enabling him to settle his account. The story is almost certainly apocryphal, but it helps explain the casinos' enviable record of debt recovery.

Many of the biggest losers are compulsive gamblers for whom the threat of being cut off is motivation enough. A New Jersey builder, David Zarin, became a regular at Resorts soon after it opened. The casino brought him one marker after another, and Zarin signed his name again and again. In 1980 alone, Resorts extended him $13.4-million in credit. Sometimes he won, sometimes he lost; before long he owed a sum in seven figures. Resorts threatened criminal action but didn't really want him in jail. He had the money in bricks and mortar, and he'd be able to liquidate his holdings more easily on the street than in prison. They told him what a jerk he was, and gave him more markers to sign. May as well have him on the hook for $3-million as $1.5-million. If he paid anything they'd be ahead of the game. If he paid the whole shot, why not take him for all he was worth? If he stiffed them, they'd have a bigger writeoff.

The Division of Gaming Enforcement, in the course of an audit, came upon Zarin's returned markers. According to New Jersey law he had not just failed to pay Resorts, he'd broken the law. By making markers negotiable instruments rather than promissory notes, New Jersey had made every judge and law-enforcement officer in the state an extension of the casino's collection department. Quite against the wishes of the casino Zarin had stiffed, the attorney general indicted him on charges of theft by deception.

When credit players do renege, the casinos have no legal recourse outside their own state jurisdictions. A Toronto sportscaster, Pat Marsden, stopped payment on two $10,000 postdated cheques he'd issued to the Dunes in Las Vegas to cover gambling losses. The Dunes took him to court, but a judge in Ontario ruled Marsden did not have to honour the cheques. Since casino gambling was outlawed by the Criminal Code, the cheques were an illegal consideration. The Dunes had no more grounds than would a drug pusher who'd found that a stop-payment had been put on the cheque he'd accepted in return for an ounce of cocaine. The same thing happened when a Florida gambler named Harry Rozany put a stop-payment on his $100,000 cheque to the Tropicana in Atlantic City. A Florida judge ruled he did not have to make good the money.

Easy credit contributes handsomely to every casino's bottom line – more than one gambler has wakened with a hangover and the awful realization he's going to have to mortgage his house – but a big cash player is a dream. He deposits cash directly into the cage. In return he's issued chips, which usually end up back in the casino's possession. No paperwork, no time lag, no stop-payment cheques. The casinos compete fiercely for high-rolling cash players. Molony was well known at Caesars as soon as it became clear he wasn't merely someone who'd blown his life savings. He was someone who came back. His free room turned into a lavish suite; the van to and from Philadelphia became a limousine.

Casino executives are part bloodhound, part monitor, part schmooze. The idea is to sniff out money and establish a "personal relationship" with those who have it. The idea is to look after them so they won't take their action next door. The idea is to get the money – every dollar. "Hey, Mr. C. How are you? Great to see you. How's Janet? How about those Giants, pulling it out in the fourth quarter. Listen, what can I get you? Come sign in at the cage. The Chateau Margaux's in your suite if you'd like to relax. Do me a favour, Mr. C. Tell me what I can do for you." The credit executive has accessed the computer: spouse's name, anniversary, favourite casino game, favourite food, favourite drink, favourite sport, favourite team, it's all there, right down to Mr. C's handicap at golf. The warmth is that of a sunning snake, the smile is purely transactional – hypocrisy of the first order. Crazy thing is, it works.

Pity the poor credit executives at Caesars trying to get a fix on Molony, radiating geniality, really working at it. "Good to see you, Mr. M. Have a good trip? How's everything up in Toronto? Those Blue Jays are really coming on." This was no twenty-thousand-credit-line jerkoff expecting to be treated like King Farouk. This was sixty thousand cash who blew every cent in a fever and, instead of slinking out, came back a week later with ninety thousand and a determined look. Tuna like that, play him right, it's promotion time. In that sense a casino is no different from an ad agency or a law firm. The crucial question is whether, if you left, you could take the business with you.

Trouble is, Mr. M. didn't get off on the bullshit that worked so well with Mr. C. He obviously wanted no inquiries of any kind. His room card said, "address on file in casino," but his patron reference card in the casino cage said only "Brian Maloney, Toronto." Lots of heavy hitters liked to play it low key, but what made the guy tick? Since a good deal rode on the answer, this became the million-dollar question. Coiffed, well-tailored men huddled in perplexed consultation. "What's with the guy on Baccarat 2?" An overweight shmuck in a rack suit and shoes that look secondhand. Can we redo your suite for you, Mr. M., different colour scheme maybe? Get the decorator in? Trouble is, he never spends time in his suite except to change his shirt or phone his girlfriend or, when the tension gets to him, throw up in one of the marble bathrooms. How about we install the big screen so you can watch the ball games in comfort? No thanks, he mumbles through his moustache, looking toward the dice pit. Tickets to the Pointer Sisters, maybe? Great show, seen it half a dozen times myself. No thanks, he says. Little you-know-what, maybe? "The only lady I'm interested in," he says, "is lady luck." So what turns the guy on? Give him the look – anything goes – and ask in your most friendly, heartfelt tone: "We're at your service, Mr. M. Sure there's nothing at all we can do for you?"

Finally, finally, he says maybe there is something he wouldn't mind. Not now, right now he wants to play. Maybe later. Later he might like something to eat.

You got it, Mr. M. What'll it be? Nice dinner at Le Posh ("combines Art Deco ambience with exquisite European cuisine")? Or the Hyakumi Japanese Steakhouse ("teppanyaki chefs prepare a seven-course dinner at tableside")? You want some iced Dom Perignon waiting for you at the best table in Primavera ("northern Italian culinary delights with the setting of a Venetian palazzo")? Name it, Mr. M., your wish is my command.

Ribs, he says. Barbequed ribs, no sauce, and a large Coke.

In Toronto, Molony was gambling more feverishly than ever. His monthly statement from Richardson's, showing his stock transactions, ran to several pages. Every day after work he drove to the track. Some nights he played craps after the races, but Beck's worries about surveillance made the game unpleasant and then something happened that made him wonder if he should be playing at all. One night Eli Koharski stepped out for a bite and returned to find Molony had won more than $20,000. Molony was impassive; Koharski couldn't suppress his excitement.

"Jesus, Brian, realize how much you've got?"

"Not enough," said Molony, throwing the dice.

Koharski's reaction, and the reaction of another man at the game, made him realize the risk he was running. The other player was a dentist who tried several times to start a conversation. Molony deflected his questions but overheard him asking Beck who the big winner was – the guy with the bushy moustache. The last thing Molony wanted was to draw attention to himself. Besides, low stakes made the game pointless. It was a way to fill time rather than make the kind of money he needed. When the evening ended Molony counted his cash, tucked it in his trouser pocket, and headed home.

That was it for the crap game.

At four in the morning, Molony let himself into the apartment and phoned the Sportsline number in Buffalo for the latest scores. He hung up before the tape ended – that gave him something to look forward to when he got up. He did the same thing with the race results in the newspaper, covering the names of the horses, revealing them one at a time from the bottom up. Didn't finish last, didn't finish second last . . .

Brenda stirred when he slipped into bed. "What time is it?"

"After one," said Molony, giving her a kiss. "Go back to sleep."

At eight-thirty he was at Bay and Richmond, perusing his accounts, instructing his credit officer, Steve Richardson, and making plans to get back to Atlantic City on the weekend. Through the spring and summer he continued to expand business at his post, attracting many new accounts to the branch. Harry Buckle had to admit that he shouldered an extraordinary workload. One afternoon Molony was meeting with a new customer when Beck phoned. The customer stepped out; Molony indicated he'd just be a moment.

"Here comes The Banker, moving up between –"

"I don't have time. Just give them to me."

"Dodgers thirty, Cardinals forty, Pirates pick, Padres pick, Reds eighty, Giants twenty. Orioles forty, Brewers twenty, Yankees forty, Twins twenty, White Sox pick, Red Sox twenty."

"Give me the home teams in the National and the away teams in the American."

"What's this crap?"

"Do I have to send you a telegram?" said Molony. "All for the max."

He was losing more heavily than ever to Beck and Colizzi and owed them almost $90,000. He bet with them individually, and jointly, imagining neither knew the other was taking his action on the side. They let him continue so long as he paid them $10,000 a week. Meanwhile he was using Epstein and another bookmaker as well, and was in debt to them. He financed his horse and sports bets, and his trips to Atlantic City, by ordering cash parcels at the branch and buying U.S. dollars next door at Friedberg's.

Friedberg & Co. was owned by Federico Friedberg, a rotund, balding Viennese Jew. He had left Austria in 1938, at age nineteen, and lived in France and Belgium before moving to Uruguay in 1951. He spent twenty years as a currency dealer in Montevideo, where he changed his name from Fritz to Federico. He knew six languages and every currency. Spend your working life in the money business and sooner or later you see just about everything. There's certainly nothing unusual about a young man phoning to get a U.S.-dollar quotation and appearing a few minutes later with a bank draft.

Molony dropped into Friedberg's three or four times a week, buying U.S. cash with a certified cheque or a draft he himself had signed. No one ever asked for identification. Molony, for his part, never engaged in small talk, never lingered, never counted the money. He stuffed it in his suit and hurried out. One day he had just picked up $40,000 U.S. when a bank customer walked in.

"What are you doing here, Brian? Supporting the competition?"

"Late for a meeting," said Molony. "Speak to you later."

He was petrified the customer had seen the cash and would let slip his identity. Friedberg's, however, took a piece of every dollar he changed. He was changing as much as $200,000 a week, a goose who laid golden eggs. Still, his hurried manner, the frequency of his visits, and the amount he was turning over made him the subject of speculation. Federico Friedberg kept a safety deposit box at Bay and Richmond. One day he happened to notice the mystery man working at the branch. The word got around; the clerks at Friedberg's, among themselves, started referring to Molony as "Mr. CIBC."

Look up at the ceiling in any casino and you'll see mirrors or one-way glass. Behind the glass is another world. The surveillance department of a casino is a closely guarded secret, unknown even to other employees. The monitor room is mission control, with a bank of screens on one wall, phones, a computer terminal, facilities for videotaping, and shelves for storing the tapes. Some things had to be taped: the passage of slot money across the casino floor, the locked chip wells on the tables at closing time, the count room. The date and time of day were automatically recorded. Other things were taped at the casino's discretion: any heavy action, in case of dispute; any suspected dishonesty on the part of a player or an employee; anything that might eventually end up in court.

Watching the games in the monitor room, or live from the catwalks through the one-way glass, you got a unique perspective on a player. If you needed to find out about him you simply accessed the computer. Key in PF11 and you got the bank report – information obtained by the casino from the patron's bank. PF5 gave you the central credit summary. PF8 gave you a summary of the player's history at the casino – what he'd taken in markers, what markers he'd paid off, what cash he had deposited. PF9, a marker rating inquiry, gave you the same information that was attached to every marker issued down in the pit, including the player's average bet, minutes played, win or loss, and his rating. Every player was rated on a scale of 1 to 6. A 6 was somebody who took markers and then walked with the chips, trying to look like he was generating big action in hopes of getting comped. The highest rating was a 1, somebody who played for consistently high stakes and put in long hours, like the portly guy who came from Toronto three or four times a month.

Every shift on surveillance you had to fill in a Game Observer's Report, recording everything that happened while you were on duty:

Security call: servicemaster shampooing rug in cage area.

Blackjack #58: Green play. Player making big bets on impulse. Inconsistent betting pattern.

Cage scan. Tape 129 stops. Tape 197 starts.

You paid such careful attention that you got to know the casino personnel, and many players, in a strangely intimate way. You might bump into a floorman at Pleasantville Plaza and he was so familiar – you knew his nickname and what brand he smoked and which cocktail girl he had his eye on – you were tempted to say hello. And only then remembered he didn't know you from Adam. He had no way of realizing you even worked for the same company.

Weird job, surveillance. Using the joystick, you could zoom in and read the watch on a player's wrist, then back off and pan one end of the casino. Using the computer, you could find out all about him. Using the recorders, you could tape him for posterity. He didn't even know you were there. Watching the players and dealers, and the people who watched the players and dealers, and the people who watched them, you sometimes got a funny feeling. Up there in the ceiling, invisible and omniscient, you felt a bit like God.

July 25. Caesars Atlantic City. Frank Hines.

8 p.m. Baccarat #3. Brian Maloney on game. Has $45,000. Has received $90,000 in markers. Bets up to $10,000.

2:30 a.m. Baccarat. Maloney still on Game #3.

Sherry Brydson was finding it no simple matter to transform a run-down hotel into an elegant women's club. Barb Elson, her partner, was experienced in dealing with contractors, but the project was huge. There were scores of decisions to be made each day. The first architect didn't work out and had to be replaced. Strikes in the building trades brought lengthy delays, and the overruns kept mounting.

Brydson was also puzzled by the bank's attitude. Strange that the CIBC took so little interest. Molony sometimes dropped by to see how things were shaping up, but no one else seemed to care how many tons of concrete had been poured, how membership plans were developing, when they hoped to open the doors. If she were a banker, wouldn't she have wanted assurance that things were proceeding? The project was eating money; her loans were growing; the bank now had a substantial stake in the club. Yet when she needed more money she had only to alert Brian, who wrote downtown and obtained an increased limit. She didn't even have to outline her plans to more senior personnel.

At least Molony seemed to understand what she was doing. He was supportive and helpful, and had become friends with Stu Butts, her lawyer. In August Brydson invited Brian and Brenda to her cottage for the weekend, along with Butts and his wife, Barb Elson and her husband, and another couple. Molony didn't want to go – two days on an island in Georgian Bay without telephones, ball games, or horses promised to be hell – but he felt he had to accept for the sake of customer relations. Maybe Brenda would enjoy herself, provided she didn't choke on the Asian food. At least it would be nice to spend time with Stu Butts and his wife. Every now and then the four of them got together socially.

Before driving up north, Molony stopped in to see Nick Beck. "Give me the home team in every Saturday and Sunday game," he said, in the storage room at the dress shop. "I'll take all the underdogs in the CFL games." He phoned Colizzi and said, "I won't be around this weekend. I want the one horse in every race, both days, both tracks. Also the one-and-one doubles and reverse wheels. And the one horse in every race at Aqueduct."

"You want to bet every race?" said Colizzi. "You don't even know who's running."

"For the maximum," said Molony. "Sir, speak to you Monday. Be good."

To see him through the weekend, Molony took all the magazines and papers he could lay his hands on. At the dock Brydson noticed he'd parked in someone else's spot. While they loaded the boat she went and moved his car. It was pure Brian – a stale-smelling mess of pop tins, McDonald's wrappers, junk mail, and old newspapers. The sun visor was broken, and the turn signal hung on its wires from the steering column.

Stepping into the motorboat, Molony showed Stu Butts what he had in his bag – a bottle of Bacardi and a dozen tins of Coke. "I know she's big on the great outdoors, but if she thinks I'm going to fight off mosquitoes for an entire weekend without this, she better think again."

"If you're not careful, she'll invite you back next weekend."

"With all respect," said Molony, "I intend to be otherwise occupied."

August 29. Caesars Atlantic City. Bob Moran.

4 p.m. Observed Maloney on Baccarat #1. Player was betting $500 to $5,000.

August 29. Caesars Atlantic City. Frank Hines.

8 p.m. Maloney has $30,000. Betting Pass line, Come, $2,000 each. Lost $5,000.

August 29. Caesars Atlantic City. Matt Wilson.

10 p.m. Very good purple action on Craps #12. Maloney on game. Has about $38,000 in front. Playing line to about $2,000.

Several times each week, through the summer and fall, Molony left the bank with two drafts. The first, payable to Richardson Securities, he used to purchase bearer bonds. On the way back from Richardson's he stopped in at Friedberg & Co. With the second draft, payable to Friedberg's, he purchased U.S. cash. At his branch he took the bearer bonds downstairs to the securities department. "Mr. Oskaner wants to sell these at market. Give me the sell order and I'll have him sign it." Then he went up to his office on the mezzanine level and put the cash in his credenza. The outing took less than half an hour. In a single trip he had bought bonds with money from one fictitious account – usually Brydson – paid down the Oskaner account, and obtained cash to use on the weekend in Atlantic City.

He was also ordering cash parcels at the branch – so many, in fact, that the tellers' supervisor mentioned it to her superior. Brian was ordering U.S. cash twice a week, said the girl, as often as Brinks delivered. "This is Bay Street," she was told curtly. So regular had his orders become that he no longer even had to alert the head teller. Twice a week she came to him. "I'm putting in the order for Tuesday, Brian. Need any cash?"

In the casino, meanwhile, Molony was becoming a mythical figure. Unlike most high rollers, he wore cheap, ill-fitting clothes. His moustache and glasses made him look like a nerd. He was also gaining a reputation as an unfailing loser. "Lock up the cash," the floormen said to one another with a wink. "Look who's back." It wasn't that he didn't know the games. He knew them inside out and appeared to gamble with a purpose. But he started playing the moment he arrived and kept at it until the casino shut down or the money was gone. You couldn't tell from his demeanour if he was winning or losing. He gave no sign of pleasure or disappointment. The Iceman, somebody called him.

Dealers are paid minimum wage and make the bulk of their income from tips, which are pooled. The dealers liked Molony even though he didn't tip. At baccarat, two hands are dealt, the player's and the bank's. The gambler bets on one or the other, or on a tie. The casino makes its money by taking a 5 per cent commission on bets won on the bank. With most players you had to mark their commission and inform them at the end what they owed. Molony kept a running total in his head. Some players used a scorecard to keep track of the hands. Molony remembered what had happened in each of the last fifteen or twenty hands. Unbelievable memory. He didn't talk much but wasn't unfriendly. He never drank. When one of the casino executives gave him a present – a jogging suit, or a gumball machine, or a Rolex watch –

he tucked it away without even looking at it. He came to play, and his intensity was something to see.

A baccarat shoe contains eight decks of cards, about eighty hands. Ordinarily it takes forty-five minutes to get through a shoe. When playing by himself, Molony got through it in twenty minutes. Before you could spread the hands for overhead surveillance and add them to the spent cards, Molony had the next hand coming. It seemed his object was to play more hands, more quickly, for more money. If you did anything to hinder him, if you were slower than necessary or made a mistake, he motioned to the floorman and you were gone. If he liked playing at your table, you couldn't help feeling flattered.

While Molony was becoming legendary at Caesars, he was becoming more elusive to family, friends, and colleagues. Everyone had a different idea of where he was on a given night and how he spent weekends. He misled without actually lying. He told Brenda he was driving down to see Doug, letting her conclude he'd be in Sarnia for the weekend. "You're kidding, Brian. You drove all that way just for dinner? And now you're going to turn around and drive back?" There was something he had to be back for, Molony said, leaving Doug to imagine a wedding or family dinner. He could not tell anyone the truth. What if somebody asked the question he, in idle moments, came perilously close to asking himself: why return to the casino again and again when logic says the house advantage is insurmountable?

One part of the answer grew out of Molony's emotional need for optimism. Once he had begun dipping into the bank, he could not admit the possibility of failure without risking the collapse of self-image. Staying psychologically intact meant deluding himself, holding to the belief that success was inevitable. In one sense each loss, each fraud, had the salutary effect of bringing the happy day closer.

As the months passed, however, as he became more deeply mired in debt and deception, he felt another looming inevitability. A branch was typically audited every twelve months or so, and Bay and Richmond was overdue. Molony didn't know when the audit was coming, but each day he failed to win back the money brought it closer. The audit had the boding weight of doomsday. When it came, he was finished. He had to keep going back to Atlantic City, he told himself, because he had to win before the audit ruined him.

Another, less evident explanation of why he kept returning and losing has to do with the nature of the casino itself. As a drain on pockets and bank accounts, it is a formidable and underrated mechanism. No institution is more deeply rooted in human frailty, and none more richly nourishes itself on self-deception. One way we calculate the probability of a future event is by recalling its incidence in the past. We remember things that happen frequently more easily than things that happen infrequently. Why, then, do casino gamblers – assuming they want to win, and given that they usually lose – keep coming back?

Partly because other variables skew the equation. Ease of recall, for example, is just as important as frequency in shaping our judgement about the probability of future events. As evidence, take the psychological study in which people were asked to judge whether "k" was more likely to appear as the first letter of an English word or the third letter – do you happen to know? The preceding sentence contains three words with "k" as the third letter, only one that begins with "k," and that's the ratio for the language as a whole. Since "know" comes more quickly to mind than "likely" or "asked" or "take," however, most people guessed incorrectly that "k" is found more often at the beginning of a word. The easier it is to recall instances of an event – even an infrequent event – the more probable we consider the event to be. This principle is exploited by every casino. A slot-machine payoff – flashing lights, sirens, and a prolonged spewing of coins – does more than obscure the fact that hundreds of other machines are not paying off at that moment. It makes the player's winning pull far more memorable than his losing ones, impairing his judgement of future probability.

Our ability to envision a future event also affects our calculation of its true probability. The sandlot quarterback who dreams of playing for the Dolphins no doubt has a higher regard for his chances than the scout who has graded hundreds of sandlot quarterbacks. In a casino, the act of envisioning a big win obscures the likelihood of its taking place. The player is encouraged at every turn to picture himself a future winner. The "Slotbusters Hall of Fame" at Caesars, around the corner from the executive offices, includes photographs of Odell Chisolm (with his cheque for $1.5-million), Geraldine Hendrickson ($1-million), Dolores Perry ($1.36-million), Frederico Morales (no teeth, but $305,708) – just plain folks who put a hit on the slots. Many casinos display the gold, the Mercedes, or the cash you stand to collect in a big win. They do not, of course, depict self-contempt, cancelled vacations, or personal bankruptcy.

Many gamblers are badly served by a faulty understanding of the laws of probability. Asked to create a random sequence of imaginary coin tosses, people tend to produce a sequence in which the proportion of heads to tails is much closer to 50–50 than chance would predict. They believe a small segment of random events will reflect the larger proportion, as does the losing gambler who believes a hot streak lies inevitably round the corner. Shown a sequence of imaginary coin tosses that includes a high number of tails, people tend to continue the sequence with a disproportionate number of heads. Many gamblers, too, assume the process is self-correcting, that deviations cancel each other out. The roulette player who watches black come up five times in a row and therefore bets the limit on red is acting on this fallacy. In truth, short-term deviations at a roulette table are not corrected by the subsequent spins, merely diluted. The chance that red will turn up on the sixth spin is precisely the same as that black will come up yet again.

Casino personnel promulgate such misinterpretations. The unifying lie in every casino – which employees perpetrate and gamblers long to believe – is that luck determines a player's fortunes. Like all gamblers, Molony was constantly encouraged in the idea that he was due, his luck was certain to change. Of course, this banter was no more serious than the greeting, "How are you tonight?" At the same time, a casino is a house of mathematics. Casino personnel are well aware that a gambler faces the same disadvantage each time he plays and that luck is merely a euphemism for short-term fluctuations in the inevitable long term. Their livelihoods are staked on the certainty that if a gambler stays long enough, or returns often enough, he'll lose everything. A dealer at Caesars, asked if he could spot a losing gambler, replied, "Sure. Anybody you see more than twice."

Nov. 21. Caesars Atlantic City. Archie Rich.

1:45 p.m. Baccarat #3. Big play – Maloney. Losing big. Left pit but has seat reserved.

Steve Richardson couldn't believe it. He got back to the branch after lunch in the employees' cafeteria at Commerce Court to find he'd missed Roger Oskaner again.

As Molony's credit officer, Richardson, a genial young Englishman in his first credit posting, dealt with most customers whose accounts Molony handled. He called about missing documentation, pointed out that an interest payment was overdue, asked if the Thursday meeting with Brian could be switched to Friday morning. An assistant manager used his credit officer as a combination serf and secretary. In this way the credit officer learned all aspects of lending and, if he was good, prepared himself for promotion. On some accounts the credit officer had more contact with the customer than did the assistant manager.

Roger Oskaner, however, Molony kept to himself. Each morning he gave Richardson the day's instructions – "Have Nette copy this, Steve, I want to get the application in this afternoon. Let's call Hardy about his pro forma – he said we'd have it yesterday. I'll need the Stillwell file before my meeting at eleven. What's your recommendation on the Thomas overdraft?" Mention was rarely made of Oskaner, even though the account was extremely active. Evidently Oskaner traded heavily in precious metals. Molony invariably handled the account himself. One day Richardson said, "I don't like this – Oskaner's way over his limit." Molony said, "I phoned downtown and got the approval, I'll do a memo for the file. Now what about that lawyer's opinion for our German friend – have we got that yet? Better give him a call."

The weird thing was that Roger Oskaner often stopped by the branch to pick up his cash. It always happened when Richardson was out. Punctually at 11 a.m. Richardson went to lunch. All the credit officers went early, so they'd be back to look after the posts while the assistant managers had lunch. Richardson usually walked down to Commerce Court, where the subsidized meal cost forty-five cents. When he got back, at noon, Oskaner had come and gone. It turned into a standing joke.

"Do you think the guy's trying to avoid me?"

"Maybe he's a Liverpool fan, Steve. Doesn't like anyone from London."

One day, returning to find that Oskaner had been in picking up cash yet again, Richardson said, "Maybe tomorrow I'll bring a peanut butter sandwich and stay at my desk. Seems like the only way I'll ever meet this guy."

"Brian, Jess Lenz. I'm the casino manager. If there's anything we can do for you, let me know."

Jess Lenz had a firm handshake, dazzling teeth, and the laser eyes you see in anyone who has spent twenty-five years watching what money does to people. He had moved to Atlantic City from Las Vegas. Like many people who settle in Nevada, he'd been on his way to California. As a young man in Chicago he had dreamed of becoming a pro golfer. Instead he found work dealing at the grind joints in Las Vegas, the Fremont, the California, learning the business before moving to the more prestigious spots on the Strip. From the Desert Inn he went to Caesars Palace as a floorman. When Atlantic City got going he was transferred to New Jersey.

The new casino developed a reputation for excellent dealers and control of the games. In large part it was Lenz's doing. He could look at a printout of the drop, spot the pit that wasn't functioning at peak efficiency, and zero in on the dealer who wasn't up to par. That's why he got a salary in six figures and a luxury car. He didn't say much – in meetings he was known for his one-word answers – and he was not a conceptual thinker, but he knew his stuff.

Many casino employees were fresh-faced graduates of one of the dealing schools. There were things they didn't teach you in dealing schools. Like how to hold a die between thumb and forefinger and flick it, spinning it on its axis, to detect "weight." Like how to spot double-number dice. Like gamblers who lay one big bet, collect, and disappear. Like shooters who don't end a roll with a clean hand – palm up. Like nicked cards and late bets and dirty dealers. Jess Lenz knew all the scams. Sometimes, after hours, the less experienced employees gathered round one of the tables and Lenz put on a clinic.

Lenz made a point of acquainting himself with the big players at Caesars. When a gambler's losses get into hundreds of thousands, you want to know everything about him. When is his wife's birthday, so we can send a little gift? How does he like his steak? What's his shirt size? Favourite colour? Wine? Song? It's worth the trouble. A hundred thousand cash represents a lot of free-drink artists nursing nickel chips at blackjack, endless busloads of arthritic widows feeding their complimentary rolls of quarters into the slot machines before piddling away their social security cheques. A cash player in six figures merits serious, personal attention. If he feels no connection to your casino he'll take his money next door.

Molony made clear to Jess Lenz, as he had to Michael Neustadter, that he didn't want attention. He was not unfriendly, but he was all business, ducking any question meant to elicit personal information. Lenz was understanding. Fair's fair. Some cash players were skimming from the grocery store. Some were laundering drug money. Records of their transactions might cause problems with wives or colleagues or the taxman. The art of being a casino host was to treat gamblers as they wished to be treated. If somebody made clear he didn't want sycophantic attention, you laid off, even if you were all the more curious about his background. You handled him with discretion. Made him think you were scarcely aware of his presence. At the same time, you did the little things that let him know he was valued.

One Saturday, while Molony was pulling bundles of cash from his pockets at the casino cage, Lenz invited him to the annual Christmas party. The party would get under way Friday evening and Caesars would be delighted if Molony and a lady friend could attend. Molony said timing was a problem. He'd be busy until six on Friday and there were no evening flights to Philadelphia. In that case, said Lenz, fly to LaGuardia and we'll send the helicopter for you. If the weather's bad we'll send a limousine. It's going to be a great bash and we'd like to have you as our guests.

Molony needed no encouragement to return to the casino but Brenda, it turned out, was dead set against going. She had grown to despise his gambling. She hated that he went away every weekend and stayed out every night. She hated that he wouldn't discuss it. When she tried to raise the subject he grew impatient and annoyed, told her not to worry, which only made her worry more. The last thing she wanted was to spend a weekend in Atlantic City. But Brian had accepted on her behalf and would be embarrassed if she didn't go with him.

For the two days they were at Caesars she didn't leave the room. He rarely left the casino. Friday night he skipped the party. He closed the baccarat pit at 6 a.m. and opened it four hours later. Each time he went up to use the bathroom or change his shirt, he put on a cheerful face. Brenda's hostility was ferocious. He hurried back downstairs and continued doing as miserably as he'd done that week on sports and horses. He had brought more than $200,000 cash. By Sunday morning he was into the money he'd set aside to pay Colizzi. When they flew back to Toronto, with their bags and their Christmas gift – a cordless telephone, compliments of Caesars – he was cleaned out.

On Monday morning he got out of the apartment before Brenda had a chance to question him. Between having to deal with her and having to walk into the bank, mornings had become an ordeal. Mondays were worst of all. Five days, in which a thousand things could go wrong, before the next respite, the next chance to right himself. Each day he half expected Brenda's ultimatum; each day he half expected to find the auditors in the branch. When that happened he was sunk. He used the half hour in the car, driving along the lake, to calm himself. For a time he had listened to the soundtrack from *Man of La Mancha* every morning, but a Melissa Manchester ballad had replaced "The Impossible Dream" as his favourite song. It got to him every time he heard it:

Don't cry out loud
Keep it inside, learn how to hide your feelings
Fly high and proud, and if you should fall
Remember you almost had it all . . .

Molony parked in the Eaton Centre and hurried across Queen Street. The department stores had done up their windows. Powdery snow blew against the glass and swirled along the sidewalks. With Christmas only a couple of weeks off, he'd been given a reprieve. Surely the audit wouldn't be sprung until the New Year. Thank heavens – he desperately needed the time. He didn't like to think how much he owed the bank; the number, out of context, was frightening. But his luck had been so bad lately it was bound to turn, and two or three big wins would put him back on his feet.

Molony headed down Bay Street, hurrying through the falling snow. He wasn't wearing an overcoat and felt the chill on his neck. When he peered through the plate-glass windows on Richmond, drawing close to see past his own reflection, his heart shrank.

Too much activity in the branch. Faces he'd never seen. At eight-thirty in the morning, it could mean only one thing.

5

THE HEAT IS ON

"Slow me down, Lord. Ease the pounding of my heart by the quieting of my mind. Steady my hurried pace with a vision of the eternal reach of time."

– Prayer To Achieve Inner Peace

Bank audits are intended to accomplish two things: ensure that proper procedure is being followed, and confirm the assets and liabilities of the branch. At Bay and Richmond, an audit meant the unannounced arrival of a twenty-five- or thirty-man team first thing in the morning. They counted the cash and the securities before the branch opened, in order not to impede the day's business. They also seized the books. The first part of an audit entails balance confirmation. The inspectors then go through the loans in detail, confirming security and collateral and giving each loan a rating of 1 (satisfactory), 2 (acceptable), or 3 (unsatisfactory).

In the United States, audits are conducted by state or federal agencies. Banks with state charters are inspected by state inspectors. Banks with federal charters – about a third of the roughly 15,000 American banks – are audited by the comptroller of the currency. The corresponding federal agency in Canada, the inspector-general of banks, is insignificant and servile. The inspector-general has a staff of only a few dozen people; his duties are "to be responsible for the administration of the Bank Act," a document written by the banks themselves in the nineteenth century and revised by Parliament every ten years.

In Canada, bank audits are conducted by the inspection division of the bank itself. The auditors are looking for sloppiness, dishonesty, and adherence to systems. A good audit improves their chances for promotion. The mood at the branch can get testy. When Harry Buckle was in Halifax, an auditor noticed a loan to someone he happened to know and dislike, and "rated" the loan (as questionable) out of personal animosity. Buckle was outraged; the two men remained at odds for years. But a Commerce man is encouraged to think of himself as part of the Commerce team, and the mood is more often one of friendly cooperation. The bank's biggest branch, Commerce Court, sometimes informed the inspection division that it didn't want to be audited on a particular date – at the time of a new bond issue, for instance, it would be in no one's interest to have the auditors counting $100 government bonds. In the U.S., such intervention would not be tolerated. There's not the same adversarial air in Canada as in the United States. Nor, perhaps, the same rigorous scrutiny.

The morning Molony peered through the Richmond Street windows and saw the auditors in the branch, his first impulse was to flee. Vanish, never to be heard from again. Poor Brenda, his poor family – such shame and humiliation. He stood in the falling snow and wondered where, exactly, he would go. The only places that came to mind were Las Vegas and Atlantic City. What would he do? Without working capital he had no way of bailing himself out. Besides, once they uncovered the frauds they'd catch up with him soon enough.

"Morning, Brian," said one of the tellers. "Coming in, or are you going to stand there playing snowman?"

He had no choice. He pushed through the door as if it were another day at the office. It was over. He'd put his bad eggs in two baskets, and one or other was sure to be looked into. Roger Oskaner owed the CIBC $175,000. His credit limit was $100,000 with full security. Not only was he a fictitious customer, he was over his fictitious limit. In branch records he didn't have any security. He didn't even have an address.

How could Molony buy time? He did a hasty memo indicating he had spoken to Credit Room and got approval for a $175,000 loan to Oskaner fully secured by government bonds. He added the memo to the loan file. He could only pray the auditors wouldn't confirm the approval or look into Oskaner himself.

The fictitious Brydson loan account was trickier. In nine months Molony had used it nineteen times and taken amounts ranging from $45,000 to $250,000. The bank's books showed her companies as owing $2-million more than she had actually borrowed. Her legitimate loans, for the Elmwood Club and her oil-and-gas companies, were in the name of Westerkirk Holdings; she was unaware the branch had a second, U.S.-dollar, account in her name. Computer-generated audit notices went out to a random sample of branch customers. Because Brydson's legitimate loans were substantial, however, she would get a personal letter asking her to confirm the audited statement. She'd reply directly to the inspection department, bypassing the branch, and Molony's goose would be cooked – if he made it that far. He had one hope. If the auditors failed to turn anything up by Friday, he'd have the weekend to win back the $2-million and Oskaner's $175,000.

In the meantime he needed cash. The Leo Sherman account?

No way, not Leo Sherman. Koharski?

Having paid off the fictitious Koharski loan, Molony could use the account again. He debited the loan account by $80,000 –

Koharski's supposed limit – and drove to the airport Saturday morning. He'd had a good week with the bookies and was carrying $170,000. The terminal was busy and the lineups were long. He cleared customs – never pleasant – and headed for his gate. At the barrier marked "Passengers Only" he waited as people fed their hand luggage through the X-ray unit and stepped through the metal detector. He had the cash divided among his pockets. He dreaded the security procedure and felt that his discomfort was obvious to everyone. The lineup inched forward. The Greek couple ahead of him were saying a tearful goodbye, hugging and kissing. The woman put her bag on the conveyor and passed through the frame. The security guard, a weary Indian fellow, signalled Molony to come forward. He stepped through the detector and set off the alarm.

"Did you forget to take your keys out?"

Bundles of American fifties were jammed into every pocket. Not ten feet away, a uniformed Mountie stood chatting to a security man in plain clothes. How could he get the money out without being seen? He stood there paralyzed. The lineup was building behind him. The Indian fellow repeated, "Pockets, sir." Molony half turned, fumbling, using his body to shield the cash. He pulled the bundles out and glanced up to find the Mountie looking directly at him: game over: when they questioned him about the currency violation they'd want to know where he worked. Frantically he freed his keys, handed them over, and stuffed money back in his pocket. It felt as if everyone was watching; but the Mountie had turned away and resumed his conversation. A little girl in line said to her mother, "That man has a lot of money."

Molony smiled at the mother, who smiled in return. He extended his arms like a scarecrow, sweating profusely. The guard ran the detector into his armpits, down his ribs, over the bulging pockets, between his legs.

"Go ahead."

Molony was halfway to the gate before he could breathe. Thank God no one paid attention to children. He was certain he'd been caught, yet he'd pulled through. It was surely a sign. Once he'd recovered his composure he began to feel purposeful and confident. The worst was finally over. This was going to be his day. Boarding the plane, he had a clear picture of himself in the casino, moving back and forth between craps and baccarat, his winnings so substantial he needed a security guard to help with them. He felt the cash in his pockets and buckled himself into his seat. If he could have had one wish, he would have asked to be transported instantly to the crap table at Caesars. Like a child before Christmas, he could hardly bear to wait.

Dec. 12, 1981. Caesars Atlantic City. Kevin Kelly.

12:05 p.m. Craps 9. Purple action (Maloney). Has almost two full racks, $100,000. Was down to $10,000, made big hand, ran it to almost $90,000. Walked.

3:45 p.m. Observed Maloney receive $70,000 in markers – 3×20,000 and 1×10,000 – and lose it all.

4:20 p.m. Baccarat 2. Maloney up $90,000. Lost it all. $20,000 marker. Lost. $20,000 marker. Lost. Going bad.

9:00 p.m. Observed Craps 10. Maloney betting $3,000 on Pass with odds and $1,500 on Come with odds. Two players on table. Maloney losing. Gets a $10,000 marker and loses that.

The week after the auditors showed up at the branch, one of the audit assistants, a young Chinese, stuck his head in Molony's office and asked if Steve Richardson was around. Richardson had gone to Commerce Court for lunch.

"He's out for an hour. Maybe I can help."

"I'm working on the Westerkirk Holdings account."

"Oh yes," said Molony. "I'm familiar with it."

Auditors try to ensure that a customer's entire activity at the branch is included in the confirmation, otherwise the customer gets alarmed: "What about my term deposits? Why aren't they on here?" The Chinese said, "I want to make sure we have everything in our confirmation letter."

"Let me see," said Molony, terrified. The auditors had overlooked both the fictitious Sherry Brydson loan account and her liquid assets. "There's more. I'm busy right now, but leave it with me if you like."

The auditors were using branch typists – not recommended procedure, but the audit turned out a huge volume of correspondence and the branch had secretarial staff available. Molony changed the heading of the letter, adding "Sherry Brydson" to "Westerkirk Holdings Inc." He included the liquid assets and had the letter retyped. The Chinese fellow was surprised he'd taken the trouble.

"Thank you for the help. Lot of work."

"No problem," said Molony.

The new heading on the letter suggested that the fictitious Sherry Brydson loan had been included in the audit confirmation. The loan card for Sherry Brydson bore the notation, "Hold mail – give to manager post #2." If the auditors came to Molony, he'd say, "Everything was included in the Westerkirk letter that went out to her," and hope they didn't bother comparing the loan balance at the branch to the loan balance in the letter.

Sheer fluke that Richardson had been at lunch and Molony had been able to doctor the letter. Thereafter he lived in terror. He didn't know how the computer isolated loans for detailed inspection, but assumed any loan in seven figures would be confirmed.

When Brydson's controller received the confirmation, she might notice the discrepancy in the name of the account. He had to get the bad loan paid off. He wasn't sure how much time he had, but days at most. His only hope was to put together a stake – a real stake – and get back to the casino over the holidays.

Leo Sherman?

No way, not Leo Sherman.

Leo Sherman was a skinny, white-haired businessman who had sold his nut business to Standard Brands for several million dollars. Alex Osborne, with his contacts and good reputation among the Jewish businessmen on Spadina Avenue, had attracted the account to Bay and Richmond and turned it over to Molony. Sherman had taken out investment loans in various corporate names. A rather self-centred, blustery fellow, he had also set up a $1-million authorized credit in his own name, seemingly for no other reason than to be able to tell his friends, "I have a million-dollar personal line of credit at the bank." In two years he had never borrowed against it. The documentation was in place, the credit fully secured; his presigned demand notes were on file.

Not Leo Sherman.

Molony liked the man. His company's motto was "Our business is nuts." He gave everybody jars of peanuts. He worked alongside his son at a big, peanut-shaped desk. He took Molony and Alex Osborne to watch the Blue Jays from the Standard Brands private box. He dropped by the branch for no other reason than to bellow, for all to hear, "Where's Molony? I want to see my banker." Sherman took him across the street for a shoeshine and invited him down to Florida. He dragged Molony along to a YMHA dinner, introduced him to his cronies, and said, "This is my banker, Brian Molony. Terrific kid. You should all give him your business."

Not Leo Sherman.

What difference did it make now? If he didn't pay down Brydson before the auditors got to it, he was sunk. He had a problem that only money would solve and Leo Sherman had a million-dollar line of unused credit. What choice was there? First big win, the money would go to retiring the loan.

How big a loan? Molony took one of the presigned promissory notes and, before he had time to change his mind, filled in the first figure that came into his head: $360,000 U.S.

Over the holiday a number of Molony's friends noticed he was drinking more than usual. Wasn't like Brian to knock back one drink and pour another. But then it was Christmas, and if anybody could hold their liquor, Brian could. After five rum-and-Cokes he behaved exactly as he had before the first. You'd have thought he'd forgotten the Bacardi.

Funny, too, that he and Brenda weren't going to Florida. It was something of a Molony tradition that the family gathered in Fort Lauderdale over Christmas. Brenda assumed they'd be going, but at the last minute Brian said he had so much to do at the branch he simply couldn't spare the time. When Brenda told her girlfriend, also a CIBC employee, the girlfriend commented to her husband that, so far as she could recall, Brian hadn't taken holidays all year. According to the Branch Management and Operations Manual, he should have taken two consecutive weeks at least once a year. Wasn't like Brian not to go by the book.

Molony spent a quiet Christmas with Brenda's family, then drove out to the farm to visit Sieg and Sheila. Sieg, too, noticed a change. He had recently come into Toronto to see Brian for more money. He and Brian's mother were both keen on an oil stock, and Sieg wanted to increase his investment loan. Brian had been uncharacteristically brusque and impatient. Sieg got the feeling he was being hurried out and wondered if Brian was embarrassed to be dealing with a country rube. He said nothing to Brian, of course, but told Sheila he couldn't help wondering whether Bay Street and the big promotion had gone to Brian's head.

On Boxing Day, Brian drove down to visit Doug in Sarnia, telling Brenda he'd be there two or three days. Doug teased him about his messy car; they talked about their jobs, and the stock market, and what had happened to some of their old school chums. On the surface things were the same as ever. Neither of them had forgotten the trip to Las Vegas. After Nicole and the kids had gone to bed, Brian and Doug got into the rum. As they were saying goodnight, Brian suddenly blurted, "I think I'm in trouble." Doug assumed he was referring to the borrowed money and asked if he could help. Brian drained his glass, chewing an ice cube, giving himself a moment. "Not unless you're a marriage counsellor. I'm in trouble with Brenda. She was planning on going to Florida."

In the morning, before anyone else was up, Brian woke Doug to say goodbye. It had snowed heavily overnight and a noisy wind was whipping the house, piling drifts against the window.

"You're not going to drive back in this weather."

"Have to," said Brian. Colizzi was in Las Vegas. "The snow's stopped. The highway's probably clear."

At the office, or in action, Molony never felt tired, but at a restaurant or in the car exhaustion sometimes seeped out of his bones. On the treacherous drive along Highway 401 he kept the windows open. The air was freezing cold but the heater made him so drowsy he feared he'd drive off the road. Toronto had missed the brunt of the storm and the plane took off on schedule.

In Las Vegas he took a cab to the Tropicana. He had almost $250,000 cash. In a few hours the money was gone. How stupid could one person be? He hadn't even got bets down on the college bowl games. He'd often had bad luck at the Tropicana and promised himself he'd avoid it. He couldn't have picked a better spot if he'd been trying to lose. Why hadn't he gone next door? It was his own damn fault, he was such a stupid idiot he could have punched himself. Lucky that Colizzi was in town or it would have been a thoroughly miserable wait for the flight home. He went to Colizzi's room and knocked.

"Who is it?"

"I need to talk to you."

"Come back later."

"Open up. It's important."

Colizzi opened the door dressed in a gold chain and a bath towel. Behind him, in bed, a pale woman was doing something with a credit card and a mirror.

"What do you want?"

"Maybe he wants a date," said the woman. "Ask him in."

"How much have you got?"

"What do you need?" said Colizzi, taking his leather pants from the chair. "Want some of that?" He nodded over his shoulder. "Not bad French."

The woman reached for her wine glass and sipped like an actress. Molony concealed his disgust, avoiding her eye while Colizzi counted out hundreds. "Thirty-nine, forty."

Molony stuffed the money in his pocket.

"You two have fun."

"You sure?" said Colizzi. "My treat."

"Maybe he'd like a line," said the woman.

Colizzi laughed. "He gets his at the crap table. He doesn't like that shit any more than I do."

Molony shut the door and shuddered with revulsion. Why would anybody waste time on a dyed stranger with bruises on her arm? You could get your oil changed anywhere. You didn't have to fly out to Nevada. Why would anyone come all that way and spend time anywhere but the casino or the sports book? They only had two days.

Finally, finally, the bad dream was over. Molony had been shooting craps for two days and nights and had won so much money he could barely carry it. He flew back to Toronto with his pockets and his bag jammed with hundred-dollar bills. He made it through customs – the final hurdle – and found, when he got to the branch, a letter waiting for him. Harry Buckle gave it to him. He'd been appointed to Commerce Court, the bank's most important branch, as senior assistant manager! An unheard-of posting for someone his age. The appointment was effective immediately; he was wanted at Commerce Court right away. First, though, he hurried down to Richardson's, purchased bearer bonds, and retired all the bad loans. No one would be the wiser. Then he raced down to King Street. He was ushered into Ross Brady's office. Alex Osborne was there, too. Both men shook his hand warmly.

"Congratulations," said Brady. "Quite a step."

"I can hardly believe it," said Molony. "I don't know what to say."

"You're most deserving," said Osborne. "Impeccable record, excellent judgement, a history of achievement. I'm proud of you. Good work."

"I just want you both to know –"

"Wake up," said Colizzi, elbowing him. "We'll be landing in a minute. You're talking to yourself."

God, was he hallucinating? He felt his pockets. He had won, he wasn't completely crazy, he'd turned Colizzi's $4,000 into $65,000. It didn't solve his problems, but at least it was a start.

Colizzi drove him home. When he let himself into the apartment Brenda kissed him and told him that friends had invited them to a New Year's Eve party.

"What did you say?"

"That we'd love to see them," she said, keeping him in suspense a moment. "But that you'd mentioned something about another party."

"I'll look after it."

Molony phoned and said, "We'd really enjoy seeing you, but I'm afraid we've already made plans for New Year's Eve. I don't see how I can change them."

"We never get to see you two anymore. Why don't you come over for brunch tomorrow?"

"Tomorrow's not an option," said Molony.

"Come for brunch on New Year's Day."

"Damn," said Molony. "I'm afraid that's not possible either. You know what it's like at this time of year."

Jan. 1, 1982. Caesars Atlantic City. Archie Rich.

4:50 p.m. Craps 12. Purple play. Maloney betting Don't Pass, Don't Come and Come at the same roll. Lost heavily and walked.

A couple of weeks into the New Year, Molony was on his way out of the branch when he bumped into Leo Sherman's accountant. He was an older fellow, semi-retired, not in the best of health. Sherman had taken him on to give him something useful to do.

"Where's Steve?" said the accountant.

Molony was in a hurry – he intended to stop at Friedberg's and Richardson Securities on his way to a meeting at Commerce Court – but Steve Richardson was away from his desk. Molony had to be polite.

"He must have stepped out. Anything I can help you with?"

The accountant produced a bank statement showing a mysterious debit to Leo Sherman's current account. Molony realized instantly what it was: a month's interest on the fraudulent $360,000 loan. The interest was supposed to accrue in the loan account so that it wouldn't show up in the current account. The accountant said he had no idea what the debit referred to. It could have been something Sherman had done without telling him. He was going to ask Steve Richardson to investigate.

"I'll look after it."

"Don't bother," said the old fellow. "You've got more important things to do. I don't mind waiting."

"What's more important than customer satisfaction?"

Molony took the statement to the discount department, explained the mistake to the clerk, and asked her to correct it.

"Our error," he told the accountant. "It's been straightened out."

"You had me worried there for a moment."

"Sorry for the inconvenience."

"It's nice to know even bankers are human."

"Thanks for dropping by," said Molony. "I have to run, I'm late for a meeting. Give my best to Leo."

Alex Osborne had invited Molony for a drink with two senior partners at Blake, Cassels & Graydon, one of the Toronto firms that handled the CIBC's legal work. This was Osborne's way of signalling to the bank's senior counsel that Molony was a comer, and of introducing him to people he might one day need to call on. Over drinks the lawyers said that Blake's was seeking ways of securing more of the bank's Toronto business. Strathy, Archibald & Seagram, a competing firm, did a good deal of CIBC work in the Toronto area and the partners were eager to know how their firm could get more involved.

When Alex Osborne was at Bay and Richmond, he held weekly seminars for his assistant managers. He spoke for an hour on a given subject and then fielded questions. Molony had found the seminars immensely helpful and suggested to the partners that bankers would profit from bull sessions in which they could ask hands-on questions about registering a security in Alberta, dealing with a London bank, assessing the collateral value of partnership agreements. How about a seminar on bankruptcy – what are the bank's legal rights and obligations when a customer declares bankruptcy? The bank assumed you'd pick these things up through experience. Why not provide the information in a concentrated but informal way? Osborne told the partners he thought it a great idea.

When the lawyers left, Osborne ordered another round. Keele and Lawrence was going to be a lot of work, he said, and he was trying to get Molony transferred up from Bay and Richmond. Molony had to appear delighted. The transfer would mean another step up the ladder, another promotion engineered by Osborne. It would mean a grade increase, from grade 9 to grade 10 or even 11, with a corresponding raise in salary. And it would mean he would be reunited with Alex Osborne.

"Nothing would please me more, Mr. O. At the same time, there's a lot to accomplish at Bay and Richmond." The implication was that Buckle was not the manager Osborne had been.

"That's no longer my first concern," said Osborne. "My main goal now is to get Keele and Lawrence straightened out."

"Speaking of goals," said Molony, "I notice Mark scored again last night."

"Let me know if you run across tickets for the Detroit game next month. We'll get a group together."

"He doesn't seem to be having many problems adjusting to the NHL."

Osborne gestured with his swizzle stick. He'd had a drink or two. "If you've got talent and you're willing to work hard, you'll succeed. I saw the talent in Mark many years ago, and I've tried to teach him the value of hard work." He raised his glass of scotch in a toast. "I like to think I've got a knack for spotting talent."

Jan. 15, 1982. Caesars Atlantic City. Matt Wilson.
1:30 p.m. Craps 5. Maloney on game. Still losing steadily.

Jan. 16, 1982. Caesars Atlantic City. Kenneth Rapp.
3:45 p.m. Craps 11. Steady purple action. Maloney has gotten $45,000 in markers and is losing.

On Friday, January 22, 1982, in York County Court, Judge George Ferguson granted the head of the Metro Toronto Police Intelligence Bureau, and those persons aiding him, an authorization to intercept private communications. It made legal the monitoring of certain specified communications either by "an electrical connection known as a 'cross-connect' or 'hard wire connection' capable . . . of intercepting telephone communications and transmitting them to a monitoring location," or by "a microphone capable . . . of intercepting oral communications and transmitting them to a monitoring location." The authorization, valid for sixty days, empowered the police to wiretap eight men. One was Mario Colizzi.

The morning after the wiretap authorization was granted, Molony flew to Las Vegas for Super Bowl weekend. He had bet $80,000 on the game with the bookies in Toronto, who'd taken the bet on condition Molony pay cash if he lost but take only half cash if he won, the other half to be applied against his outstanding tabs. Roger

Oskaner had been busy, and Molony had another $140,000 U.S. in his pockets. He promised himself he'd put $130,000 on San Francisco the moment he arrived in Las Vegas. The 49ers, he believed, were a good bet, and winning $130,000 U.S. and $80,000 Canadian would be a first step toward paying off his loans.

It was a beautiful winter day in the desert, bright and warm, the mountains brilliantly etched against the blue sky. At the sports book in the Barbary Coast, Molony asked the maximum bet they'd accept on the Super Bowl and was told $500,000, and $500,000 more every hour thereafter. He'd had good luck at mini-baccarat in the Barbary. If he put $70,000 on the game he'd have twenty-four hours to run the other $70,000 up to half a million. Put half a million on the Super Bowl at 6–1 odds – a round-robin parlay, guessing which team would score more points in each quarter and whether the total points would be over or under the casino's prediction – and he'd turn the half million into $3-million. More than enough to repay his outstanding loans. Just like that, the anxiety of the past fifteen months would dissolve like a child's phantom.

Molony asked for orange juice and sat down at the mini-baccarat table. Half an hour later the $70,000 was gone.

How could he have been so ignorant? He'd promised himself he'd put the money on the Super Bowl. He didn't even have the self-discipline to keep his promise. A weakling and a fool. He deserved to lose. It was only Saturday afternoon and he barely had cab fare back to the airport. Depression was empty pockets in Las Vegas. In action, his focus was as pure and absolute as the desert sky. Broke, he became unpleasantly aware of the taste of thawed shrimp, the chemical basis of the orange juice, the stricken expressions of the people around him. You saw many emotions in a casino but happiness wasn't one of them. Losers were distraught and winners wanted more. Losing made Molony ache the way broken hearts made teenagers ache. Not because he'd lost but because he couldn't play. Nothing made him feel so deeply the vacancy that lingered after he'd told himself how much he had to be thankful for – good health, brains, work he enjoyed, a woman who loved him, family and friends. The things that, in others, added up to a rich life. The things that, in him, got sealed away, by a complex routing, in some inaccessible station of the heart.

Molony flew back to Toronto and watched the Super Bowl at Eli Koharski's townhouse. Early in the game Cincinnati got inside the 49ers' ten-yard line and failed to score. Koharski, who had the Bengals, yelled at the television.

San Francisco led 20–0 at the half. This was exactly what Molony had foreseen. Exactly what he'd wanted to happen. He'd won his first-half bets. Why, then, when the game resumed, did he find himself cheering for Cincinnati?

"I thought you liked the 49ers," said Koharski. "Bet it both ways, or what?"

Molony didn't want the Bengals to win, but the game lacked intensity. There was something profoundly unsatisfying about it. God, what a baffling enterprise. He was getting what he wanted and it was not what he wanted. He had to have victory but hungered more deeply for drama. Where was the consummation in this helpless passion? Cincinnati scored twice and he had all the drama he wanted. Late in the game the Bengals got within five points. If they recovered their onside kick and scored another touchdown, they'd win the game.

The 49ers recovered the kick and won 26–21. Koharski stomped around, kicking furniture and cursing. "Those bastards cost me five hundred bucks!"

Molony sat impassively on the sofa, amused by Koharski's performance. He himself had won $70,000 on his parlays in Las Vegas, breaking even on the trip. He'd won $80,000 in Toronto, but the bookies would keep half the $80,000, plus the weekly $10,000, plus next week's $10,000. Molony would collect only $20,000 Canadian. Driving home, he felt sick, despondent, persecuted. How was he ever going to disentangle himself? Even the things he did right turned out wrong. Who else could have backed the winning team, bet heavily, and barely broken even?

Monday night he met Colizzi in the parking lot at the racetrack to collect the $20,000. In his new Cadillac Seville, Colizzi patiently wet his thumb and counted out hundred-dollar bills.

By the sixth race Molony had lost the $20,000. Between races he found Beck and Colizzi by the concession booth. Beck was eating his program. Sunglasses almost hid the swollen discoloration around his left eye.

"Here comes The Banker, ready to make his move."

Colizzi made a pistol of thumb and forefinger and pretended to shoot him in the head.

After the last race, cursing himself, Molony made his way through the shivering crowd and the sea of worthless tickets. Talk about a bad night. He'd not only lost his Super Bowl winnings, he owed Beck and Colizzi another $25,000.

"Brian, Larry Woolf. If there's anything you need, please don't hesitate to ask."

Larry Woolf was a compact man in a pinstripe suit and button-down shirt. He was from Shelly, Idaho, and had a trace of the military in his manner, a legacy from his days as a sergeant in the U.S. Army. After receiving an honourable discharge in 1966, he attended the University of Nevada-Reno. He put himself through college by working as a keno writer at Harrah's, joining the casino full-time after graduating in American history and literature. He dealt all the games – blackjack, craps, baccarat, roulette, and poker – then rose to boxman, floorman, pit boss, shift boss, and finally manager of the pit department. He joined Caesars in 1979, six months before the new casino opened, and moved his wife and two children to New Jersey.

Woolf was trim, polished, and low-key, a Mormon who could calculate drop percentages in his head while carrying on an urbane conversation. He was the perfect mix of the old breed – he once dealt five-cent craps, and few things attract more lowlife – and the new. An avid reader of the latest books on corporate excellence and management technique, he was quite at home in any boardroom. He was thirty-nine. His neatly trimmed and blowdried hair showed the first signs of grey. Behind his wire-rimmed glasses were those laser eyes ubiquitous in the industry.

At Caesars he had climbed quickly. He'd been taken on as casino administrator but soon moved up to assistant vice-president of casino operations and then vice-president. Peter Boynton, the president of Caesars, was Woolf's boss, but among casino employees there was no mistaking who ran the gambling operation. It was Larry Woolf who had made Caesars one of the most dependably profitable casinos, and it was Woolf to whom Molony was referred when he wanted to get his limit raised above the $10,000 table maximum. Molony had seen a group of Orientals playing baccarat for sums far in excess of the posted limit and wondered how he too could get his limit bumped.

One casino, The Horseshoe in Las Vegas, boasts that it will accept any bet on any game, but every other casino in Nevada and New Jersey imposes a betting limit. The limit prevents a gambler from doubling his bet every hand until he wins, and it insures against the hot streak that could seriously affect profits. Albert Ngan, a Chinese who sometimes gambled with Molony, lived at

Caesars for several weeks and played baccarat every day. At one point he was up more than $3-million, enough to raise sweat on the brows of the casino executives. Anything can happen on a given hand, in a given hour; casinos grind out their profit on longitudinal play, repetition. Albert kept at it until he'd lost his winnings and a good deal more, but not before giving Larry Woolf a few more grey hairs. Not that Brian Molony was a candidate to put a hit on, take the money and run. He was an automatic loser. Spend enough time in a casino and you can spot them at a glance – the ones who don't drink, don't notice the tits and ass, don't care about eating or sleeping or anything but the next hand. Even if Molony did get lucky he'd be back.

"Your limit's based on how much you bring," said Woolf. "We'll calculate your limit per hand at five per cent of the cash you have on deposit."

"If I brought $300,000, I could bet $15,000 a hand."

"If you need help making any arrangements, just let us know."

Early in February, 14 Division of the Metropolitan Toronto Police asked Craig Law for help with the bookmaking wiretap. Law was a stocky sergeant in the Morality Bureau, a methodical man with back problems and a tendency to put on weight. He ran the anti-gambling squad and knew as much about bookmaking, and the people engaged in it, as anyone in Toronto – which storefronts in Chinatown hid the fan-tan games, which clubs on College Street saw money change hands, which hotel was home to the illegal dice game.

Morality work involves endless hours of surveillance. It's no occupation for the restless. Craig Law was imperturbable. Because of his tenacity and his burliness he was known, though not to his face, as The Bulldog. He had built his own cottage near Parry

Sound, working carefully and patiently on weekends and holidays for nearly fifteen years. Patience was key. When somebody applied for surveillance, you asked him in for 2:30 and let him sit until 4 o'clock. If he started pacing or drumming his fingers, he probably wasn't right.

One of Law's best surveillance men was a forty-year-old constable named Ron Andrews. Andrews didn't look like a cop – balding, with a limp and the beginnings of a pot belly – but a cop was what he'd dreamed of becoming in his boyhood in east-end Toronto, and when they turned him down as undersized he got a job as a tool-and-die maker to build himself up. At the age of twenty-eight he made the weight. For five years he wore a uniform, walked a beat, worked the cars, old clothes, and the front desk at 55 Division. When word got around that the force was putting together a SWAT team, he applied and – a bit to his own surprise – was accepted by the new Emergency Task Force.

Andrews enjoyed the rigorous training and mental discipline. He liked the intensity and camaraderie of the gun team. The work was demanding and exciting. Each shift brought five or six calls – someone was brandishing a weapon, or holding a hostage, or barricaded in a house. The satisfaction came with a safe resolution, but not every incident was satisfying. One night the team was called to a rooming house off Queen Street, where a drunk was threatening people with a .22 rifle. The man turned out to be a holdup artist who had become a police informer and, not coincidentally, an alcoholic. Booze had addled his wits: no amount of talking would separate him from his weapon. Finally the gun team teargassed the house.

Andrews was in the hallway when the fink came unexpectedly through the bedroom door, wild-eyed, rifle trained on Andrews' heart. Andrews backed off, talking through his gas mask and watching the fink's trigger finger. When the finger turned white, Andrews fired. His twelve-gauge Remington short barrel was fitted with a shot diverter, which fanned the pellets. Andrews knew about shotguns from duck hunting and his ETF training, but he wasn't prepared for what the Remington did to the fink. It lifted him off his feet and slammed him, face down, back up the hall. It took off one finger and blew away one shoulder, but it was the four pellets in the fink's liver that killed him. He died a month later of lead poisoning.

The fink was convinced, up to his death, that he had murdered a policeman. It turned out his gun had jammed. The rifle was in good condition, the ammunition new. Nobody could recall another instance of rim-fire shells jamming a .22 automatic. Such things make you wonder if maybe there isn't somebody up there looking out for you. Make you imagine what it would be like for your kids to have no father. Make you realize you survive a finite number of such encounters.

Shortly after the shooting, Andrews went on another gun-team call and ended up wrestling a hood with a .45 automatic pistol. When they fell to the ground, Andrews took the man's full weight on his left knee. The knee joint shattered, and Andrews underwent extensive surgery. Bone had to be taken from other places and used in reconstruction. Andrews was lucky to walk again. When he tried to resume running, to get back in shape for the gun team, the staff sergeant said maybe he was asking too much of himself. The staff sergeant happened to know of a temporary opening in Morality. That's where Ron Andrews got to know The Bulldog. When a permanent spot opened up on the anti-gambling squad, Andrews made the change.

It was very different work, but then Andrews was a different man from the one who'd joined the force. He and his wife had a busy household – two children, plus assorted cats, dogs, and birds – and a cottage up north. He enjoyed getting away for the weekend and spent as much time with his family as he could. He no longer prized some of the things that had once seemed so important. A rack of antlers hung over his fireplace, a splendid trophy, the first moose he had ever shot and the last. Take the life out of such a magnificent animal and you deaden something in yourself. You learn to be satisfied just watching it in the wild.

Andrews didn't know much about gambling. He never bet, and preferred snowmobiling and racing hydroplanes with his son to the sports that drew action. Ordinarily this would have been a formidable handicap. Every wiretap demands interpretation – nobody ever says, "Let's buy an ounce of heroin from Rick and then shoot him" – and bookmaking wires sound especially like gobbledygook. Bookies do as much as possible on the street. They assume they're being tapped and speak cryptically. An inexperienced monitor could easily listen to a conversation and miss its import.

Andrews lucked out on his first authorization. The bookie, George, was expanding his clientele. He took the time to explain to new bettors how bookmaking worked. Andrews, sitting eight-hour shifts in a tiny, windowless room, got an instant education. George taught him about favourites and underdogs, odds and spreads, nickels and dimes. When he came off that wire and moved onto the next he knew what to listen for.

When The Bulldog was approached by 14 Division, he thought immediately of Ron Andrews. On previous investigations Andrews had got to know a good deal about the Colizzis. The family was originally from Bari, on the Adriatic coast in southern Italy. Mario had come to Canada in 1952, at age seven, with his mother and two brothers. The father had emigrated the year before. Mario's older brother, well known to police, had run the gamut of illicit enterprise. Mario's younger brother also made a living that did not require a social insurance number, though he lacked the brains and drive of the eldest son. Mario himself was also well known to police.

The Colizzis had extensive contacts in the underworld. To eavesdrop Mario was to tap into a network that stretched from Montreal to Buffalo, from the prisons in the Kingston area to the mob families of Hamilton and Niagara Falls. Someone who knew the cast of characters could extract that much more meaning from references and allusions. Ron Andrews began monitoring live calls. He went back through the log and replayed the conversations marked "nothing relevant noted," to make sure nothing relevant had been missed. He drew up a flow chart, placing Mario Colizzi at the centre of a web linking all the people he spoke to or mentioned.

The authorization rooms were on the second floor of a two-storey brick building at 60 Richmond Street East. The rooms were part of the Intelligence Bureau which, for bureaucratic reasons, had its own anti-gambling unit. A certain antagonism had developed between the two anti-gambling squads, and when Morality needed an authorization room they were usually assigned to Room 8.

All the authorization rooms on Richmond Street were cramped and uncomfortable, but Room 8 was the worst. It contained a desk, chair, filing cabinet, typewriter, phone, and a bank of Uher 4000 reel-to-reel tape recorders. Starkly lit and poorly ventilated, it was smaller than most prison cells. Someone had taped a picture of a window to the wall.

Thanks to the growing frequency of his visits to Caesars and growing size of his bets, the unlikely roller from Toronto had become as familiar to employees of the surveillance department as he was to the dealers and casino executives on the floor. Molony imagined he was attracting little notice, but his name was turning up more often than ever on the Game Observer's Reports:

Feb. 6, 1982. Caesars Atlantic City. Archie Rich.

2 p.m. Baccarat 3. $40,000 marker Maloney. Ran it up to $110,000. Lost back to $40,000 and walked.

3:45 p.m. Baccarat 3. $30,000 marker Maloney. Ran it up to $150,000. Sent $80,000 to the cage. Still playing.

5:45 p.m. Baccarat 3. $20,000 marker Maloney. Lost all and walked.

Feb. 6, 1982. Caesars Atlantic City. Jim McCarthy.

6 p.m. Observed Craps 11. Purple action Maloney. Pass line with odds. Player has approx. $5,000 and receives $10,000 marker. Player betting Don't Place for $3,000 inside. Maloney lost $15,000 and left.

7 p.m. Observed Craps 11. Maloney receives a marker for $20,000. Betting Pass line also with maximum double odds. Also betting $3,000 coming with maximum double odds. Also betting behind the inside number Don't Place. Player is losing. He receives $10,000 more in a marker and starts betting the Don't Pass with odds and Don't Come behind also with odds. Player is losing. Received another $10,000. Made a Pass line bet and left the game with approx. $8,000.

9:30 p.m. Observed Craps 12. Maloney received $10,000 marker. Player is one from stickman. Maloney is betting purple in the Don't Pass $4,000 with double odds $8,000. Also pressing odds 2nd paying vig. Also betting Don't Come with odds. 2nd Don't Place. Maloney started winning, then lost and left.

Feb. 6, 1982. Caesars Atlantic City. Frank Hines.

10:30 p.m. Baccarat 3. Maloney on game. Received $10,000 marker. Bets up to $2,000. Was up to $25,000. Now has $8,000.

12:30. Baccarat 2. Maloney on game. Bets up to $10,000. Was up to $90,000 at one time. Now has $30,000.

3:30 a.m. Craps 10. Maloney now on game, next to 3rd base dealer. Received $40,000 marker. Bets $2,000 Pass line – odds. Buys 4–10, $2,000 each. Places inside numbers, $2,000 each. Lost $30,000 while I observed game. Went to Craps 11. Received another $30,000 marker. Betting same pattern. Left game with approx. $15,000.

Alex Osborne rounded up tickets for his son's first professional game at Maple Leaf Gardens and dropped into the get-together in the Hot Stove Lounge beforehand. He was in fine fettle, laughing and telling stories about Mark's childhood. Molony noted that he was actually responsible for Mark's success in Detroit, having signed Mark's passport application. Jeremy Brown, a radio commentator, bank customer, and friend of both Osborne and Molony, wanted to bet a dollar on Detroit.

"Don't bet with friends," said Molony. "Think how bad you'd feel if you took your banker's money."

Before the hockey game, Osborne told Molony he was still trying to get him up to Lawrence and Keele, but that Harry Buckle was resisting the move. Molony had hoped Osborne might have dropped the idea. If Osborne succeeded in arranging the transfer, Molony would have no choice but to accept it. He'd be given two weeks' notice and then his accounts – legitimate and fraudulent – would be turned over to another assistant manager.

"Couple of months down the line might be better than now in any case. Still things to be done at Bay and Richmond. Shall we go sit down? It's almost game time."

Alex Osborne couldn't have had a happier night. Not only did Mark score Detroit's first goal in his first NHL appearance at Maple Leaf Gardens, he was named first star. After the game, when Mark skated out to acknowledge the applause, Osborne leapt to his feet, clapping and cheering. Molony was delighted as well. Thanks to Mark's goal, he'd won his $10,000 bet with Colizzi.

The out-of-town scoreboard had more good news. Molony had won every game. Three good days in a row. It was starting to turn around. The months of anxiety had been the dues required in any grand endeavour. At last he was on his way to bailing himself out. He'd halved his debt to Beck and Colizzi, and at lunch the day before Colizzi had paid him $60,000. He already had U.S. cash for Saturday. If he could just keep the streak going at Caesars. He'd start with craps. He'd move to baccarat as soon as he lost three bets in a row. Maybe he'd never leave the crap table. Maybe this would be the weekend he'd pick up the dice and never put them down, play day and night without –

"– evening like this."

"Pardon?" said Molony. Everyone else was standing, trying to file past him. He was still in his seat.

Downstairs, amid the exiting crush of people, Osborne said, "Tell the others to wait here. I want to congratulate Mark. Then I'd like to buy everybody a drink."

Feb. 20, 1982. Caesars Atlantic City. Kevin Kelly.

10:40 a.m. Craps 10. Maloney lost $4,000 on two rolls and walked.

11:25 a.m. Baccarat 3. Heavy purple. Maloney $10,000 a hand; as high as $70,000. Loses all but about $12,000. Goes to Craps 12. Loses the $12,000 and walks.

2:45 p.m. Craps 11. Purple play. Maloney betting Pass line, odds, and Don't Place. Lost $20,000. Went to Baccarat 3, got $20,000 marker.

4:15 p.m. Maloney walked with $105,000.

Sit wires eight hours a day and you become expert on the human voice. You can tell many of the same things a spectrograph reveals – whether someone's tense, or lying, or disguising his voice. The same voices turn up again and again, and you become as familiar with inflection, with the tiny hesitations and changes in pitch, as a therapist or a lover. You also get to know a good deal about individual lives. A wiretap is relentlessly intimate. To eavesdrop everything a person says on the phone is to know that person better than anyone he talks to. Each caller gets a single piece of the puzzle. You get all the pieces. Everyone deals in gaps and distortions. Some people say one thing to one caller, the opposite to the next. Eavesdrop the same voices day after day and you find yourself forming clear opinions about people you've never seen.

One fellow who often spoke to Mario Colizzi was a certain Mr. Brown. He was different from Colizzi's other contacts. He was impatient on the phone, articulate and well educated. He probably held a responsible position at work. He was quick at mathematics and versed in all areas of gambling – horses, card games, football, basketball, baseball. He addressed Colizzi with a curious politeness, though in his voice you could sense distaste. "Sir," he would say, "I'll see you out there tonight. Be good."

Colizzi often spoke to another well-known bookie, Nick Beck. Someone owed them both substantial sums, though he regularly gave them money. The two bookmakers frequently groused about this someone and discussed who should get the next payment. Sit wires eight hours a day and you get a gut feeling for who's being talked about. Maybe it's timing – one discussion ends and ten minutes later the line lights up again. Maybe it's a phrase in one conversation – "Atlantic City" – that recurs in the next. Andrews couldn't swear, but he had a feeling the someone who owed money to the bookmakers was Mr. Brown.

Each morning, Andrews took the streetcar to work, bought two bran muffins and a coffee, signed himself into the authorization room, and played back the overnights. He noted each call in his log, monitored the live calls, and did preparatory work for future authorizations. Every so often he stretched his legs, to keep his bad knee from stiffening. The more often he heard Mr. Brown's voice, the more convinced he became that something was stirring beneath the surface. He had a feeling the day might come when he'd need to put all the Mr. Brown calls together.

Each time Mr. Brown spoke to Colizzi, or Colizzi and Beck alluded to the fellow who owed them money, Andrews put a red star beside the entry in his log book.

By the time the audit inspectors got to the Oskaner loan, Molony had retired it. Using money from the fictitious Sherry Brydson account, he had purchased bearer bonds from Richardson Securities, sold the bonds to the bank, and credited the proceeds to Oskaner. In this way he had repaid Oskaner's supposed debt to the bank. When the inspector checked into it and found some troubling details, he was able to shrug and move on.

Roger Oskaner, $175,000. Authorized limit: $100,000. No security. Did the audit officer forget to include it? No authorized credit. Better get the Oskaner file. Not much here. Personal financial statement and a twelve-line memo. That's all? Where's the manager's approval? What's the status of the loan now? Oh, paid off. Good. Don't have to check further. Stamp it. Satisfactory loan. Two branches behind and I'm still on the O's.

With the fictitious Brydson account, Molony was on even thinner ice. When he started using it, her legitimate loan account had been well secured and not much used. Recently, though, as she continued making oil-and-gas investments and proceeded with construction of the Elmwood Club, the Westerkirk account had been active. She was thinking of buying an oil rig that would have to be towed from Australia; she was looking at another exploration deal; she was continually revising the estimate of the final cost of the Elmwood. She had liquidated her holdings and was now several million in debt to the bank. Molony, meanwhile, still had $2-million in fraudulent loans in her name. To the audit inspectors, who spent days going through her massive file, it looked as if Brydson had borrowed well in excess of the value of her security.

Even so, the inspection department was reluctant to classify her loans as risky, not wanting to raise hell at Commerce Court. Classify the Brydson loan and the inspector would undoubtedly hear from a vice-president who'd been trying to land Thomson business. So the inspection department delayed classifying the loan and sought to avoid doing so. The audit inspector told Molony, "If you can get this authorized within three weeks, I'll rate it a two. Otherwise, I'm going to have to give it a three." Eager to help solve the problem, Molony wrote to Special Loans asking for another increase in her authorized limit – he would appear to be acting at Brydson's request. If Credit Room agreed to the increase, the inspection department would be off the hook.

One of the other assistant managers at Bay and Richmond was on good terms with someone in Special Loans. Molony told the other assistant, "If you happen to be talking to your friend, find out what's happening with Brydson." A few days later the fellow came to Molony's office. "I've got Special Loans on the line. They're turning down the Brydson increase. Want to talk to him?"

Molony asked the assistant's friend to read the letter. "We find the customer is overextended at present borrowing levels. The available security causes us concern. We're therefore not prepared to approve . . ." The branch would not be instructed to call the loan, but the application for an increased limit was being deferred. Special Loans was saying, in effect, see if you can't get more security and then try us again.

Special Loans would now write to Credit Room; Credit Room, in turn, would write to the branch. Credit Room would undoubtedly say not only that it was unprepared to authorize the increased credit, but that it wanted to see Sherry Brydson's loans reduced to reflect the available security. Credit Room would suggest either that the branch reapply for a lower line of credit, or that the Thomson family be asked to guarantee the difference. In a few days, Molony would have a major problem. If Credit Room told Harry Buckle, "Get this loan down to $7-million," Buckle would simply pass along the bad news to Brydson. The apologetic messenger. Nothing he could do. Credit Room had laid down the law.

To which Brydson would say, "What do you mean, get it *down* to $7-million? The loan now stands at $6.6-million."

6

LUCK OF THE IRISH

"All fortune is to be conquered by bearing it."

– Francis Bacon

Ron Andrews sometimes had to leave the little room with the picture of a window on the wall. As well as running wiretaps, the anti-gambling squad of the Morality Bureau was always working on future investigations. One tap might yield two or three spin-offs. Somebody had to find out whom the voices belonged to, where the traced numbers led. Physical surveillance requires inventiveness as well as patience. In one investigation Andrews was able to discover that a bookmaker worked out of a highrise. He knew which building but had trouble determining which apartment. One evening he took his son with him. The boy was selling raffle tickets to raise money for his hockey team. When the bookmaker got home, Andrews and his son managed to get on the same elevator. The boy started his sales pitch. When the bookie reached his floor, they got off with him and accompanied him to his apartment door.

One day Andrews returned to Room 8 to find that another monitor had logged two calls on Mario Colizzi's line. Andrews rewound the tape and put on his headphones. In the first call, Beck and Colizzi were complaining about somebody. Andrews felt sure it was Mr. Brown.

"He said he was going to go away and pick something up," said Colizzi. "He never went away, so I put on the stall for him. He's probably mad at me. Fuck him."

"Yeah."

"They all get mad at me. How did he do, good or bad?"

"He lost."

"Oh, that's good. A lot?"

Beck asked, "What's going on with this guy?"

Colizzi said he didn't know, the guy had phoned his father at least six times. "With me, he wants to play, you know. He never has money to give me. He said he was going to go away and get it, he didn't go away and get it and he wanted to keep playing. No way."

"So that means he's lying then."

"He's always lying."

They talked about which of them should get paid first. Beck pointed out that there was another IOU for twenty-five.

Andrews listened carefully. Twenty-five hundred? Or twenty-five thousand?

"It looks like the party's over, doesn't it."

"Yeah, that's what I think," said Colizzi. He said he had given Mr. Brown the slip at Greenwood. He said that Mr. Brown had phoned his father, but that he'd turned off his beeper. "Plus I had a good excuse anyways, my little niece's birthday party."

"Sounds like it's all over for him," said Beck.

"Sure, if he don't give it's all over. Am I going to play for fun? I might get caught and arrested for fun?"

Beck suggested giving Mr. Brown a free holiday if he paid off.

"We got to send him to a place where there's no gambling," said Colizzi.

"He'll find something to do."

"Send him to Devil's Island," said Colizzi.

Andrews put a little red star beside the log record of that call, then ran the tape ahead. Mr. Brown had called Colizzi not long afterwards. The old man answered the phone.

"Is Mario there, please?"

"Just a moment. *Mario, telefono!*"

"Hello," said Colizzi, "I had a little problem. The ex-wife got arrested, drunk driving and everything, so I had to get the kid. I had the kid for the weekend."

"You can't pick up the phone and phone me."

"Phone, you wouldn't have been there. You said you were going to go up there, then this happened."

"Well, I said –"

"I went up there by the sixth, seventh race, ask Freddy. He said you were there mad and you left. Then I came home and my father said you'd phoned all day."

"He said he could get hold of you."

"I left the beeper at home, thought I had it with me, that's what he said, phoned the beeper, I said I left it here. I thought you were going to go away, too. The weekend."

"Even if I go away," said Mr. Brown, "I call you first."

"What am I going to do, the kid comes first. I wish I'd get him forever. She's getting fourteen days in jail and six months, her second time."

"Drunk driving?"

"Yeah, second time, she'll probably do weekends. I'll get the kid every week, it's good."

Mr. Brown was planning to go to Atlantic City. Colizzi was worried that they weren't getting together. Mr. Brown wanted to meet on Thursday instead. Colizzi said, "Thursday, I'm busy Thursday, I might have to go to Buffalo."

"One second you're looking after the kid. The next thing you're going to Buffalo." Andrews detected something new in Mr. Brown's voice, an undertone of contempt. This was a man who did not like being jerked around. He said he'd looked like a fool at the track, searching for Colizzi when he wasn't there.

"You were seventeen short," said Colizzi. "Seven plus the ten."

Seven plus ten. If it's hundreds, you don't say ten. Seventeen thousand dollars short? In a week? Plus another IOU for twenty-five thousand? Was Andrews getting this straight?

"Don't worry about the other one," said Mr. Brown.

"I'm not worried about nothing."

"Well, don't upset me!"

"What do you want to do," said Colizzi, "you want to keep going?"

"Yeah!"

"You want to keep on going?"

"Yeah!"

"When do you want to stop?"

"Whenever you feel uncomfortable."

"I feel what?"

"Uncomfortable."

"I don't know what you're talking about. Listen, can I see you tonight? We'll talk about it."

They agreed to meet at the track before the first race.

Ron Andrews put a red star beside that call, too. Then he rewound the tape, slowed it down, and listened to the conversation again.

What to do about Sherry Brydson? In the wake of the audit at Bay and Richmond, this delicate question weighed not just on Brian Molony but on Harry Buckle as well. How heavy a hand ought the bank to use in dealing with a member of the Thomson family? The ideal solution would be to obtain from John Tory the family's guarantee. Molony arranged a meeting with Tory so that he and Buckle could feel him out. Tory, it turned out, was unprepared to extend the guarantee. Sherry's disbursement from the trust she could do with as she wished. She had wanted to spread her entrepreneurial wings independent of the family and that was her prerogative. Tory indicated to Buckle and Molony that the bank was to treat her exactly as it would any other customer. He made clear, though, that the CIBC was to do nothing rash before consulting him. The bank had the idea the Thomson interests would not allow Brydson to embarrass herself, but that direct support would be provided only in case of dire need. All of which brought Harry Buckle – and everyone else at the CIBC – back to where they'd started. What to do about Sherry Brydson?

Because Molony and Brydson's lawyer were on good terms, Buckle took them for a meal at the National Club. Perhaps Brian could induce Stu Butts to go back to Brydson and make clear the bank's concerns. Perhaps that would prompt her to increase her security or find some other way of appeasing the bank. The three men discussed the situation at lunch and again, a week later, at a meeting in Molony's office. Molony, fearing that either Butts or Buckle would mention a figure, kept changing the subject, piping up with non sequiturs about the Blue Jays, the bad weather in New England, and the erratic performance of the Canadian dollar.

"The key point," said Buckle, "is that the building, in its present condition, simply isn't –"

"Wasn't that your phone, Mr. Buckle? I know Stu has to get back, so perhaps we should end here and talk again in a day or two."

Buckle didn't mind ending the meeting. This was something Brian could look after. He seemed to get along with Brydson's people, and he was the only one who really knew the details of the loan account. Besides, Buckle had other things on his mind. He was about to head off for three weeks of golf in Florida and South Carolina, and he hadn't yet packed.

The weekend Harry Buckle headed south, Ron Andrews drove north through a snowstorm to The Bulldog's cottage. He and The Bulldog both made a point of developing friendships outside the force. All too easy to socialize with other cops, to fall into the embittered, myopic cynicism that was one of the occupational hazards. Andrews and The Bulldog were close friends, though, and often went snowmobiling together. On Sunday the conversation got around to the 14 Division wiretap. The sixty-day authorization was almost up, and nothing solid had grown out of the investigation.

"I think we should keep an eye on Mario Colizzi," said Andrews.

"What have you got?"

"I don't know. There's something behind this Mr. Brown. I don't know what, but something."

"Think we should obtain a new authorization?"

"Just a feeling I've got," said Andrews. "I can't tell you more than that."

Obtaining a new authorization meant starting over, putting together an affidavit. It meant a new round of physical surveillance on the subject. You had to be able to say where he went and who he met. You had to document that his phone was busiest at the hours when gambling was normally carried out. You had to take the affidavit to a crown agent. Only if it were airtight did you get your authorization right then. Bookies thought it was easy – almost automatic – when in truth it was often a pain in the neck. You basically needed enough to arrest him then and there. The wiretap gave you documentary evidence to take to court, icing on the cake.

There was also the expense. Bell charged $50 a day for each line, and one authorization might cover twenty lines. A thousand a day added up quickly, and The Bulldog's budget had no fat. But The Bulldog himself had worked more than a hundred authorizations. He knew the importance of listening to the monitors, encouraging them to form their own opinions, letting them steer the investigation. That's why his men turned up more quality stuff than the Intelligence gambling squad – individual contributions to the group effort. Mario was still booking, no doubt about that; they had the grounds for a new affidavit. It came down to Andrews' gut instinct, and The Bulldog put great faith in instinct.

"See what I can do," he said.

On March 11, 1982, Judge H. R. Locke of York County Court granted an authorization to intercept the private communications of a number of men suspected of illegal betting and conspiracy to bet illegally. One was Mario Colizzi.

It was now more or less understood, by their friends if not by either set of parents, that Brian and Brenda were living together. He had moved in to the twenty-third-floor apartment on a trial basis. He gave Brenda $300 a month and she looked after the bills. Two hundred was half the rent; the other hundred was for phone, cable, and sundry items. They split everything. When the phone bill started including page after page of long-distance charges to the Sportsline number, Brenda simply gave it to him without a word. He paid it himself. She pointed out that he earned a better salary than she did – $33,000 to her $23,000 – but he wouldn't hear of contributing more than half the total cost. Indeed, when she raised the subject, saying she sometimes spent more than her $300 share, he chastised her for not budgeting more carefully. The next day he sent flowers and a card saying he was sorry.

Brian was less than tidy, and his clothes tended to collect on every chair and door frame. If Brenda objected, he explained that he was airing them out. There was no arguing with him. His mother had spent her life picking up after the Molony boys and he expected her to do the same. It wasn't a big deal, not something she'd ever really got upset about. That was just Brian. But she was more unhappy than ever – tired of spending night after night and weekends by herself – and reminders of his selfishness added to her resentment. Gathering up the dirty clothes, waiting for the elevator down to the laundry room, she wondered why she'd become so involved with him in the first place. The Brian she lived with wasn't the same Brian she'd been drawn to.

If anyone else criticized him, she stood up for him. When one of the girls at work suggested that Brenda was getting the short end of the stick, that Brian was using her, she vehemently denied it. Secretly, though, she wondered if it were true. What was she going to do? The strain was affecting her sleep, her work, her whole life. Between chatting on the phone with girlfriends and visiting her parents, she fantasized about issuing an ultimatum. She would have done it, too, except she was afraid to imagine his answer.

One evening, putting his socks away, she came on a bundle of U.S. cash. The sight of the money terrified her. It was like the airline tickets she'd accidentally opened, like Colizzi's low, faintly accented voice on the phone – it took her fear out of hiding and stuck it right under her nose, so blatant she couldn't pretend it wasn't there. What was Brian doing with so much American money? Had he got himself in debt to them? Was he discharging the debt by carrying money across the border? Is that why he was always going away?

That night Brian got home at one-thirty. He'd had good success at the races and was looking forward to checking the scores and the stock quotations. The sight of Brenda in her flannel nightgown, stone-faced, not even watching television, nearly made him turn around. She asked him about the money. She wanted to know why he had it, where it came from. Was it his? Was he in some kind of trouble? He gave splendid, evasive answers, but she wouldn't let him get away with it. She had promised herself for months she'd straighten this out – get some real communication going or else break it off completely.

"Where is this relationship headed? Where do you want it to go?"

Brian seemed puzzled. "In what sense?"

"Nothing changes. When I tried to talk to you before Christmas you said your problems would be settled by February. Now it's March and you're going away more than ever. What are you doing?"

"I'm looking after things the best way I know how."

"What are you looking after?"

"I've told you. I've got financial responsibilities. I'm under a lot of pressure at work. Buckle's away. I've got an important meeting coming up. They're my problems and I'll deal with them."

"I have two thousand in my savings account. You can have that if you want."

"I appreciate the offer, but I'll deal with this myself."

"I could cash my RRSP. Almost three thousand. I could give you almost five thousand dollars altogether."

"Brenda, I can't take your money. Just let me deal with it."

"Do you owe more than twenty thousand?"

Brian laughed, as if the question were preposterous. "Where did you pick that number? Out of a hat?"

"I don't know where. Answer me. Do you?"

"I want you to let me deal with my own problems. And please stop worrying. There's nothing to worry about."

"Don't tell me to stop worrying! I just worry more."

He shrugged and turned on the TV.

She got up and shut it off. "Why do you have to go away?"

"If you want more time together, come with me," he said, turning it back on, changing stations. "I told you before, you can come anytime you want." She hated Atlantic City, hated gambling. But now she couldn't say he hadn't made concessions, offered to include her. Her anger turned into hopelessness.

"Just tell me one thing," she said, resigned now, more curious than accusing. She felt chilly, and tucked her bare feet under herself on the chair. "Please tell me why you have to keep going back."

She may as well have asked a bull, in its bright necklace of blood, why it kept lunging at the cape. The question was central to Molony's essence but one he himself was unequipped to answer. He believed he kept going back because he had borrowed a huge sum and gambling was his one chance of recovering it. He thought of himself as forced to gamble to extricate himself from the financial web in which he'd entangled himself. The casino games at Caesars offered his only hope of redemption.

Craps and baccarat are indeed games, as pinochle and checkers are games. As in any game, agreed-upon conventions organize the activity. To subscribe to those conventions, to participate in the game, is to cut yourself off from the world. The variables that orient you in the outside world – climate, geography, hour of day – vanish when you step into the casino. The Tropicana in Las Vegas at four on a blistering afternoon is the Golden Nugget in Atlantic City on a foggy night. The Tropicana is the Golden Nugget, New Jersey is Nevada, four o'clock is eleven, and money is chips – these are what the American sociologist Irving Goffman calls the "transformation rules" that give new meaning to existing perceptions.

The casino insulates those who play the game, and its power to render you inattentive to the outside world makes it a marvellous escape. What better way to forget the office, the mortgage, the pressures of family and career? Most people find a few days in Las Vegas or Atlantic City a wonderful tonic. They're free to live by their own schedule, behave as they wish, enjoy the glitter and self-indulgence. They return to their lives restored and content.

Unhappy people, though, grieving people, desperate, bereft, fragile, rejected, downhearted, frightened, unfulfilled, lonely, and insecure people find a casino less restorative than analgesic. In the casino, life's complications are set aside. The more painful the complications, the greater the casino's allure. If the gambler has low self-esteem, if the outside world has given him a poor self-image, he has the additional comfort of being stroked. He is recognized and catered to. His ego is bolstered, his vanity flattered. Every gambler tells himself his object is to win, but his true object may be the avoidance of pain. Playing and losing is better than not playing. Winning is better than losing, sure, but only because it allows the gambler to keep playing.

Goffman has said that all games "display in a simple way the structure of real-life situations. They cut us off from serious life by immersing us in its possibilities." Once Molony entered the casino, he found it self-contained and complete. Within its framework anything could happen. He could witness the impossible – twenty straight passes at the crap table, the bank winning ten times in a row at baccarat, someone down to his last chip cashing out for a million dollars. Not just witness the impossible, but accomplish it. The chosen someone could be him. Going to the casino was not like going to the movies – mere escape into entertainment – because his presence helped dictate the construction of events. He did gamble to escape, clearly, but gambling was more than that: it was an existential act. Each time he threw the dice he forged his fate. No matter that his fate was pre-ordained, that anyone else could have predicted a disastrous end. Swept away by his defiance were the limitations, frustrations, and ambiguities of daily life, a grey plain across which other people spent their lives trudging. This was (1) not satisfactory, (2) acceptable, or (3)unsatisfactory. This was black and white, win or lose. Molony had found the way to take himself off the grey plain, knowledge so powerful it's usually available only to those able to master it. He happened on it through a defective brand of self-possession and was unequipped for mastery. Fail to master powerful knowledge and you're at its mercy.

In a casino, the conventional distinctions by which people organize themselves – appearance, social standing, race, religion, dress, occupation – are set aside. Few places are as egalitarian as the crap table. Nothing counts but money. If you have enough to play, you're part of the game. It doesn't matter how you came by the money or how you're perceived by the outside world. Your achievement at the table becomes the basis of your standing, as achieved success is the basis of capitalistic society. The casino reflects the North American ideal – make money at the game and you're a winner. Even if you're a loser ("anybody you see more than twice"), the casino allows you to gain status according to the amount you lose and the way you comport yourself. The brilliance of the casino is twofold. It allows you a measure of dignity while taking your money, and it conditions you to return and lose more money.

More than anyone else, the Harvard psychologist B. F. Skinner has shaped our thinking about conditioned behaviour. Skinner is the main proponent of the view that human behaviour is shaped by its consequences. Pavlov's conditioning was based on association. His dogs, accustomed to hearing a bell when presented with food, began salivating at the sound of the bell even in the absence of food. Skinner looked instead at how a particular behaviour was reinforced. He believed that our thoughts and rationalizations are mere gloss on the true reason we do what we do. He argued that behaviour, if positively reinforced, will be repeated; if negatively reinforced, will eventually be extinguished.

Skinner's ideas are by no means universally accepted – he makes a quick, unexamined extrapolation from rats and pigeons to human beings – but behaviourism provides, at the least, an intriguing way of looking at the world. Regard a casino in behaviouristic terms and you find all the elements Skinner deemed crucial to the conditioning process. The first is an environment that's carefully controlled. Skinner's rats and pigeons were confined in highly simplified, barren environments – "Skinner boxes." The casino environment – stimulatory music and colour schemes, constant temperature and lighting, no clocks or windows – is as deliberate as the uptempo Muzak segments programmed to coincide with unproductive work periods in offices and factories. And while the gambler, unlike the lab rat, is free to leave this contrived setting, he is subtly discouraged from doing so. Everything he might want – food, drink, entertainment, shopping, recreation, sleep – can be obtained under the same roof. It's easier to stay than to leave. Architecturally, hotel-casino complexes contrive to bring you again and again to the gaming tables. Go from the coffee shop to your room, the pool to the newsstand, the showroom to the front doors, and you pass through the casino. There are few places to sit down other than at the tables. To get from Caesars' casino to the Boardwalk in Atlantic City, you pass through two sets of doors. The tinted exterior glass makes even the sunniest day appear overcast and dismal.

Skinner found that one key to successful operant conditioning is timing. Conditioning is most successful when the consequence immediately follows the behaviour. In the casino a bet is placed, it's won or lost, the next bet is placed. The same behaviour is repeated over and over; the reinforcement is immediate. The most effective reinforcement schedule, Skinner discovered, is intermittent positive reinforcement. If a behaviour is always reinforced, the animal doesn't repeat it immediately: a food pellet can be obtained any time. If it's never reinforced, the behaviour gradually dies out. Behaviour is most firmly reinforced, in other words, when the reward does not come each time the behaviour is repeated but does come, eventually, if it is repeated often enough. Every gambler wins sometimes but never knows when the next win will come. Though unable to predict when he'll be rewarded, he's been conditioned to expect that, sooner or later, he will be.

Like every gambler, Molony lost more often than he won. Is losing not negative reinforcement? According to behaviourism, shouldn't gambling be extinguished? Often it is. Many people gamble, lose, and swear off gambling. Suppose, though, that the reinforcing consequence of placing a bet is not winning but feeling the intense excitement of having money at risk. If stimulation is the reinforcement, the gambler, as he loses, is conditioning himself to continue gambling. Psychologists have done laboratory experiments in which an electrode was implanted in the pleasure centre of a rat's brain. In the rat's cage was one bar that could be depressed to release a food pellet and another to stimulate the pleasure centre. The rat opted for pleasure again and again; depressing the pleasure bar was its final act before dying of starvation.

"I have to go back," Molony told Brenda. She wanted nothing more than the truth, but how could he share it with her? The tortuous complications of his life were his own doing. What kind of person would drag an innocent into them? "It's something I have to clear up. It won't take much longer."

"Brian, don't you see? I don't know if we can go on like this much longer."

"You'll just have to trust me. I know what I'm doing."

March 13, 1982. Caesars Atlantic City. Frank Hines.

10 p.m. Brian Maloney on game. Received two markers for total of $45,000. Bets up to $10,000. Lost $30,000 while I observed game.

3:30 a.m. Baccarat 1. Maloney still playing. Bets up to $20,000.

On the morning of St. Patrick's Day, Bert Mills walked briskly from Commerce Court up to the branch at Bay and Richmond. Mills was a distinguished-looking, grey-haired man who didn't quite fill out his dark blue suit. He was a vice-president in the bank's credit division. Since Harry Buckle was away, Mills asked the acting manager, John Galbraith, to brief him about the Sherry Brydson meeting. Galbraith knew little about it and introduced Mills to Brian Molony.

"Perhaps you could bring Mr. Mills up to date."

Molony told Mills that Brydson had requested a meeting once it became clear that the bank was unwilling to make further loans in the absence of more security. Brydson felt that if she could talk to someone senior in the bank, said Molony, she could explain exactly what she was trying to do.

"How much more do they want?"

"A million to a million-two should do it."

"We'd better get over there," said Mills, looking at his watch.

"I'll just use the men's room first."

It was a lovely morning, with a hint of spring in the air. Crossing Bay Street to the Thomson Building, Molony felt like a man walking to the gallows. The day before, in desperation, he had done a memo to Credit Room claiming that the Bank of Montreal had agreed to take over part of Brydson's loan. Craziness. It would only draw questions about how the business had been allowed to slip away.

In the spacious boardroom on the twenty-fourth floor of the Thomson Building, Mills and Molony shook hands with Brydson and her people. "Is it warm out?" Stuart Butts asked Molony. "I can't believe how hot your hand feels." The atmosphere was tense. Brydson's people wondered if the bank had decided there would be no more money. That would be inconvenient enough, but there was an even more disquieting possibility. Had the decision been made to call the loan? Absurd to go this far and then pull the plug, but why else would the meeting have been called? Why would a vice-president be getting involved?

Brydson's people sat on one side of the table, Mills and Molony on the other. John Tory sat slightly apart, an observer. Molony had to find a way of directing the meeting. He was terrified not only of a possible reference to the amount of Brydson's loans, but also to any allusion to the Bank of Montreal.

"Why don't you tell us about the club," he suggested. "How's the membership drive going?"

"We'd prefer to follow our agenda," said one of Brydson's people, distributing xeroxed sheets around the table.

Molony was so anxious he could barely make sense of the financial projections. Was it possible? He went through the projections again. Miraculously, there was no reference to the loan balance.

"Perhaps you could explain the membership projections," he said. Could they not hear his heart thumping? "How exactly do you plan to attract these members?"

Brydson's original plan had been to sell shares in an oil-and-gas company and offer club membership as a bonus. This approach had tax advantages, allowing members to write off their investment. But the deal became so convoluted – the Ontario Securities Commission would require scores of documents from each investor – that it aroused suspicion; then federal legislation was passed that erased the tax benefits. Having spent $370,000 developing the prospectus, Brydson had to trash the whole scheme. The new plan was to raise money through annual memberships. Molony asked how these memberships would be sold. Brydson mentioned a number of marketing ideas, and Molony asked for elaboration. Membership didn't bear directly on financial matters: he could have talked about membership all day.

Brydson's people couldn't grasp the point of the meeting. Mills kept saying the bank had serious reservations. Brydson replied that the bank had been kept apprised all along: "The facts are the facts. You have our financial statements. We've been keeping you up to date on the projected opening date. Now, as you know, it looks like there's going to be a strike in the building trades, which is why we've had to set the opening back again."

"The situation is unacceptable," said Mills. "The bank has concerns about these projections and the available security. Mr. Tory, we would frankly appreciate the assurance of your support."

Tory, an impeccable diplomat, replied that the project had to be assessed on its own. If, through unforeseen circumstances, Sherry's affairs reached crisis point – a purely hypothetical situation – then yes, of course, some form of support would be seriously considered. The salient fact, though, was that this was a business proposition, to be looked at without reference to external factors.

Mills was frustrated. Why wouldn't Tory say, "We stand behind it. If this thing blows up, we'll write a cheque."

Brydson's people were frustrated. Why wouldn't the bank articulate its concerns? Here was its chance to say, "We're not happy with the reporting procedures," or, "We're not persuaded by these financial projections." But Molony only asked for more information and Mills only shook his head and repeated that the situation was unacceptable.

"I can't make the plumbers work any faster," said Brydson, exasperated. "It seems to me you have two choices. You either support us until we can get the doors open and have some hope of making the money back, or you help yourselves to a partly completed project. I can't see any other options. I can't snap my fingers and make the problems go away."

"As I say, we have concerns about the available security."

"You have the security of the building," said Brydson. "I don't understand why that isn't enough."

To Brydson, the building was securing $4-million in loans. To Mills, it had been securing up to $6.5-million. The discrepancy hung like a guillotine above the boardroom table, miraculously invisible to everyone but Molony.

Mills asked if the appraisal on the building had been done recently. Brydson said it was a few weeks old. Mills asked Molony what the bank's own appraisers had to say about it.

"We don't have a Kinross appraisal," said Molony. "That's a very good point. Perhaps we should get their thoughts before we go any further. I'll arrange it this afternoon. Once we have that, we'll all be in a better position to assess the situation."

Brydson left the meeting angry, baffled, and upset. If they thought there was a problem, why didn't they make clear what it was? If they thought she was mishandling the project, why didn't they send in a management consultant to look things over and protect their investment? What had been the purpose of the meeting? Simply to scold her?

Stu Butts said to Molony, "Is it chilly in here? Your hand is ice cold."

Mills, aware that Tory represented all the corporate concerns beneath the Thomson umbrella, said, "Good to see you. Why don't you come up to the fifty-sixth floor one day and have some lunch."

"Good to see you, too."

"Interesting meeting," Molony said in the elevator. "What are your thoughts?"

"I don't know about that women's club," said Mills. "Some of those projections seem very optimistic. Now they're talking about changing the health spa and adding boutiques? If you ask me, the whole thing seems a bit farfetched."

On Saturday morning, Molony drove to the airport with a haunted sense of mission. He did not feel well. He had not been sleeping. When he did slip under, he found himself back at the boardroom table trying to explain the $2.5-million discrepancy, sputtering, mortified, a disgrace. This was the weekend. It had to be. He had survived St. Patrick's Day by the skin of his teeth and didn't know how much longer he could hang on. He cleared customs and was making for his gate when he noticed a man headed his way who looked remarkably familiar. The man had Alex Osborne's bulky build and round face, but was dressed in white trousers and a floral shirt.

"Hello there, Brian."

"Good to see you, sir. What are you doing here?"

"Might even be the same thing you are," said Osborne, teasing. "Not catching an airplane by any chance, are you?"

"Just surprised to see you," said Molony, acutely aware of the $238,000 cash in his various pockets. He must have looked like the Michelin man.

"How's everything at Bay and Richmond?"

"A bit hectic lately."

"Thanks again for your information."

The two had stayed in close touch. Molony had mentioned on the phone that a Keele and Lawrence customer had turned up at Bay and Richmond, looking for a loan. Osborne had been after a personal statement from the customer for some time, and was surprised Molony had been able to obtain it. Molony had passed along the financial information Osborne had been looking for.

"Glad I could help, Mr. O."

"I've told Ross Brady at Commerce Court that he should get you transferred down there. I can't get you up to Lawrence and Keele. Our friend Buckle won't oblige."

"I appreciate that," said Molony. "Where are you off to?"

"Just a little holiday. How about you?"

"I have a sick aunt in New York. I'm kind of the family representative, I guess. My mother and father are tied up this weekend. I've been to see her a couple of times. She's not at all well. I thought I should spend some time with her."

"That's very good of you."

"I think that's my flight," said Molony, shaking Osborne's hand. "Have a good trip. Speak to you when you get back."

When Molony's plane put down at LaGuardia he hurried through the terminal and down the escalator. The limo would be directly outside. Instead of going all the way to the exit he pushed through a safety door. He'd misjudged. He was in a maintenance area. Three men sat by a forklift, passing a reefer. Molony was suddenly aware he was white. He turned to go back through the door, but it had locked shut behind him. The men were eyeing him. One stood up and said something. The others, unhurriedly, got to their feet. Molony started walking in the other direction, so quickly the bundled money made his pockets flap; he held his suit jacket tight to his sides. He emerged at the cab stand and found himself facing two lanes of oncoming traffic. By the time he'd made it back to the limousine he was soaked with sweat.

The driver opened the door for him, as if passengers did this every day.

"Mr. Molony?"

"Sorry I'm late."

Molony locked the doors and gazed out the tinted window. He was looking not at the Manhattan skyline but at nearby cars, peering inside, memorizing licence numbers. Many of them had New Jersey plates. A grey Oldsmobile followed the limousine off one freeway and onto another. It pulled out to pass when his driver did; it seemed to be keeping a steady distance. What if it was someone from the casino, an employee or another gambler? In New York twenty dollars was worth killing for. What would someone do for a quarter million?

Before long the limousine was tearing along a deserted stretch south of Newark. The Oldsmobile had been left behind. Molony was all for getting there, but this was ridiculous. Something didn't seem right. The driver was nervous and preoccupied. He was a man Molony hadn't seen before – a big, black, handsome, unhappy fellow, a movie star stuck behind the wheel. When he glanced at Molony in the mirror, Molony wondered if he knew about the cash. Everybody must have known. The casino executives knew, and word got around. Toronto. Glasses and a bushy moustache. Cash player, pulls it out of his pockets. They were in the middle of nowhere, a stretch of decrepit warehouses and factories. What if he'd been set up? The driver would pull off, claiming engine trouble. He'd open the hood, his buddies would appear, all over in ten seconds. Molony felt the cash and tried to think of the money he was going to win at Caesars. This was going to be the big weekend. Monday he'd square himself with the bank. At the very least he'd win enough to pay down Brydson. The awful feeling was sheer paranoia. He was getting as bad as Beck. He'd start at baccarat, five thousand a hand, stay until he lost three in a row, then move to craps –

"Stopping for coffee."

The driver was already slowing – how could Molony tell him no? Ahead, on the left, was a dilapidated diner set off by itself. The driver parked around the side, asked if Molony wanted anything, and said he'd be right back. The moment he stepped out, Molony locked the doors. He looked all around – nobody in sight, just a few parked cars – and began stuffing cash under the front seat, between cushions, anywhere he could. Would it be horrible, something out of *The Godfather*? Where would they come from? The back of the diner? One of the parked cars? Would another car pull up alongside?

Two men emerged from the diner, hesitated, and headed his way. One wore work clothes; the other carried an oversized briefcase. Terrified, Molony crouched on the floor and prayed they'd walk by. They could have it all, he'd fish it out for them, but what if they didn't stop at robbery? How could he have been so idiotic, packing sums that people would kill for? This was his last chance to bail himself out. If they took his money he wouldn't even be able to report –

Crack! Crack-crack!

Molony nearly jumped out of his skin. Someone was knocking on the windshield. They knew he was in there, no use hiding. He peeked over the seat, expecting to see a gun. It was the driver, pointing at the locked door and shrugging.

Molony didn't say a word the rest of the trip. When they got to Atlantic City he retrieved the money he'd hidden. Still shaken, he hurried into Caesars. He hadn't counted the money and realized he might have left a bundle under the passenger seat. He hurried back outside but the limousine was gone. At the cage he pulled cash from every pocket and piled it on the counter. Signing the customer-deposit receipt, he could barely grip the pen. He was racked with convulsive shudders and pretended he was chilly. Was he losing his grip? Was this what happened when you had a nervous breakdown?

He headed for the baccarat pit and asked the floorman for a marker. The computer printed it out. Molony signed the marker and was issued chips. He fondled the chips a moment, deliberating, then bet the bank. His panic had subsided, he felt better. He felt fine. Actually, he felt great. He'd stay with baccarat until he'd won half a million or else lost three hands in a row. He was waiting for the shuffle when Jess Lenz sat down beside him.

"Nice to see you, Brian. Have a good trip?"

"Not really."

"That so? Anything I can do for you?"

Yes, said Molony, there was. He worried about carrying so much money, frankly, using the same procedure each week. People knew he brought large parcels of cash. He also disliked taking money through customs. Was there a way of transferring funds directly from Toronto?

Lenz said he thought so, but wanted to speak to the attorneys. He went off to find Larry Woolf. Woolf had just been promoted again, to senior vice-president, which made him responsible for the hotel and the food and beverage departments, as well as casino customer development, casino administration, and casino operations.

Woolf took the matter to Bill Hessel and Linc Ebert in the financial department. Like Lenz and Woolf, Hessel and Ebert were Nevada hands who had moved east when Atlantic City got going. Hessel, a thin, nervous, chain-smoking man, was the casino controller. Ebert, whose glasses, moustache, and corpulence gave him a certain resemblance to Molony, was director of cage operations. They said a transfer procedure was already in place. Molony could wire funds directly to the Caesars account at Midlantic Bank in Atlantic City.

Jess Lenz went back to the baccarat pit and, at the next shuffle, informed Molony of the procedure. "All you have to do is take the funds to your bank, Brian. They'll wire them to our bank."

Never. American law required banks accepting cash deposits of $10,000 or more to obtain identification. The bank would want to know who was wiring the money. Besides, Canadian banks got skittish when American currency showed up. There had been a rash of counterfeit U.S. bills in Toronto. Walk in with pots of U.S. cash and the next thing you'd feel a tap on your shoulder.

Molony mumbled something about tax problems.

Jess Lenz got the picture. Maybe Mr. M. was concerned about anonymity – lots of heavy hitters were. Maybe Mr. M. had his own reasons for not liking the idea. That was Mr. M.'s business. Lenz said he'd look into it further.

Molony, stifled at baccarat, gathered his dwindling pile of chips and headed for the dice pit.

March 20, 1982. Caesars Atlantic City. Frank Hines.

12:45. Craps 9. Brian Maloney on game. Betting real good. Laying 4 and 10, Don't Place, 6 and 8 or 5 and 9. Also betting $2,000 in Come, *up to $5,000 in Field. Switches between Don't and Pass Line. $2,000 double odds. Was up to $70,000. Now has $45,000.*

When Mario Colizzi told Molony he was going to Las Vegas for a few days, to get away from the cold and pick up a suede jacket, Molony asked him to make some bets at the Barbary Coast. Colizzi stopped by the apartment on his way to the airport. Molony met him in the lobby.

"You should come with us," said Colizzi. In the freezing cold he was wearing white slacks and a Hawaiian shirt. "You work too hard. You don't look good. You need to relax."

Two men Molony didn't know were waiting in the Seville. "Some of us have jobs, Mario."

"Few days, big deal."

"Sir, phone me when you get there," said Molony, handing him an envelope full of U.S. cash.

"I'm not taking that," said Colizzi. "Want me to bet, send me the money."

Molony had to add another stop to his noon-hour circuit. On Monday he hurried down to CNCP Telecommunications on Front Street. The office was cramped and understaffed; there was a lineup. He waited restlessly while the clerk prepared the wire transfer. Molony had arranged, through Michael Neustadter, a complimentary room for Colizzi at Caesars Palace in Las Vegas. The funds were sent in care of Caesars, to be released on presentation of Colizzi's Ontario driver's licence. Molony paid with a CIBC bank draft, drawn on Roger Oskaner's account – since it had got by the audit inspector he was able to use it again – and then hurried up to Richardson Securities.

He was no longer dealing only in stocks and bonds. He had moved into options and commodities, speculating on copper, tin, soybeans, pork bellies, and the Canadian dollar. To Jim Surgey, who was having an excellent year, it seemed a natural enough progression. Options and commodities meant feverish action and greater risk, of course, but also the possibility of substantial profit. Brian's people were more active than ever in their stock and bond dealings: the monthly statements for the "Brian Molony in Trust" accounts – one in U.S. dollars, the other in Canadian – sometimes ran to ten pages. Brian himself was remarkably cool, considering the sums involved, and had a keen understanding of the connection between interest rates and the value of the dollar. He seemed quite at home dealing in dollar futures. Indeed, as Surgey remarked to his secretary, he had something of a flair for it.

"Enclosed herewith are five demand promissory notes in favour of your bank. You or any officer designated by you are hereby authorized and requested to complete one or more of these notes by filling in the date and rate of interest . . ."

The letter was the standard assignation form provided by customers opening a loan account. Molony had applied for an authorized credit of $3-million in the name of a fictitious company called 499726 Ontario Ltd. Every new company in Ontario is assigned such a number; most convert the number to an operating name. Molony had looked up the most recent numbers, to be in the ballpark. Signing the assignation, purportedly on behalf of 499726 Ontario Ltd., he didn't even bother disguising his distinctive signature. He was taking the corners on two wheels now, almost out of control, claiming the loan was secured by the liquid assets of a wealthy retired fellow whose account he didn't even handle. Insanity, but he had to do something and couldn't imagine what else to do. He had run the fraudulent Leo Sherman loan account over its $1-million limit. He'd created another fictitious account in the name of Kernwood Limited and made loan advances of $920,000 and $490,000. There was still tremendous heat on the Brydson loan account. Interest was coming due on all the outstanding loans. And Harry Buckle was about to return from holiday. If he could just make it back to the casino . . .

Using two of the fraudulent promissory notes, Molony put through loan advances of $1.8-million and $1.1-million to the numbered company. He placed the money in term deposits. If downtown refused to approve the $3-million credit, he'd be guilty of having advanced the money prematurely. At least he'd be able to say yes, true, but it's in term deposits: it hasn't left the branch.

The term deposits served another purpose. Molony intended to use the 499726 money to pay down the Brydson loan. Having claimed that the Bank of Montreal had assumed part of her loan, he had to get the balance down. He couldn't simply take money from one customer's loan account and apply it against another customer's loans. That would surely arouse suspicion. Rolling over the term deposits for a couple of days would open up a bit of room between the two transactions.

Then, abruptly, the retired man whose assets were securing the 499726 loan moved his business. Evidently he'd found a less busy branch where the staff could spend more time humouring him. Disastrous: the security for a huge, fraudulent loan had evaporated. Molony could only hope that Buckle, going through the backlog of work after his holiday, wouldn't notice. In another way, though, the customer's departure was a blessing. At least he would no longer be in the branch. There was less possibility that a chance remark to him, or by him, would expose the fraud.

As soon as downtown authorized the 499726 loan, believing it fully secured by assets now with another branch, Molony cashed the term deposits and applied the proceeds against the Brydson loan. He also phoned Atlantic City to say he'd be coming down on Friday night. Jess Lenz said he'd book a suite and see to the transportation.

"Have you found out how the funds might be transferred?"

"We have, Brian, but I don't want to talk on the phone. Don't worry about your trip – you won't have to take the limo. We'll have a plane pick you up at La Guardia."

On Friday Molony put through another loan to the numbered company, for $300,000. He used the proceeds to pay down the Roger Oskaner loan, buy U.S. cash for himself at Friedberg's, and send more money for sports bets to Colizzi, whom he'd talked into staying in Las Vegas. Again he went to CNCP and waited while the girl prepared the wire transfer. The largest sum Western Union would transmit was $2,000. Colizzi, in Las Vegas, had to sign for receipt of forty-five separate telegraphic money orders. Each bore the slogan: "Western Union – Fastest Way to Get Money Around."

Molony returned to the branch, worked into early evening, then raced out to Pearson International, just making his flight. On arrival at LaGuardia he phoned Sportsline for the basketball scores, then got a taxi. When the driver found out he was only going to the private terminal, he wanted a flat five bucks. Molony was outraged.

"I'm only going half a mile."

"Leave here, man, I got to go all the way around and get back in this line, understand?"

"Extortion," said Molony.

The aircraft was a chartered Cessna 200. To take off, the pilot had to cross the runways used by the commercial airliners. Molony peered out: a jumbo jet seemed about to land on top of them. The pilot didn't even flinch. Molony crouched down, terrified. Was he losing his marbles? He drew a deep breath and closed his eyes, trying to calm himself.

It was a half-hour flight to Pomona Airport, where a stretch limousine was waiting. When Molony walked into the lobby at Caesars, one of the credit executives greeted him and accompanied him to the cage. Molony pulled bundles of cash from his pockets and signed a customer-deposit receipt. Jess Lenz approached him by the baccarat pit and said he had good news.

The casino had an even faster way to get money around.

7
APRIL FOOLS

"There's a little more to the casino business than the play at the tables. First and foremost, we have to be objective. By that I mean this business is about money, and all money looks alike. Am I right?"

– Elmore Leonard, *Glitz*

The Manulife Centre, at Bay and Bloor Streets in Toronto, occupies a prime city block and includes three levels of underground parking, three floors of retail outlets, sixteen floors of offices, fifty floors of apartments, and a rooftop bar that commands a fine view of downtown. The apartments attract well-heeled urbanites; the retail floors attract shoppers from Bloor Street and the nearby Yorkville district to its forty boutiques, agencies, theatres, restaurants, and banks.

One of the banks with a branch in the Manulife Centre was the Bank of Montreal, Canada's third largest (after the Royal and the CIBC). The branch maintained two accounts – one for Canadian dollars, the other American – in the name of California Clearing Corporation. The company was incorporated in 1966 and was also licensed to do business under the name Charles K. Peterson. Branch records showed the account holder's address as 3570 Las Vegas Blvd., Las Vegas, Nevada.

On the Las Vegas Strip it's not easy spotting street numbers, but somewhere behind the computerized fountains and neon arpeggios and mock-Roman facade of Caesars Palace you may find 3570, or perhaps MMMDLXX, bolted to a stucco-and-chicken-wire column. California Clearing Corporation was a dummy company set up by Caesars for casino patrons wishing to deposit cash for future use or pay down gambling debts. Caesars maintained such accounts in many places, including San Francisco, New York, Chicago, Houston, Mexico City, Hong Kong, London, and Singapore. Think of Caesars Palace as a kind of central vacuum system, sucking in lost bets through concealed outlets in the world's major cities.

New Jersey law prohibits Atlantic City casinos from maintaining bank accounts outside that state. As alumni of Caesars Palace in Las Vegas, Jess Lenz and Larry Woolf were aware that Nevada had so such prohibition. In the baccarat pit at Caesars in Atlantic City, Lenz told Molony about California Clearing Corporation. To forward money, Molony had only to alert the Caesars office in Toronto that he was making a deposit in the CCC account at the Manulife branch of the Bank of Montreal. The money would be credited to Caesars Palace in Nevada, which would transfer it to the sister casino in New Jersey. Once the deposit was confirmed in Toronto, the money would be made available to Molony in Atlantic City.

Molony thanked Lenz and spent the weekend gambling in Atlantic City. "Brian," Lenz said to him, shaking his head, after watching a feverish run at the crap table, "you're worse than the Arabs." Colizzi was still betting sports for Molony in Las Vegas. On Sunday afternoon, when Molony ran out of cash, he called Colizzi, who was about to return to Toronto. Molony asked him to stay in Nevada, the only place in North America where you can gamble legally on sporting events. The NCAA college basketball championship would be decided in New Orleans the next night. Molony wanted to bet the game – North Carolina versus Georgetown – and told Colizzi he'd wire more money.

On Monday morning, at Bay and Richmond, Molony instructed that $200,000 be advanced to Roger Oskaner and $120,000 to 499726 Ontario Ltd. He picked up bearer bonds at Richardson Securities, sold the bonds to the securities department of his own branch, bought U.S. cash at Friedberg's, and went down to the CNCP Telecommunications office on Front Street. There he sent off more money to Colizzi, this time in care of the Barbary Coast. He paid for the transfer with a CIBC draft, showing the money as being sent by Roger Oskaner.

A day survived moved him a day closer to the casino. He stayed late at the branch, locked the doors and picked up Brenda at her branch. They drove out to the townhouse of friends in Scarborough. Phil and Louise had invited them to play hearts. Brian, as usual, insisted on Swiss Chalet – Phil and Louise rolled their eyes. Shortly after everybody had taken their places at the table, Brian glanced at his watch. "Mind if I turn on the TV? There's a game I wouldn't mind following." Out the corner of his eye he watched basketball. North Carolina had been favoured by 1½ points over Georgetown, and he'd given the points to bet the Tar Heels. North Carolina had to win by at least two points for Molony to win his bet.

The game was as tight as the spread; the lead shifted back and forth through three quarters. Molony was outwardly indifferent, as usual, but rum and Coke loosened him and as the final minute ticked away he couldn't restrain himself. His enthusiasm was infectious; the others cheered when the Tar Heels took the lead, groaned when they fell behind. With fifteen seconds to go, Michael Jordan hit a jump shot that put North Carolina ahead, 63–62. The others clapped and hollered.

Not Brian. The Hoyas would work the ball up court, playing for the final shot, running the clock down. They'd win or lose by one point on the last play of the game. He was sunk. Then, unbelievably, Georgetown turned the ball over. James Worthy intercepted a pass, giving North Carolina possession with only a few seconds left. He was saved! Georgetown had to foul intentionally, giving North Carolina two free throws. Sure enough, one of the Hoyas fouled Worthy, the Tar Heels' best player and a 90-per-cent shooter from the line.

Worthy had to hit only one of two free throws for the Tar Heels to win by two. He dribbled, set, and lofted the ball. It caught the rim, rattled the backboard, circled the rim, and rolled out.

"No," said Molony.

The referee bounced the ball to him, and Molony knew he'd miss again. He knew as surely as he knew his own name. Worthy dribbled and shot. The ball hit the front rim and bounced back.

"Fuck! I can't believe it!"

None of them had ever heard Brian swear. Not even Brenda had seen him express anger. Phil wondered how much he'd bet on the game – must have been hundreds.

Worthy and the other North Carolina players were jubilant. Their team had won the NCAA championship by a point; by a point, Molony had lost $250,000. The closing spread added salt to the wound. If he'd waited until game time, he could have bet the Tar Heels even. He would have won by a point. A half-million-dollar reversal. Unbelievable. Why him? Why, in the midst of the most gruelling test of his life, had he been singled out for misfortune? He fought an impulse to drive his fist through the tabletop.

"Clubs are played, Brian."

"Excuse me."

In the bathroom he removed his glasses and studied himself in the mirror. His skin was pasty, his breathing came in ragged gasps.

His mouth filled suddenly with saliva. He knelt at the toilet but nothing came. At the basin he splashed water on his face and felt better. At least the game had been a thriller. Losing by an inch was more intense than winning by a mile. God, what a ride. Close your eyes on a roller coaster and you can't tell whether you're hitting bottom or going over the top. All you know is what you feel, and you feel things that people who stick to subways and buses will never feel . . .

Molony flushed the toilet for the others to hear. Funny how he'd known Worthy would miss the second free throw. If he could have bet, right then, he would have bet his life. He dried his face and put his glasses back on. The others were waiting for him. He took his seat, avoiding Brenda's eye, and picked up his cards.

"What did you lead?"

"Clubs," said Phil.

"Anything wrong?" said Brenda.

"What's the matter?" said Louise. "Your team won."

A couple of days later, on Thursday morning, Molony arrived at work to find his office done up with streamers, his drawers taped shut, and the wildlife prints on his wall upside down. His phone rang. He picked up the receiver and heard only a dial tone. Two girls, watching across the mezzanine, couldn't help giggling. "April Fools!"

Where was the old Brian? The one who would have had an instant comeback. As a credit officer he'd been unfailingly genial, thriving on work, cheering up the others with a joke. Remember the time he phoned Ralph's credit officer, knowing that Ralph was out of the branch? He pretended to be Ralph's biggest customer and said he was pulling his accounts because he could never get in touch with anyone who knew anything about them. Remember the stunned look on poor Terry's face, and Brian's mischievous grin, and the way they laughed about it afterwards? Whatever happened to that Brian? Remember the way he'd acted on Monte Carlo night, when blackjack tables were set up downstairs and he showed all the girls how to play? "When you want another card say, 'Hit me! Hit me again!'" Like a big kid. Remember the party in his office every Christmas, when he'd buy eggnog and invite everyone in to drink the booze his customers had given him? He'd changed since Osborne got him the promotion, no doubt about it. Maybe Buckle was less keen on him, but Buckle had brought his own man across the street and it only stood to reason. That didn't mean Osborne hadn't made a wise move. Now, though, two years later, some of the girls who'd seen Brian's gradual transformation wondered if it had been such a wise move after all. He was twenty-six going on forty. He seemed to bear the weight of the world. Had Osborne overestimated his capabilities? Had Brian bitten off more than he could chew?

From his gaily adorned office, Molony phoned Michael Rosen at the Caesars office in Toronto. He said he intended to deposit $400,000 in the California Clearing Corporation account. Most was for his own use that weekend in Atlantic City, but $40,000 was for Mario Colizzi at Caesars Palace in Las Vegas. Rosen told him to notify Mrs. Locke at the Manulife branch of the Bank of Montreal when he made the deposit.

Molony took out one of the numbered company's forged promissory notes. He filled in a sum – $490,000 – and took the note down to the discount clerk. The proceeds were credited to the account of 499726 Ontario Ltd. In the foreign-exchange department he told the girl to prepare a draft for $400,000 U.S. He told her to debit the cost to the 499726 loan account, and to make the draft payable to California Clearing Corporation. Wonderful name – how many upstanding dentists, carpet kings, and Rotarians had found it convenient to make cheques payable to California Clearing Corporation rather than Caesars Palace? Charles K. Peterson had a nice ring to it as well.

When the girl put the draft on his desk, Molony considered taking it himself to the Manulife Centre. No. The subway was too slow and a cab would cost at least five dollars. Nor could he afford to leave his office. This enterprise was as tense and complex as a space launch; his phone was mission control; to leave it unattended would be to invite disaster. Didn't the Bank of Montreal have another branch in the concourse of the Thomson Building across the street? He looked up the number, phoned over, asked for the accountant, and got Tim Rochford.

"I'm an assistant manager at the Commerce," said Molony. "We have a substantial draft here, $400,000 U.S., which a customer wants deposited in one of your branches. Can you telephone-transfer it? What's the procedure?"

Rochford had been promoted a few weeks earlier and was still feeling his way in his new job, which made him responsible for all lending, personal and consumer, in the branch. "I'll have to check on that," he said. "Can you give me your number?"

"I'll hold," said Molony.

Rochford returned after a minute. "If you can tell us the branch, we'll telephone-transfer it up."

"Manulife branch," said Molony. "To the attention of a Mrs. Locke."

"You'll deliver the draft here?"

"Yes. It will be credited today, I presume. They certainly wouldn't want to lose a day's interest."

"If you'll get it here, we'll transfer it right away."

"What's the charge on that?" said Molony.

"Hold on a second. That would be sixty dollars."

"Sixty dollars! I'm better off sending it up by cab."

"Whatever you like."

"Seems like a lot for a telephone transfer. Guess it doesn't matter – it's the customer's money."

Molony phoned Mrs. Locke at the Manulife branch and said he was with the Commerce at Bay and Richmond. "One of our customers asked us to transfer funds to an account at your branch – the California Clearing Corporation account. You'll be getting a telephone transfer from your Thomson branch."

"Fine."

"It's a large sum," said Molony, faltering. He hadn't given his name, he could hang up. "Uh, four hundred thousand U.S."

"Oh," said the woman, "six or seven million flows through that account every month."

So much for customer confidentiality. Molony sealed the draft and a covering note in an envelope, addressed it to Rochford, then realized he'd failed to include the name of the remitter. What if the Bank of Montreal called to ask, "Who's the CIBC customer depositing this money in the California Clearing account?" The foreign-exchange girl was nowhere in sight. Molony slipped down to her desk. He had to use her typewriter so the typeface would match. In the upper left corner of the negotiable copy of the draft, he typed: "b/o M. Colizzi." He was about to head across the street when Harry Buckle walked into his office.

"Is this yours, Brian?"

Molony's heart leapt. For a year and a half he had kept track of all the bad loans in his head, but it had become impossible. There were too many, and he'd done too much juggling. That morning on scrap paper he had listed them and added them up, to see where he stood. Buckle, catching up on his work, had asked for a file. In putting the file on Buckle's desk, Molony had inadvertently included the list of fraudulent accounts. How could he have been so stupid? The $400,000 was on its way to the casino, his salvation already in place. This was going to be the weekend, he knew it, if only he could catch up to the money. After all the grief, the heart-stopping moments and miraculous escapes, was this how it would end? With the manager waving his own list of $7-million in bad loans?

"Is this yours?" Buckle repeated.

The handwriting was unmistakable. As Molony tried to answer he swallowed involuntarily, choking on the word "Yes."

"You left it on my desk," said Buckle, and walked out.

April 3, 1982. Caesars Atlantic City. Frank Hines.

2 p.m. Craps #12. Brian Maloney is only player on game. Has $20,000. Lost that. Received another $30,000. Was betting Don't, $5000 double odds. Plays 4, 5, 9, 10 for $5,000. Don't. Places 6, 8 for $5,000. Left after going broke.

3 p.m. Baccarat #1. Heavy purple play. Maloney was down to $10,000. Ran it up to $120,000. Maloney ran a $40,000 marker up to $100,000. Switching back and forth between craps and baccarat.

3:20 p.m. Baccarat #1. Purple play. Maloney lost all. Got a $20,000 marker, lost it and left.

4:08 p.m. $50,000 marker. Maloney. Lost. Moved to baccarat #2. Got $40,000 marker. Lost. Moved to craps #11. $15,000 marker. Heavy action, switching from Don't Pass to Pass line. Action fast and furious. Was up to $80,000. Walked with $20,000. To baccarat #3. Lost it all and walked.

The following week Molony put through a loan of $990,000 in the name of DCL Customs Brokers Ltd. There was no such company.

He handled the account of Danzas Canada Limited, however, which had a $1-million authorized line of credit secured by a Swiss bank guarantee. If questioned – "What's this DCL loan? Why is there no authorized credit?" – he'd say it was actually Danzas. He instructed the foreign-exchange girl to issue a draft to California Clearing Corporation in the amount of $800,000 U.S. The cost of the draft – $986,150 Canadian – was debited to the DCL Customs Brokers account. As he'd done the previous week, he waited until the girl was elsewhere, then slipped down to her desk. On the negotiable copy he again typed: "b/o M. Colizzi."

Molony phoned Michael Neustadter at Caesars in Atlantic City and said $800,000 was being deposited in the California Clearing Corporation account. It would be in Colizzi's name, he said, but was for his own use at Caesars Palace in Las Vegas, where he planned to spend the Easter holiday with Brenda, Phil, and Louise. Neustadter had already arranged a complimentary suite and given Molony the name of a vice-president at Caesars Palace. Molony worried that Neustadter would question the size of the transaction, but he simply thanked Molony for the call. Molony said he'd phone later to confirm.

His shirt was soaked through. In the men's room he washed his face and hands, pulling himself together. Then he called Tim Rochford across the street to say the same customer wanted to make another telephone transfer to the Manulife branch. He put the $800,000 U.S. bank draft in an envelope, addressed it to Rochford, and took it across the street himself. He told a clerk, "I was asked to drop this off for Mr. Rochford," and hurried out. No use worrying. It was out of his hands. Nothing to do but return to the correspondence, files, and message slips on his desk.

Harry Buckle, meanwhile, was still making his way through the work that had accumulated on his holiday. One of the many things requiring his attention was Molony's position description. Having blocked Molony's transfer to Lawrence and Keele, which would have meant a promotion and a raise, Buckle was putting in for a grade increase so Molony would receive the same raise at Bay and Richmond. The position description was a standard form. Under the heading "Knowledge and Skills," Buckle wrote of Molony: "Broad knowledge of bank's credit requirements and services. Capacity to communicate and negotiate with senior executives of large corporations." Under "Personal Characteristics," Buckle described Molony as having "good judgement and proven ability to make decisions. Personable, alert, aggressive, and industrious." Among the things Buckle included under "Description of Duties" were: "Supervise authorized credits to ensure compliance with credit terms and provisions" and "Participate in development and growth of all areas of branch business by way of expansion of existing business and development of new business."

The day before Molony left to spend Easter weekend with the $800,000 he had sent to Las Vegas, Harry Buckle signed the position description – recommending promotion from grade 9 to grade 10 – and sent it downtown.

Caesars Palace, on the Las Vegas Strip, is an unabashed monument to excess and corruption. Built by Jay Sarno, himself an ardent gambler, financed partly by the Teamsters' pension fund, run initially by executives with direct ties to Mafia families, Caesars has attracted the attention of every major law-enforcement agency in the United States. Dozens of its owners, officers, and employees have been investigated – and, in many cases, indicted – for stock fraud, bookmaking, skimming, and conspiracy. When the company applied for a licence to operate in New Jersey, the Casino Control Commission insisted that two principal owners, the Perlman brothers, dissociate themselves from the corporation. Many Las Vegas casinos are surrounded by a criminal aura; ever since it opened, in 1966, Caesars Palace has been considered one of the most unsavoury.

The place looks like something devised by Walt Disney and Bob Guccione. A giant marquee announces the current showroom star – over the years the headliners have included Diana Ross, Sammy Davis Jr., Bill Cosby, Joan Rivers, and Frank Sinatra. Fountains gush alkaline water fifty feet in the air. Rows of cypress trees line the drive to the parking lots. Pedestrians enter the Temple of Diana, off Las Vegas Boulevard, and take the automated walkway to (but not from) the casino. The place is monumental and shaped vaguely like the Roman Forum. Its white stucco exterior is bathed at night in blue-green light, which glows behind the cement grillwork that covers the building.

Inside, the gaudy sumptuousness is unrestrained. The colour scheme leans toward rich reds and purples. There's marble everywhere – columns, balustrades, and twenty-foot knockoffs of such statuary as the *Venus de Milo*, *The Rape of the Sabines*, and *Winged Victory of Samothrace.* The brass and crystal chandeliers suspended from the ceiling of the casino are purportedly the biggest in the world. The cocktail girls wear mini-togas and artificial falls of hair. The restaurants have names such as Bacchanal, Cafe Roma, and the Ah So steakhouse; one of the cocktail lounges, Cleopatra's Barge, rocks gently on the mechanical waves of its own lagoon.

When Phil and Louise saw the accommodations Brian had arranged for Easter weekend, they exchanged a glance. The suite included two large bedrooms and a spacious livingroom-diningroom. The beds were on raised platforms, the walls covered with velvet, the bathroom glasses wrapped in gold metal foil. The carpeting must have been three inches thick. The ceiling above the sunken tub in the bedroom was mirrored. How much was all this going to cost?

The women spent the weekend sitting around the pool, window-shopping at Gucci and Ted Lapidus, feeding quarters into slot machines. The men went off to gamble. Brian told Phil, "The only way to learn Las Vegas is on your own. See you later." Around seven everybody met for drinks, dinner, and a show. Brian signed all the food and bar cheques, billing everything to the suite. Once the women had gone to bed, the men went back out gambling.

Over the weekend a number of things happened that Phil found perplexing. He wanted to bet the Blue Jays' home opener, so Brian took him across the street to the Barbary Coast. One of the smaller places on the Strip, the Barbary is tricked out in mock Victoriana meant to evoke turn-of-the-century San Francisco – fake antique stained glass and cocktail waitresses in frilly garters. At the sports book Phil tried to bet the Jays. Too late: the first pitch had already been thrown. When Phil said the clerk had refused his bet, Brian had a word with the manager. Presto – they took the bet after all. Now that, said Phil, is what I call pull. Brian, obviously uncomfortable, shrugged: "Your bet isn't going to break the bank." Phil puzzled over the incident, though, especially when something curious happened that evening. While they were all at dinner, a stranger approached Brian and said, "Hear you had a big win today." Brian, embarrassed, excused himself from the table. And Louise told Phil something Brenda had told her. That afternoon Brenda had gone across to the Flamingo, to try the slots there. She spotted Brian playing craps. When she went up behind him and touched his arm, surprising him, he told her he didn't want to see her. Playing with anyone you know, he said, was bad luck. He hadn't even said it nicely, he'd snapped at her, then apologized to her back at the suite.

The next day Molony got a call from Albert Ngan, the high-stakes gambler from Hong Kong whom he'd met at Caesars in Atlantic City. Though on cordial terms, the two men were hardly bosom buddies. Albert knew no more about Molony than that he was from Toronto and played baccarat for exorbitant stakes.

"How are you, Brian?"

"You're the last person I expected to hear from."

"Why don't you come here? They'll fly you back in time to see the Bucks and the 76ers. They say we can meet Dr. J. at half time."

Evidently it irked people at Caesars in Atlantic City to think of Molony spending the weekend in Las Vegas, even if he was at the sister casino. They'd taken the wrong tack to lure him back. Though Molony had discussed the NBA playoffs with Albert and bet the series heavily, he had no interest in attending a game or meeting Julius Erving. He didn't enjoy being a spectator, no matter how much was at stake, since it meant three hours without access to other scores and race results. He had no intention of leaving Las Vegas, not during the run he was enjoying. He had indeed had a big win at the Barbary, and he'd hit a rare streak at the crap table, one of those magic interludes when you practically tell the dice your number. In his first twenty-four hours he'd won $600,000.

Molony told Albert no thanks. He changed his shirt, went to the Dunes, and won $100,000 in half an hour. He crossed to the Barbary to check the scores and won another $100,000 at mini-baccarat. Nothing spectacular, just steady good fortune. All he had to do was keep it going. On Tuesday he'd pay down at least some of the bad loans. Maybe all of them. Maybe he'd be able to put the whole wretched escapade behind him.

Brian had a reputation for near-misses at the airport; on the last day Brenda reminded him, "We need to leave at least an hour before our flight." The others gathered back at the suite, packed and ready, but there was no sign of him. Brenda fumed. Brian had checked them in and had to sign them out. Phil imagined he was on a roll and didn't want to break it off. Finally, half an hour before the flight, Brian let himself into the suite. They hurried down to the desk. When Brian checked them all out, Phil asked how much their share was.

"Two fifty," said Brian.

"Come on. Two hundred and fifty bucks for everything?"

"We're on a special deal. Let's go."

If the plane hadn't been held they would have missed it. The dirty looks from other passengers only added to Brenda's simmering resentment. On the flight home, Phil asked her how she'd done. She'd lost twenty dollars on the slots. Louise had dropped forty but at least had got a tan. Phil said he'd won on the ball games but lost more than $1,000 in the casino. He asked Brian how he'd made out.

Ordinarily, no matter how intense the action, Molony knew at any moment exactly how much money he had. This time he'd lost so furiously it took him a moment to figure out where he stood. He'd asked the Barbary Coast to send $538,000 across the street to Caesars Palace, and instructed Caesars to transfer the balance of his account to New Jersey. He'd have $948,000 in Atlantic City. Was it possible? He'd run the original $800,000 to well over $2-million before hitting the cold streak. After three days of spectacular good fortune, had he really won only $148,000? Had he really lost more than a million dollars in the last two hours?

Better to look on the bright side. He'd snapped his losing streak. He had Atlantic City money in place. He'd proven the big win was possible. If he could hang in long enough, it was inevitable. Maybe he hadn't redeemed himself, but he'd taken a first step. Maybe he could get down to Atlantic City before the weekend.

"Sir, I got out with my shirt," he told Phil. "The important thing is that we all had a good time." He nodded at Brenda, who was glumly turning the pages of a magazine. "Well," he said quietly, "almost all of us."

April 14, 1982. Caesars Atlantic City. Al Wilson.

9:05 p.m. Baccarat 1. B. Maloney sits in with $70,000 marker.

9:10 p.m. Maloney gets $70,000 marker.

9:55 p.m. Maloney taps out. Walks to Craps 11. Gets $50,000 marker.

10:20 p.m. Baccarat 1. Maloney with $70,000 marker. Gets $60,000 marker. Table gets $300,000 fill. Maloney now has $650,000. Walks.

11:30 p.m. Baccarat 1. Maloney back. Gets four $50,000 markers. Loses. Walks.

3:00 a.m. Craps 11. Maloney strong purple play. Walks with $90,000 to Baccarat 1. Bets as much as $40,000 per hand. Winning heavily. Sends $300,000 to cage and walks.

April 16, 1982. Caesars Atlantic City. Matt Wilson.

10 p.m. Maloney on Baccarat 1 with about $75,000. Left with about $50,000.

3:55 a.m. Craps 11. Maloney has approx. $80,000 betting Pass, Place, Come, and Don't Place. Also betting hard ways and buys 4 and 10. Left game with approx. $65,000.

At six o'clock Saturday morning, just before the casino bell signalled the end of play at Caesars, Molony put $10,000 on the bank at baccarat. That left him a single $500 chip, a purple, which he bet on a tie hand. Player won. Cleaned out. Every dollar was gone of the almost $1-million he'd sent from Las Vegas.

"Bad timing," said the floorman. "Just when it was going to turn around."

Molony went up to his suite and vomited in one of the marble bathrooms. He drank some water, composing himself, and headed for the limousine stand. Good timing, really, losing his last chips on the last hand. Losing all your money wasn't like losing most of it and having to scale down. Losing most of it left you full of self-loathing. It made you think back over the mistakes you'd made, the little promises you'd broken, the pathetic rationalizations. Losing everything was pure. It gave you a surge of aching, almost overwhelming despair, but only for a time. Once you got through that you were liberated from what had happened. You were forced to look ahead, to wonder how you'd go about starting all over again. You had nothing to regret. You had nothing.

At the magazine stand in the concourse, Molony picked up a newspaper to read on the plane. He gave the clerk a Canadian quarter. The tag on her blouse said her name was Darlene. She turned the coin in her hand.

"This ain't no good."

"It's a quarter," said Molony.

"I can't take this."

Molony checked his pockets but didn't have an American quarter. He had no American change. He offered the girl another nickel, Canadian, but she didn't want it.

"Come on," said Molony. "Thirty cents Canadian is worth twenty-five American."

"How my supposed to know that?"

"Here, I've got a dime. Thirty-five cents Canadian. You know that's worth more than a quarter."

"I don't know nothing about that," said the girl.

"Need a quarter?" said Larry Woolf, who happened to be on

his way to the lobby. He stopped and dug in the pocket of his suit trousers.

"Kind of you, sir," said Molony, folding the newspaper.

"My pleasure," said Woolf.

On Monday, April 19, Molony put through a loan of $1.12-million, crediting the proceeds to the account of the numbered company. Madness. The numbered company was already over its supposed $3-million limit. But Molony could think of no other way to raise money. What difference? He had to win it back before the next return of irregular liabilities. Each month the branch had to report any loans not in accordance with authorized terms and conditions, or obtain an exemption from Credit Room. He had no idea how he'd finesse the numbered company through. If he could just get back to Atlantic City, get on a roll . . .

Molony told the foreign-exchange clerk to prepare a draft for $920,000 U.S., payable to California Clearing Corporation, and to debit the numbered company's account. She brought the draft up to his office. While she was at lunch he went back down to her desk and typed Colizzi's name on the negotiable copy. He sealed the draft in an envelope and had it delivered to the Bank of Montreal across the street. He then phoned Michael Neustadter in Atlantic City. He was making a deposit in the California Clearing Corporation account – nine hundred and twenty thousand, he said, and swallowed. What if Neustadter balked? What if Neustadter told him, "Sorry, Brian, that's it. We don't want to see you anymore."

What if he couldn't gamble?

"Great," said Neustadter. "We'll pick you up in New York. What time should the pilot be there?"

When Michael Neustadter got off the phone with Molony, he advised both the financial department and the casino cage at Caesars to expect the $920,000 deposit through the U.S.-dollar account at the Manulife branch of the Bank of Montreal in Toronto.

A few hours later, Linc Ebert, the director of cage operations and Molony lookalike, received the transmittal form from the sister casino in Las Vegas indicating the $920,000 was on deposit. The form, however, showed the deposit as being in the name of "M. Colizzi."

Ebert spoke to Bill Hessel, the chain-smoking casino controller. Hessel didn't see how the funds could be released to Molony. He went to Larry Bertsch, the chief financial officer of the company. Bertsch, a blunt, irascible man, agreed that funds forwarded in the name of Colizzi couldn't be released to Molony. Hessel called Michael Neustadter in the casino.

"We got a problem, Mike."

"Like what?"

"The Toronto funds have been transferred, but they're in somebody else's name."

Neustadter explained the trouble to Larry Woolf. The two men tried to persuade Bill Hessel to release the funds. Hessel said no. What if Colizzi walked in and said, "Where's my money?" What was the casino supposed to say? "We gave it to your friend Molony?" Suppose Colizzi said, "Who's Molony?" No, the cage couldn't release it unless Mario Colizzi accompanied Molony, presented identification, and signed the money over.

Neustadter brainstormed with Woolf. There seemed no choice but to contact Molony and ask him to bring along his friend. Partner. Colleague. Whatever the hell Colizzi was. Talk about frustration. Million-dollar tuna on the line, begging to be landed. In Las Vegas you'd haul him in and say, "Welcome aboard, Mr. T.

see you. What can we do for you?" Here, according to the were supposed to say, "Sorry, sir, we really can't help you, ›ut contravening subsection this of paragraph that of the ;gulations." New Jersey and its goddamn Casino Control 's just going to swim off to a more accommodating boat.

:adter phoned Michael Rosen at the Caesars office in Toro. o and asked him to relay the bad news to Molony. But Molony was already en route to the airport and couldn't be reached. Neustadter phoned Pearson International but got no response to his page. What now? This was turning into a full-fledged cockup. A hasty meeting was convened in the second-floor, corner office of Peter Boynton, the president of Caesars.

Boynton was a hefty, easygoing man who worked out each day at the spa. He was not a typical casino executive. After studying political science and doing graduate work in finance, he'd worked for an aerospace manufacturing company and a national brokerage firm. He'd entered the gaming industry through Caesars World in Century City, California. Caesars World owned 100 per cent of Desert Palace Inc., the company that owned and operated Caesars Palace in Las Vegas, and 86 per cent of Boardwalk Regency Corporation, the company that owned the Atlantic City operation. Boynton dealt with stock analysts, put together financial reports, and did liaison work with the subsidiaries before being put in charge of preparing the company's entry into Atlantic City. He helped determine the structure and staffing requirements of the proposed hotel, and in 1979 joined Boardwalk Regency Corporation as vice-president operations. He oversaw everything but the gambling side until 1981, when he was named chief executive officer and assumed total responsibility.

Boynton was more at home on Wall Street than in the dice pit. His tastefully decorated office might have been that of an insurance executive. It featured only one allusion to the corporate aegis. Instead of a clock marked by combinations of dice, or a wall of photographs of himself shaking hands with celebrities, he kept a model of the Caesars helicopter on a side table. One of his children was emotionally disturbed; he served on the board of the special school the boy attended. He'd also served on the Atlantic City Casino Hotel Association, an exercise in public relations. He was just the sort of gaming executive the Casino Control Commission liked to see in its jurisdiction.

But he wasn't a casino man, and he was viewed by people who worked for him as out of touch. A casino responds to action the way a teenaged boy responds to sexual instinct. The moment drives everything. If someone's betting big money, keep him in action even it means violating the regulations, stonewalling the Casino Control Commission, making an end run around your own president. Get the money now, face the consequences later. In its first few years of operation Caesars had committed literally thousands of regulatory violations. The fines were always minor compared to the wins.

Nobody wanted to miss out on $920,000 cash. Peter Boynton, Larry Woolf, Michael Neustadter, and Bill Hessel were joined by the two Jemm oldtimers, Milton Neustadter and Roy Goldberg. The problem discussed around Boynton's coffee table was how to accommodate Brian Molony without violating CCC regulations and, more important, federal law. The Casino Control Commission maintains an office in every casino, but nobody was about to ask for an interpretation of the New Jersey regulations. For the moment, the fewer people who knew about Brian Molony the better.

Bill Hessel maintained that the funds couldn't be released. Maybe Colizzi's coming down with Molony and all we'll have to do is hand him a pen. Fine, but what if he's not coming? Then we haul his ass down here. Or we send somebody up to Toronto to get his signature on a customer-deposit receipt and a release authorization. Any problem with that? Well, actually, cage transactions have to be performed in the cage. True, but all we're doing is moving the cage to Toronto, right? Once the cage has the signatures up there, the money can be released to Molony down here. Wait a minute, is he still a cash player if we do it that way? Or does that make him a credit player? The distinction was important because the casino was obliged to have on file detailed financial information, including bank references, for credit players. Sure he's still a cash player – "cash," in the regs, means cash or a cash equivalent, and the transmittal form from Caesars Palace is arguably a cash equivalent. Let's get a jet ready to go, just in case.

Hessel wanted a casino employee to accompany the cage person on the flight to Toronto. He wanted it made perfectly clear that the procedure had been agreed upon by both departments.

When the meeting broke up, Michael Neustadter went off to charter the Learjet. Larry Woolf had the documentation prepared and instructed that Molony's computer number be changed. There were terminals throughout Caesars, and anyone could find out how much he was depositing and betting. No reason why the whole world had to know about Brian Molony.

Bill Hessel, meanwhile, went to the casino cage. He spoke to Jane Blackton, the supervisor. How would she feel about flying up to Toronto that evening? She asked what for; when Hessel told her, she explained she had a fear of flying – could he maybe ask Claire Lodovico instead?

Lodovico, an assistant cage manager, had spent fifteen years with First National State Bank in Ventnor before joining Caesars in 1979. A divorcee, she lived in a tiny bungalow with her cat and felt privileged to work in the gaming industry. It was more lively than the bank, and the money was better. She didn't want to jeopardize her position. Still, the idea of flying to Toronto made her nervous, and she questioned the appropriateness of leaving the cage to perform a cage transaction. Hessel reassured her: he'd just come from Boynton's office, he said, where that very question had been resolved.

Lodovico's close friend, Katherine Campellone, a credit executive, was chosen to represent the casino department. The two women were briefed by Hessel and Woolf.

About eight o'clock, Brian Molony walked into Caesars. Michael Neustadter and Larry Woolf met him and said they needed to talk. One of the mirrored panels by the cage opened to reveal a private office. The two men explained the problem to Molony.

"I don't understand the difficulty," said Molony. "Wasn't it transferred the same way the last two times?"

Woolf and Neustadter exchanged a glance.

"We'll look into that," said Woolf. "The immediate concern is that we can't release the funds that came through today."

"This is ridiculous. What's the solution?"

"One possibility would be to fly Mr. Colizzi down here to sign over the funds."

Out of the question. Colizzi didn't know his name was being used and would have been stunned by the sums. Well, said Molony, actually, he wasn't sure he'd be able to get in touch with Colizzi.

Woolf and Neustadter got the picture. What if we fly casino personnel to Toronto, Brian? Colizzi could sign off up there.

Molony thought it over. Maybe, he said, but he wanted to see the documents Colizzi would be asked to sign. It was essential, he added, that Colizzi not be made aware of the amount of the transaction. Any forms had to be blank when he signed them, the details filled in later. And the Caesars people were not to answer any questions Colizzi might ask. All questions were to be referred to Molony himself.

Sounded perfectly reasonable to Woolf and Neustadter.

Molony asked them to step out while he made the call. A few minutes later he emerged from the office. Colizzi, he said, would be at the American Airlines ticket counter at Pearson International in Toronto. Terminal One. He'd be wearing tan slacks, a brown and black leather jacket, and crocodile boots. Molony repeated that he was not to be apprised of the sum involved.

Unable to gamble, Molony wandered through the concourse to the lobby, past the black marble walls and oversized sculptures. A roar came from the casino and Molony hurried back to see what was going on. A whole table in the dice pit was on a roll. Painful, being a spectator. He went over to the casino lounge and stood listening to the bar band a moment. Dreadful music – strange he'd never noticed. He walked past row on row of slot machines and pushed through the doors to the Boardwalk. He had never been out here before. The air had a salty tang. The huge Caesars sign was engulfed by a red aurora. The darkness seemed to move in time to a low, rhythmic roar, not unlike the sound from the crap table. Garish light from the hot-dog stands and souvenir shops on the Boardwalk spilled across the sand, revealing the water's ragged edge. The roar was the surf, breaking, receding, and breaking again.

Molony went up to his suite and turned on television. Killing time, knowing that downstairs dice were being thrown and cards dealt, was a kind of exquisite torture. To be so close to the purest concentrate of the energy that sustained him – action, they called it, but the word didn't do it justice. Action was passing a finger through the flame. He sandpapered the fingertip, exposing every nerve end, then held it perfectly still and turned up the heat, filling the void of his life with distilled sensation. How long can the scream go unuttered?

Molony ordered up ribs, no sauce, and a Coke, but found he had no appetite. He phoned Brenda and asked what she was doing; she knew better than to ask the same. He kicked off his shoes, then put them on again. He wanted to be ready when the word came. He sat listlessly through game shows and soap operas and a Jimmy Cagney film until 1:30 a.m., when the phone rang. Neustadter.

"Good news, Brian. Your money's waiting for you."

April 19, 1982. Caesars Atlantic City. Michael Francis.

1:45 a.m. Craps 11. B. Maloney receiving markers for $50,000 and $60,000. Player betting Pass, Don't, Come, Place, Field, and Don't Place for $10,000-plus per bet. Player left game for Baccarat 1.

3:00 a.m. Baccarat 1. B. Maloney receiving $50,000 and $100,000 markers and betting up to $50,000 per hand. Went back to craps for awhile and returned. Player had up to $500,000. Back down to $300,000. Player went to Craps 11 with $100,000.

3:35 a.m. Baccarat 1. Maloney betting as before. Had $800,000. Moved to craps with $150,000 approx.

3:45 a.m. Craps 11. Maloney betting as before. Lost the $150,000 and returned to Baccarat 1.

3:50 a.m. Maloney betting as before. Had $790,000 and returned to Craps 11 with $90,000.

3:55 a.m. Maloney betting as before. Left game with $90,000. Took $897,000 back from Baccarat 1.

At six-thirty in the morning, about the time Molony stepped off the Learjet that returned him to Toronto, Ron Andrews stepped off the streetcar that took him to work. He bought two bran muffins and a coffee, walked down to Richmond Street, signed in, and unlocked the little room with the picture of a window on the wall. Each night, before the Uher 4000s went on automatic, the last man set the counters at zero. Andrews checked the counter on Colizzi's line and found it had been a busy night. He opened the log book, put on his headphones, and played back the tape.

The first call was incoming. The machine did not record the hour – sometime after 8:12 p.m. The old man answered. The operator told him she had a collect call for Mario Colizzi from Brian Molony. "*Mario, telefono!*" Colizzi came on.

"How are you?" said Brian Molony.

The hair stood up on Andrews' neck. That voice. He'd heard it a hundred times. Mr. Brown!

"Not bad, you?"

"Not so good. I'm in Atlantic City. Trying to get you some money."

"I thought you weren't gonna go no more."

"Well, you know what tomorrow is. What I have to do, remember the, ahh, I really can't talk to you on this line."

Sure you can, Mr. Brown. Brian Molony. Come on, keep talking.

"Call me at the hotel. Room 4800. In five minutes. Can you go outside?"

"Am I gonna reverse charges to you?"

"If they'll accept it."

"In the payphone?"

"Room 4800 in five minutes."

"Did you talk to Nick?"

"No," said Molony.

"He said he didn't give me nothing, he says you're going to give me money, you're gonna give his. I says, 'You're all wrong, Nick, it's something else that we're doing, me and him.'"

"I gave you yours," said Molony.

"But how about the other thing with him, I was a partner with him too, wasn't I? Why are you gonna give me half?"

"Twenty-five," said Molony. "Another twenty-five."

"He didn't give me half."

"Why?"

"Because he says you're gonna give mine to me and yours to him, he told me, he says –"

"No," said Molony.

"OK, I'll talk to him tomorrow."

"Phone me in five minutes."

You don't need to go to a payphone, Mario. Stay where you are. Talk to Mr. Brown.

"Is it very important?"

"Very!" said Molony.

Andrews phoned The Bulldog to tell him he'd put a name to Mr. Brown, hoping it might ring a bell. The Bulldog said no, he'd not come across a Brian Molony that he could recall. Andrews stretched his legs – his bad knee was stiffening – and ran the tape ahead. The next call was Colizzi phoning Molony in Room 4800.

"Everything's OK."

Damn, he had gone out to phone. Now he was back home.

"I know," said Molony. "They just phoned."

Molony apologized for having wakened Colizzi's father. He said he'd tried to page Colizzi at the airport. Colizzi said he'd already left. Molony said, "I'll see you tomorrow."

Who's the "they" who had phoned Molony? What had Colizzi been doing at the airport? Why had Molony phoned Colizzi's father? Why was Molony meeting Colizzi that day? Was Molony bringing something back, maybe?

Andrews logged the calls and put red stars beside them. On the Canadian Police Information Centre terminal in the Intelligence

Bureau he keyed in "Maloney, Brian," tapping into an Ottawa data bank, available to police across the country, of information on several million Canadians, from murderers to secretaries with outstanding traffic tickets. The computer wasn't yet programmed to kick up alternative spellings. Even if Molony had had a criminal record or an outstanding parking tag, Andrews would have drawn a blank.

In mid-morning, Colizzi's line kicked in with a live call. Incoming. Andrews hit the "record" button and slipped on headphones, not wanting to miss a word. The old man answered. "*Mario, telefono!*" Molony tried to apologize for having woken him the previous night. "*Telefono! Mario!*" When Colizzi came on, Molony asked him to apologize.

"That's OK, my father, he's got no place to go."

"I feel bad about it. One-thirty in the morning, nobody likes to be woken up."

"Where are you, at home?"

"At work," said Molony. "I've been here two and a half hours."

"They were two ugly broads come up here."

"Two of them?"

"Two, really ugly, had to sign something, ugly broads, one was about seven feet tall, she says, 'He told us you were a good-looking Italian.' What do they want, good-looking Italian, you tell them I was a good-looking Italian?"

"Sure."

"Oh, were they ugly, two old, ugly broads. One was worse than the other."

"They thought they were in Disneyland," said Molony. "They loved it, flying to Toronto. On the way back they got picked up in the limo. The driver said they tried every button in the damn thing."

"The two old broads? That tall one, was she rough!"

"She would have eaten you!"

"Eaten me! She looked like a man. Ugly man, too. See what I do for you?"

"Well," said Molony, "I appreciate it."

"The things I do for love. Did that other creep call you?"

"No, I haven't, I won't, I won't phone him."

"Guy thinks I'm going to rob him."

"You know, he just wants."

"I've been mad all week, too," said Colizzi.

Molony said he'd cancelled a lunch so they could get together. Colizzi offered to make the reservations.

Why had Colizzi been mad all week? Who were the two women? Why had they flown up to Toronto? What had Colizzi signed?

Andrews entered the call in his log. He was putting a red star beside it when the line kicked in again. Incoming.

That jumpy voice. Nick Beck, phoning to tell Colizzi, "I just spoke to him now. So I says to him, like I says, I thought since it was such a small amount I couldn't believe you weren't going to give us each one, right?"

"This'll be two today," said Colizzi. "I'll keep this one today."

"Yeah, you get that, I was going to tell you yesterday you should get it. I'll talk to you after."

Andrews put a red star beside that call, too, then thumbed back through his log. Busy day. Busy month. Red stars galore. Sit wires eight hours a day and you get a feel for when something's about to break. You know, the way fishermen know when the weather's about to change. You don't know what's coming, exactly, but you know it won't be long.

Molony had left $190,000 on deposit at Caesars when the casino closed on Tuesday morning. Better to look at it that way than to dwell on the $730,000 he'd lost. On Wednesday morning he phoned Atlantic City, billing the call to his home, and told Michael Neustadter he'd be down again that night. Neustadter said they'd send the jet to Toronto. What time would he be at the airport?

"Six," said Molony, then remembered it was bowling night. He'd missed the past couple of weeks and Brenda would hit the roof if he missed again.

"Make it eight," said Molony.

"Eight o'clock," said Neustadter. "Look forward to seeing you."

After work Molony drove to the bowling lanes. He hated bowling. Brenda loved it – she kept her bowling and softball trophies on the sideboard – and it was something they could do together. How had he got himself into this? He'd gone one Sunday afternoon with Brenda and her parents. Brenda, an excellent bowler, had whipped him. Not one to take such things lightly, he said that if he put his mind to it he'd beat her within three months.

"Why don't you join the team and prove it?"

So Molony found himself part of the bank's bowling league. At least it was Wednesdays and there was usually hockey on the TV in the adjoining pool room. The early league started at seven o'clock. Ten teams, six players per team. The evening was as much a social exercise as a competition. Ordinarily everyone bowled quickly but this night not quickly enough. Molony urged the others to speed it up; he launched his own second ball before the pins had settled from the first. The Caesars people had no way of getting in touch with him. What if the plane didn't wait? What if he got out there just in time to see it take off?

What if he couldn't gamble tonight?

The moment he'd finished his last frame he said, "I have to go."

"Don't you even want to know the scores?"

"Can you get a ride with your brother?"

"Mom was talking about going out afterwards. She and Dad suggested we all get something to eat."

"I've made plans, Bren. Sorry."

Tears brimmed in Brenda's eyes. She gave him a wounded, searching look. There was something else in her now, despair, perhaps, at her growing certainty that he would never give this a proper chance. Such a shame because they could share something rare, she was sure, if only he would allow it.

Molony knew she was about to say they needed to talk, but talk was the last thing he needed. He had a chartered Learjet at the airport and money in his name at the casino. He unlaced his rented bowling shoes and felt for his keys.

"I may be late. See you in the morning."

April 21, 1982. Caesars Atlantic City. Frank Hines.

10:40. Baccarat 1. Maloney received over $500,000 in markers. Lost it all. Bets up to $60,000. Went to Craps 11. Received another $100,000. Lost that. Back to Baccarat 1. Started to win some back. Now has $250,000 on table. Cards are changed after every shoe.

On Thursday morning Molony was flown back to Toronto on the Learjet. He got home just in time to shower and go to work. On Friday morning he arranged to return to Atlantic City that evening. He'd left $635,000 on deposit – a relief to think he could gamble again without having to use Friedberg's or Richardson's or the bank's own securities department. Though he was operating on almost no sleep he felt energized and cheerful.

He was on his way out, to check progress at the Elmwood Club and have lunch with Sherry Brydson, when he bumped into Jim Surgey, his broker. Surgey occasionally stopped in at Bay and Richmond to drop off bonds or pick up a draft. Molony, fearing he might say the wrong thing, hustled him out of the branch. Surgey, a tall fellow who seemed to regard the world from a long way behind his glasses, inquired after Brian's health. He mentioned a stock he liked and invited Brian to lunch at the Military Club. Molony wondered why he'd dropped by. Was he fishing for an explanation of why his activity at Richardson's had dropped off? Molony apologized that he was in a rush. Surgey took his leave, then stopped, reaching in his pocket.

"I almost forgot, Brian. I'd like you to have this."

He handed Molony what looked like an antique medallion.

"Very generous of you, sir. What is it?"

"It's from the 1880s, when all the banks used to print their own money. That particular coin was minted by the Bank of Montreal. I enjoy antique coins, but I thought it would be more appropriate for a banker to have that. A little token. I hope it brings you luck."

April 23, 1982. Caesars Atlantic City. Frank Hines.

1:15 a.m. Craps 11. Brian Maloney on game. Came with $60,000 in purples. Has up to $40,000 on layout at any given time. Lost whole $60,000. Went to Baccarat 1. Received over $500,000 in markers. Losing pretty good. Lost over $350,000 while I observed game.

8

THE LAST TIME

"Take therefore no thought for the morrow: for the morrow shall take thought for the things of itself."

– Matthew 6:34

On Sunday night Molony couldn't sleep, and his fitfulness kept Brenda awake. Toward dawn she dropped off. When the clock-radio woke her he was already out of the shower. She stepped in, and by the time she stepped out he was leaving. She hated that he couldn't get out fast enough. She thought of him tossing in bed – he had moaned aloud – and asked if anything was wrong. He paused, agitated, and for a moment she was hopeful. But he avoided her eye, looking for his keys, and said, "Meeting." She cinched her towel, enraged, exhausted. What was the point? She said, very calmly, "We need to talk."

"Right now is out of the question."

"Why is it always out of the question?"

"We'll talk soon," he said, slapping his pockets. If he got out before she started crying he could pretend not to have noticed. "Not changing the subject, but have you seen my keys? Here they are." Again he paused. "Oh, poor thing. Think we've got problems? Had a look at Mexico's foreign debt lately?" He kissed her cheek. "Talk to you later."

In the parking lot Molony found that his car had been burgled. Someone had jimmied the lock and forced the glove compartment. He kept money there for the racetrack; they'd got $15,000 U.S. Had other cars been burgled? He reminded himself to phone the police from the bank and snapped *Man of La Mancha* into the tape player. On the way downtown he turned it up so loud it was almost painful. To fight the unbeatable foe. To soothe the unbearable jitters. He parked in the Eaton Centre and joined the hurrying crowd on Queen Street. The mere thought of the branch knotted his stomach. Rounding Simpsons and catching sight of it made him gag with pain. Ulcer? Should maybe see a doctor, pay attention to what he ate. Through the glass he sought unfamiliar faces. One of the girls unlocked the door for him.

"How are you today, Brian?"

"Fine," said Molony, instantly better, as if here, inside, the air were pure oxygen. All weekend the data centre had been updating loan-status and customer-status lists. There was a deluge of interbranch mail and head-office directives. Securities people were preparing to meet with messengers, and tellers were moving cash from the safe to their drawers. Molony took the stairs two at a time, hung up his jacket, and answered his ringing phone. His stomach had subsided. He reviewed his accounts, dictated correspondence, huddled with Steve Richardson. By ten, when the doors opened, he'd done half a day's work. Between meetings and loan-activity approvals and cheque approvals he took calls.

Could I come see you, Mr. Molony? A mutual friend said you'd be the person to talk to about an investment loan. Morning, Brian, OK if I'm a day late with my car payment? What if I drop it off before lunch tomorrow? Hi, Brian, any word from downtown about the $600,000? If I don't have the deposit Friday I could lose the building. Mr. Molony? Credit Room here. About the Kaminsky application. Hey, Brian, I've got a pair for Texas and the Blue Jays – interested?

Molony said no thanks, he had other plans. He phoned Atlantic City, asking the operator to bill the call to his home. He reached Michael Neustadter.

"It's Brian. I'm coming down tonight."

"What time do you want the plane?"

"Six o'clock." Molony swivelled his chair and lowered his voice. "Million four this time," he said, half expecting Neustadter to express alarm, or the need for authorization. What would he do if it happened?

"Fine," said Neustadter.

"Can you send somebody? It's in Colizzi's name again."

"We'll have someone on the plane. Listen, why don't we do a blanket power of attorney? Save a lot of trouble."

"Just bring paperwork for this one. Blank. Probably be the last time we do it this way."

"Shall I call when we receive notification of the funds?"

"More convenient if I get back to you," said Molony. "I'll call later on."

A million four, had he said that? A seven-figure draft was daunting, so he instructed the girl in the discount department to advance two sums, $900,000 and $520,000, to the U.S.-dollar loan account of Elm Street Holdings. He had simply renamed the fictitious Sherry Brydson loan account, in order not to have to create new documentation. The girl asked about notes.

"Do dummy notes," said Molony.

When she brought him the loan forms and dummy notes, Molony took them down to the foreign-exchange department. The clerk was a middle-aged black woman. They joked back and forth as Molony told her he needed two drafts. "Here are your debits. Bring me the drafts and all the documentation."

She prepared the drafts in favour of California Clearing Corporation, signed them, and took them up to Molony. He countersigned and, when she took her break, slipped back down to her desk. On the top left corner of the negotiable copy of each draft he typed: "b/o M. Colizzi." He sealed the drafts and a covering note in an envelope, addressed it to Tim Rochford, and had the messenger take it to the Bank of Montreal.

The messenger, an old fellow in a maroon jacket, dropped it off across the street. Rochford recognized Molony's cramped, backhand writing. The procedure had become so routine he passed the envelope to the girl who did telephone transfers without even opening it.

"Good morning, Mr. Molony's office."

"Good morning. Is Mr. Molony there, please?"

"I'm sorry, sir, he's with a customer."

"Tell him Mr. Colizzi phoned."

"I will, sir. Goodbye."

The call was outgoing. In the tiny room on Richmond Street with the drawing of a window on the wall, Ron Andrews had a new number to trace. Over the years he had monitored bookmakers talking to people from just about every profession – doctors, lawyers, elected officials, other policemen. The moment he discovered who the subscriber was he got on the phone to The Bulldog.

"You know that fellow Mario's always talking to? Guess where he works. Not three blocks from here."

In the midday twilight of the casino, Michael Neustadter found Linc Ebert by the baccarat pit. He told Ebert that Molony was going to deposit a million four in the Toronto account. It was in Colizzi's name, he said, so somebody had to get signatures again.

Ebert phoned Claire Lodovico at her little bungalow in Margate. How would she like to go back to Toronto? Fine with her – she was learning to enjoy limousines and Learjets. She said she'd be at the casino in an hour.

Ebert also called Las Vegas. As soon as Caesars Palace got the transmittal form indicating funds had been deposited in Toronto, Ebert wanted it forwarded by telecopier to Atlantic City. As for the money itself, Caesars Palace was to send a cheque to Caesars in Atlantic City via Federal Express the next morning, Tuesday.

Ron Andrews was at the typewriter, working on the affidavit for an upcoming wiretap, when the return call came. His chair had wheels, and he almost launched himself through the wall in his hurry to hit the "record" button on the Uher 4000. He slipped on headphones. Molony was going away that night and wondered if Colizzi wanted to go with him.

"Where you want to go?"

"South."

"For how long?"

"Till tomorrow morning."

"Are you going to bring something back for me?"

"Well, either that or you don't have to come down. I just need your signature again."

"Again! How much you got? Maybe I'll go by myself and pick it up."

"It's not that much."

"How much you got in my name?"

"About another, ah, thirty, forty."

"In my name, then you don't pay me."

"Well, it's not, it's, most of, it's from before."

"Oh, from before. What, you say tonight? Come back?"

"Tomorrow morning. Four in the morning."

"Oh no, I don't want to go to, you know what I mean, it's my beauty sleep, all night, four in the morning. Man, are you tough! This is what you need to do, you need me, right?"

"Well, I don't need you there. If I can just take you out to the airport. Like last time."

"Not again! You do this to me, eh? All night!"

"Not that late, you can sign it at six."

"I can sign it?"

"You don't have to go down there, but I have to phone them. Tell them to bring somebody up."

"I don't want to do this no more. I don't know what you're doing to me, OK?"

"It's nothing out of the ordinary. It's nothing."

"How long is this going to keep going?"

"This should be it, unless I win."

"Oh, if you win, that's OK!"

Colizzi agreed to meet him at a spot called Christopher's Ribs near the airport. Molony said he'd recognize the car.

"I got another car. A dark BMW."

"Jesus Christ! A new car every time."

"The other one was no good."

Molony asked to be reminded of Colizzi's pager number in case of a mixup. They agreed to meet at quarter to six.

In the tiny room with the drawing of a window on the wall, Ron Andrews called The Bulldog at home.

"I've got something, Craig."

"What do you have?"

"Remember that thing last week, Atlantic City, the women? It's starting to come together."

The Bulldog drove down to Intelligence. Andrews played the call for him. A meet. An airport. Bring something back. I don't want to do this no more. Maybe I'll go myself and pick it up. Sooner or later on any authorization drugs usually turn up, and The Bulldog had a feeling they'd stumbled onto a drug deal. Andrews agreed.

"What we've got to do now," said The Bulldog, "is gather all the calls where he's talking, or they're talking about him. Put them together on one tape. I want to get some people in."

All the calls with red stars.

Andrews made a master copy and The Bulldog played it for his boss. Staff Sergeant Brian Wilson was noncommittal: maybe there was something there, maybe not. The Bulldog called in an old friend on the RCMP drug squad. He didn't feel strongly one way or the other. The Bulldog called in somebody from Intelligence, somebody from Fraud, somebody from the Commercial Crime section of the RCMP, and before long there were ten guys in the tiny room with the picture of a window on the wall. The Bulldog wanted to cover the meet at the airport, but he needed surveillance, and Intelligence controlled Mobile Support Services. Surveillance was expensive – add up cars, gas, radios, inside help, and salaries and you're looking at $4,000 or $5,000 for an eight-hour shift – so you better be damn sure you weren't going fishing. The Bulldog was sure, but he was having a hard time persuading the others. One of the Intelligence guys said flatly, "There's nothing here."

The Bulldog, a man of almost infinite patience, found his patience tested. When his boss asked how long he intended to work on the authorization, he said he didn't know. Frankly, he didn't care.

"I'm not authorizing any overtime."

Something big was going down at Pearson International – maybe a serious drug deal – and everybody was talking budgets and overtime. The Bulldog knew Andrews' instincts had been honed over thousands of hours of interception. He wanted support, but if he didn't get it he'd damn well cover the meet on his own. He made a heated little speech.

"This man has sat this project start to finish. He's sure there's something going on. I respect his judgement. If we let it go, we'll be making a mistake. I intend to cover the meet and I want mobile support, goddamn it!" The Bulldog had never made a bet in his life. "I'll bet you ten dollars we're onto a drug deal."

The Intelligence guy said fine, you're so goddamn gung-ho? Go ahead, cover it. "And by the way. You're on for the ten bucks."

The Bulldog called Ron Stewart at Mobile Support Services. "I need a surveillance crew. I want to do some observation on Mario Colizzi. He's meeting somebody near the airport later this afternoon. I'm not sure what we've got, but something."

Stewart, an old buddy, called a crew off another job to make them available. The Bulldog, in a rental Ford, went out to the airport to brief the others and cover the meet himself.

Somebody had to coordinate the phones and the radios, so Ron Andrews stayed behind in the tiny room with the picture of a window on the wall.

In mid-afternoon Molony called Caesars to confirm that the $1.42-million was on deposit. Neustadter said there'd been no notification. Molony was baffled and alarmed – no bank lets $1.42-million sit around. "I'll get back to you," he said, and went to find the messenger. The envelope, said the messenger, had been delivered right away. Molony called the Thomson branch. The lady said yes, the money had been sent by telephone transfer as soon as it arrived. She had done it herself. He called the Manulife branch. The lady said no, they had not received a deposit in the U.S.-dollar account of California Clearing Corporation.

"Just a moment." Molony put the call on hold. He fought nausea and tried to think. How does a million four get lost over the phone? What if they started backtracking? He'd put the loan through without even alerting his own credit officer. What if Steve Richardson took the call?

What if he couldn't gamble tonight?

Good Lord, the artillery he'd dodged, a year and a half of full-out bombardment, only to get hit by a stray? A clerical error at the Bank of Montreal? The trick was not to panic. He opened the line and affected an impatient, authoritative tone. "Speak to your Thomson branch, will you? Let's see if we can't sort this out right away."

"If you'd like to give me your –"

"I'll get back to you. Half an hour."

Molony phoned Atlantic City. Neustadter sounded as cordial and businesslike as ever, but now there was an undertone. Irritation? Impatience? Suspicion?

"What's the problem, Brian?"

"My understanding is that it was looked after some time ago."

"We've got the plane ready to go. I can't authorize it without the confirmation."

As a child, Molony had loved the circus at Maple Leaf Gardens. He'd especially loved the clown who did the juggling act, a symphony of lofted balls and whirling hoops and spinning plates. It must have required absolute attention, yet the clown made it seem offhand. Molony longed to throw him a baseball – "Here, catch!" – to cause the moment's lapse that would bring it all crashing down. Now he was the juggler, and the Bank of Montreal had tossed him the ball. On top of everything else it was one of the busiest banking days of the month. Between meetings he found a moment to call the police, who said they'd had no other reports of car burglaries near High Park. Did he want to file a complaint? No thanks, said Molony, and called the Manulife branch.

"Commerce here. Straightened out that telephone transfer yet?"

"Yes. It ended up in the Canadian- instead of the U.S.-dollar account. It's been properly posted now. Sorry for the trouble."

"No trouble," said Molony, slumping in his chair. His neck was knotted, his shirt soaked through. "Would have been fun trying to balance that."

At Caesars Palace in Las Vegas, Betty Butler, an accounting clerk, was returning from lunch when she bumped into Dan Cassella, the vice-president finance and treasurer of Desert Palace Inc. He told her there was a large chunk of money in the Toronto U.S.-dollar account and they should obtain the use of it as quickly as possible. Butler called the Manulife branch and said a large sum had been deposited in the FX 276 account.

"What's the fastest way of getting it down here – wire?"

"It's too late today, it's almost four o'clock here. We could wire it in the morning, but it might take a couple of days. The cheques you write usually reach us a day or two after they're written. That would probably be fastest, especially if you can get the cheque deposited in our bank out there this afternoon."

They agreed to do it that way. Desert Palace Inc. would write itself a cheque, drawn on the Manulife account, for deposit in the First Interstate account in Las Vegas. Seemed the best solution, even though it meant the $1.42-million for Molony's use that night in Atlantic City would in fact spend the night in Toronto.

When Molony arrived at Christopher's Ribs, near the airport, Colizzi was parked in the far corner of the lot, facing the exit, engine running. They spoke through rolled-down windows, Molony in his battered Electra, Colizzi in his new BMW. One plainclothes officer who had them under surveillance had to remind himself which was the bookie and which the banker.

"I don't like this," said Colizzi.

"It won't take long. Follow me."

But Molony had forgotten a bag and didn't like clearing customs without one. It looked fishy. He turned into a travel agency and told Colizzi he'd just be a moment. Inside, a black-haired girl was sitting at her terminal. Molony asked her what a plastic travel bag cost.

"I don't know. We usually give them away. I guess you could have one for five dollars."

"You just said you usually give them away."

"Yes, but to customers."

While an unhappy bookie waited outside, and a Learjet waited at the airport, and a surveillance team waited at the far end of the plaza, and The Bulldog wondered what the hell was slowing the parade, Molony haggled over the price of the bag. Five dollars was exorbitant. Two was fair, he said, and two more than they usually got. Finally the girl just shrugged her shoulders.

Molony threw the bag in his car and led the way to the airport. He drove beyond the Avitat terminal and parked on the far side of a hangar. Colizzi pulled up beside him.

"Why you parking so far away?"

"This is where I park when I leave it overnight," said Molony, who didn't want casino personnel to see his car.

"I don't like this," said Colizzi.

In the Avitat terminal Claire Lodovico was waiting. She and Colizzi exchanged pleasantries. "I have the papers for you," she said, and he scribbled two signatures. The customer-deposit receipt was undated, and gave no indication of the nature or amount of the transaction. The second document read in full: "I hereby release all funds under the name Mario Colizzi to be paid to Brian Maloney." The space for a witness signature was left blank.

The plane was being refuelled, so Molony and Colizzi went back outside and waited in the BMW. Colizzi was pleased with his new car, and he showed Molony the features. Before long Claire came out and signalled that the plane was ready. Colizzi sped off, and Claire and Molony boarded the jet.

Canada's such a lovely place, said Claire, Toronto's such a nice city. Oh, look, Niagara Falls! Molony read the paper and wished she'd shut up. He had things to consider. His limit, for example – he had to get it raised. He'd talk to Larry Woolf about that. Five per cent of $1.42-million was $71,000. Maybe they'd go for $75,000 a hand.

Claire stopped chatting long enough to eat the food laid on for Molony. He put aside his paper and gazed out at the falling night and through the buzz of anticipation he began to put in perspective the $9-million he'd already embezzled. It had simply been dues, a harrowing apprenticeship, the price he'd paid to get where he was now – in the eerie quiet of a Learjet, slipping through twilight toward Atlantic City and $1.42-million and the casino he was going to put it to once and for all . . .

Shortly after the jet took off, the pilot filed a new flight plan. The Bulldog was informed that the plane's destination was no longer Buffalo but Atlantic City.

He sped over to Terminal One, parked illegally, and hurried in to the Air Canada counter. He wasn't sure he had enough money for a ticket, and if the investigation didn't work out he'd have trouble with the expense claim, but he'd cross that when he came to it. Turned out there were no direct flights to Atlantic City. You had to change in Philadelphia, and the next flight wasn't till seven in the morning.

The Bulldog still had the car – Molony would return to it sooner or later – so he drove back to the Avitat terminal and made a phone call. Charley Maxwell was an old buddy whose work in Intelligence had made him as well connected in Atlantic City as anyone on the force. In the late 1970s, when the casinos got going, Toronto money started moving down in a big way. Maxwell had taken a special interest in Paul Volpe, a Toronto mobster, and Angelo Pucci, his money man. In the course of monitoring their activities in Atlantic City, he had got to know a New Jersey State Police intelligence officer named Bill Kisby. They traded favours. Maxwell told The Bulldog he'd see what he could do.

The Bulldog parked his rental Ford across from the private terminal, between the Electra and an all-night greasy spoon. He got a burger and a coffee, returned to his car, and did what he'd done a thousand times before. He sipped from a little hole in the plastic lid, tuned in CBC Radio, and waited.

In the room at Caesars that made you feel a bit like God, an employee of the surveillance department recorded the swing-shift activity on a Game Observer's Report:

April 26, 1982. Caesars Atlantic City. Ronald P. Hardee.

6:20. Det. Bill Kisby, DGE, *requested John Connors call him at 641-7476.*

6:21. Called John Connors' residence. Advised Mrs. Connors to have John call surveillance when he arrives home.

7:01. John Connors called. Advised him to call Det. Kisby at 641-7476.

7:43. Corporate attorney Robert Reilert requested John Connors call him at 340-5790.

7:44. Called John Connors and advised him of Reilert's request.

7:52. Larry Bertsch, V.P., requested to speak to John Connors. Advised Bertsch that Connors was at home.

Just before the Learjet touched down at Pomona, shortly after eight o'clock, two New Jersey State Police officers crossed the floor at Caesars, heading for the casino cage. Detective Richard Rementer and Investigator Grant Valente identified themselves and asked to see the patron reference cards for Brian Molony and Mario Colizzi. Jane Blackton, the cage supervisor, took the cards from the wall file. The two men studied them, then called her over.

"Are these guys credit players?" said Rementer.

"No, strictly cash."

"Mind explaining this? I can't follow your posting system."

Blackton ran her finger across an entry. "This indicates a deposit of $360,000 on April 1. This is a deposit of $920,000 on April 19. This –"

"Nine hundred and twenty thousand dollars cash?" said Rementer.

"That's right."

Rementer looked at Valente. Valente whistled.

When the black stretch limo turned into Caesars, people stopped to see who'd get out. Every gambler once sat beside Mickey Mantle at the blackjack table or saw O. J. Simpson hailing a cab. Molony himself shot craps beside a short, sloppy guy with cigars sticking out of every pocket and a blonde at his side. The man borrowed and repaid a thousand dollars before Molony realized it was Mario Puzo. That was part of the allure – who's in the limo? Joan Rivers? Frank Sinatra? Donald Trump?

This time it was just a pudgy guy clutching a plastic travel bag. Molony tipped the driver a dollar he had set aside for the purpose and headed for the desk to pick up his key. He gave the porter his bag and another dollar. The porter said, "You be wanting those plain ribs later, sir?" Molony made for the casino and, in the concourse, saw Larry Woolf heading his way.

"Good to see you, Brian. How are you tonight?"

"Everything all set at the cage?"

"Why don't you sign in and we'll go upstairs to see Albert. He's having dinner and wants to see you."

At 8:41 p.m. Molony signed a customer-deposit receipt for $1.42-million. The presigned Colizzi customer-deposit receipt was filled in and time-stamped more than an hour later. The casino processed the credit, in other words, before processing its source, to create the paper record that permitted the issuance of markers to Molony. A sticker was affixed to Molony's card indicating cash as the source of the credit, even though the $1.42-million was earning a day's interest – several hundred dollars – at the Bank of Montreal in Toronto.

Molony went up to the Japanese restaurant and drank orange juice while Albert, his wife, and a credit executive ate dinner. Molony was eager to discuss limits. He said to Woolf, "Let's think in terms of $75,000 at baccarat."

"Fine," said Woolf.

Molony cursed himself. He should have asked for more. They agreed on a $15,000 limit at craps with double odds and a $15,000 buy-in on each number, double odds. Molony took his leave, trying not to seem impolite. In the baccarat pit his table was staffed and waiting. A crap table was also staffed and roped off. When the eight decks of cards in a baccarat shoe have been exhausted, the cards must be shuffled in a prescribed manner. It takes a few minutes, and Molony didn't like to wait. He sat down at the baccarat table, nodded, and asked for a $120,000 marker.

"Good luck, Mr. M. Let's hope tonight's the night."

April 26, 1982. Caesars Atlantic City. Matt Wilson.

9 p.m. DGE *Det. Grant requests taping of B. Maloney's play throughout this evening. Hold tape for them for review. Advised Joe of request.*

9:30 p.m. Maloney on baccarat #1. Archie watching play. Tape started.

10:00 G. Smith wants to know if we are taping both Baccarat 1 and Craps 11 when Maloney is present. Told him we are and advised Joe. Also Smith would like a copy of the tape for L. Woolf.

April 26. Caesars Atlantic City. Peter J. Miller.

9:00 p.m. DGE *present in monitor room.*

9:35 p.m. Pat O'Neil called. Advised Brian Maloney is on Baccarat 1. Started tape #121. Notify Matt Wilson.

9:49 p.m. Gary Smith called. Requested if surveillance is taping Brian Maloney. Advised Matt Wilson.

9:51 p.m. Matt Wilson advised to advise Gary Smith that we are taping Maloney. Matt Wilson was advised by Joe Mancari. Gary Smith advised Larry Woolf wants copy of tape.

Molony felt clear-headed and confident. When the next branch return of irregular liabilities came through, any one of the bogus loans – Elm Street Holdings, DCL Customs Brokers, Kernwood, or 499726 Ontario Ltd. – could spell doom. The juggling, the anguish, the surreal and tortuous vicissitudes of eighteen months had come down to a simple truth. Tonight was the night. He'd win because he had to win.

Right away it started happening. He won the first hand, lost the next, won two, lost two. Then it broke for him. Often, gambling, he had the feeling he was participating in what the cards did, influencing them, and he felt the sudden certainty the bank would win 9–8. He bet the bank, and bank won 9–8. He switched to player, and player won. Back to bank twice in a row: bank won twice in a row. He had started with 240 purple chips, and as the pile grew he bet increasing amounts. He put 150 chips – $75,000 – in two racks and moved them from player to bank as the impulse stirred him. A crowd had formed around the pit, and Molony became aware of the undercurrent of noise, the oohs and aahs when he won or lost. He had the sensation of being part of the crowd, jockeying to watch a taciturn, unfathomable man playing baccarat, changing his bet from player to bank, from bank to player, back among the spectators, straining to get a good look, a stranger to himself.

By the time he glanced at his watch he was up close to half a million dollars. Why the break in the game? He signalled the floorman – let's pick it up – then realized the dealer didn't have the purples to pay off. Molony had cleaned out the table. The floorman told the dealer, "Give him a marker."

Molony looked up over his glasses, sly innocence. "Sure you're good for it?"

The dealer – a silver-haired fellow who had worked three years to earn what Molony was betting on a single hand, years of sore backs and bogus smiles and headache-inducing concentration, of taking flak from floormen and invisible scrutiny from overhead and animosity from the players – the dealer thought this was hilarious. He laughed aloud. The floormen laughed, the cocktail waitress, everyone who worked at Caesars laughed, and it wasn't the phony laughter that follows money around. Molony liked that. He liked it so much he stood up from the table to make the feeling linger. Everyone was watching. He himself seemed to be watching. Why was the man on his feet? He needed to make sense of his actions, so he stretched and asked for an orange juice.

When he finally lost three in a row, he'd won half a million in an hour, turned $120,000 into $620,000. His deposit gave him almost $2-million. He was finally on the way. He knew it. Tonight was his night at baccarat. Time to see if it was his night at the crap table as well.

The Bulldog was on his fourth coffee when Charley Maxwell came over the radio. "Your man is at Caesars in Atlantic City. He's betting tens of thousands of dollars a hand. He's known there. He's lost millions in the last year."

The Bulldog was still thinking drugs. It took a moment to compute. "We've got a bank thief, Charley. Boy, have we got a bank thief."

"I'm going to head home now."

"Thanks for your help. Appreciate it."

Molony was simply a spinoff from an ongoing wiretap investigation. The Bulldog needed a marked car and uniformed officers. A routine police stop would allow the Morality and Surveillance guys to stay out of sight. If word got around that Molony had been taken down by the anti-gambling squad, every bookie in the city would be on alert. Question now was, who might be willing to make a couple of calls, wake people up, get them in early? The Bulldog had spent eleven years in uniform with Staff Sergeant Ron Brenham, and the last he'd heard Brenham was at 13 Division. The Bulldog called 13. Brenham happened to be working the midnight shift.

"A voice from the past."

"Got something big here, Ron. I need a car with two uniformed men."

"I'll send them out. Where are you?"

Sergeant Wayne Artkin and Constable Tom McDonald were put on special detail. The Bulldog gave them a radio and told them he'd probably ask them to stop a Buick Electra, licence NBJ 309, to confirm the driver's identification and search the vehicle. He said he couldn't be sure when the driver would return, but sometime toward morning.

"I'm off at six," said Artkin.

"I go to seven," said McDonald.

"Let me get you a coffee. You want a coffee? Maybe you'll make a little overtime."

Molony did not feel well. His stomach had seized and he was running a fever. Was he getting the flu? Tossing chips on the layout, he lost his balance and had to grip the table to steady himself. He threw the dice, a fierce, reflex motion, banking them sharply off the rubber. The chorus of moans made him look up: a crowd had formed six deep behind the velvet rope that cordoned off his table. The stickman raked in his chips. He reached for more but there were no more.

"Another fifty thousand," he said, and the floorman handed him a marker and a pen. He lost it all and left the dice pit.

"Give me a hundred," he said, in the baccarat pit. The floorman handed him a marker and a pen.

"Hundred more," he said, three minutes later, and the floorman handed him a marker and a pen.

"Another hundred," he said, one minute later. "Can't we speed it up?"

"Do you want to sign in advance, so you don't have to wait?"

"If it will speed things up," said Molony, taking the marker and the pen.

"Give me a hundred," said Molony, twenty-two minutes later, and the floorman handed him a marker and a pen.

"Hundred," he said, three minutes later, and the floorman handed him a marker and a pen.

"Another hundred," he said, twenty minutes later, and the floorman handed him a marker and a pen.

"Give me a hundred," he said, nine minutes later, and the floorman handed him a marker and a pen.

Two hours later Molony deposited half a million in chips at the cage, keeping $150,000 in chips. He asked the girl for his balance. "Nine hundred and seventy thousand," she said. He hurried back to the baccarat pit and lost the $150,000 in two hands.

"Give me a hundred," he said. The floorman handed him a marker and a pen. Molony said, "No disrespect to the dealer, but can we not speed up the game?"

April 27. Caesars Atlantic City. Shelly A. Jones.

3:41 a.m. Larry Woolf called and requested pictures of Baccarat 1. Large amount of purple checks. Started special tape #183 (Mon B).

Finally it was turning around. Molony wasn't winning, but he'd stopped the hemorrhage. For half an hour he'd played even, winning two, losing two, winning one, losing two, winning another. Then he won four in a row, betting the bank, and felt the exquisite certainty that he was embarked on the streak he'd been waiting for all night, all his life, a rampaging bull he'd ride into the ground. He gestured to the floorman – faster, let's move it – and then, hearing the bell that signalled closing, he almost collapsed under the fearsome weight of his own anticipation.

"Sorry, Mr. M., we've got to end it."

The exact wrong moment. Always the exact wrong moment. He never really lost, just kept running out of time.

"Could I see another hand, what would have happened?"

"Go ahead."

Molony stood up, raised his palms to show there was no bet, and reached for the shoe. Player, bank, player, bank. Natural bank, nine against eight. He would have bet player. He would have lost. He racked his chips and, accompanied by a security guard, headed for the cage. The crowd opened for him. People cleared their throats and turned away, trying to make themselves invisible. An elderly lady whispered, "Did you see how much he lost?"

"Shhh," said her husband. "He can hear you." Certain things about the casino, about losing, women didn't seem to understand. The man smiled apologetically. Molony smiled in return.

April 27. Caesars Atlantic City, Shelly A. Jones.
4:08 a.m. Special tape #183 (Mon B) stops.

Molony told the cashier to deposit the racks of chips and cash the rest. He went to his suite, splashed water on his face, stared in the mirror. Hadn't he been through enough? How much did he have to endure to earn the streak that would turn a year and a half into one of those nightmares that jerk you upright, terrified, and then, by the time you awake, dissolve into a phantom so harmless you can't believe you felt such grief? When he most needed to win he'd hit the cold run of his life. Looking in the mirror, seeing his hunched shoulders and ravaged face, he wanted to weep. He thought of weeping, but what would weeping accomplish? Would it get the money back? Would weeping pay down the loans? If he wept, would that wash Colizzi's name off the documentation? Would weeping guarantee a win? Would it make him a better handicapper? No, of course not. What would be the logic behind weeping? He collected his bag and went downstairs. The casino was empty except for floormen doing counts at the chip wells and maintenance people vacuuming cigarette ash out of the carpeting. Molony headed for the lobby and found Larry Woolf waiting by the limo stand. Dinner was on the counter – ribs, no sauce, and a large Coke. The limo hadn't arrived.

"You had it going there for a while," said Woolf.

"That's the way it goes."

"It's bound to turn around."

"What's it like out?"

"Nice enough night," said Woolf. "The weather's pretty good here this time of year. I like the Nevada climate myself. You don't get the humidity. What's Toronto like these days?"

Molony tried to think. Nothing came to mind.

"Shouldn't the limo be here by now?"

"Would you like me to check on it?"

"Give it another minute. Here comes one, is that it?"

"Sure is. Have a good trip back."

"Probably see you later in the week."

"Look forward to it," said Woolf, extending his hand. "Hey, wait a second." He fetched the Styrofoam packet and plastic bottle from the counter. "You almost forgot your dinner."

The Bulldog was tidying his rental car when the Learjet touched down in Toronto. He stuffed empty cups, hamburger wrappers, and chicken bones in his garbage bag, chastising himself for having overeaten. It was nearly the first of the month, he'd start a diet on the first. He wiped his hands and got on the walkie-talkie.

"That's the plane," he told the others. "He'll be out in a couple of minutes. We'll maintain visual contact and see where he's going. I'll stay between the surveillance vehicles and the marked car. I'll let you know when I want you to move on him."

Molony unlocked the Electra, threw his bag in back, and headed home. A million dollars, God, what a beating. He squinted into the rising sun and tried to adjust the visor, forgetting it was broken. No way he could go back tonight, think he was crazy. Lose a million one night, come back the next? No, Wednesday at the earliest. Only how would he do it? He'd left $390,000 on deposit, and the $75,000 limit was good all week. But he needed more to work with and couldn't ask Colizzi to sign off, not again. Major problem. Maybe the $390,000 was enough. Meanwhile there were more pressing problems to deal with, if only he could put his mind to them . . .

He swung onto Lakeshore, already humming with commuters and eighteen-wheelers. Beyond the breakwater, the lake seemed molten. A billboard flashed the date, temperature, and time. The twenty-seventh, good Lord. All the loans needed an interest payment. If interest weren't paid by day's end the loans could raise suspicion. Nine million? Ten? What's a month's interest? He began to calculate . . .

. . . missed the exit, had to turn into the park. Why Colizzi's name in the first place? Stupid, but if he tried to change it now it would cause suspicion. No, good idea, the right decision. Otherwise they would have called about the first one. If his line had been busy and the call had been routed to Steve Richardson? Better some name than no name at all, but why Colizzi? At least he was helpful enough, or greedy enough, to put his signature on blank documentation. Still, of all the names to . . .

. . . rearview mirror, wanting somebody to pull over. Me. Damn. Everybody ignored the park limit, not a soul around and you're supposed to crawl along. Uniformed constable with that air of relaxed alertness. My lucky day. Night. Morning. Whatever. Waiting, engine idling, Molony became aware of how long he'd gone without sleep. He'd feel better after a shower.

"How are you this morning, officer? What's the problem?"

"You were travelling thirty in a twenty zone, sir. May I see some identification?"

May I ask where you work? Would you mind telling me where you're going at this hour? Where you've been? How long you've been away? How did you make out? How much money do you have with you? Do you not have to work today? When will you sleep? Mind opening the trunk? Mind if we look in your car? Is this your bag? Mind if we open it? What are these envelopes? Anything in your pockets? How much is this? Do you have any more?

So often had Molony felt the sinking certainty, so deeply had the near-misses ingrained his sense of infallibility that even though the car contained, among other things, dozens of securities-transaction slips from Richardson's; the business cards of Michael Neustadter and Robert T. Catarra of Business Jet Airlines; a note with Michael Rosen's name and number and the figure $1,420,000; a dozen Caesars customer-deposit receipts from April 26, April 22, and April 20, in amounts ranging from $20,000 to $1.42-million; a memo in Molony's hand re "two U.S.-dollar drafts to California Clearing Corporation"; customer copies of CIBC bank drafts in amounts ranging from $60 to $920,000; CIBC debits in amounts ranging from $60 to $1,123,044; the remains of a $5,000 Caesars bill wrapper; a Caesars passbook showing Molony's room number as 4823-24-25; and $29,514 in Canadian and American currency – even as Artkin and McDonald waded, with growing incredulity, through this damning morass, and The Bulldog, out of sight, wondered what was taking so long, Molony, oblivious to the park's first joggers and dogwalkers, still didn't realize it was over.

Artkin went back to the cruiser and got on the walkie-talkie. The Bulldog said, "Arrest him for theft." Even as Artkin opened his notebook and read the words taped to the inside cover – "You are arrested on a charge of theft. Do you wish to say anything in answer to the charge? You're not obliged to say anything unless you wish to do so, but whatever you say will be taken down in writing and may be given in evidence against you" – Molony still didn't realize it was over. He'd straighten it out at the station. They'd seen the denominations of the bearer bonds on the Richardson's slips and assumed the bonds were stolen.

Artkin and McDonald had a little problem of their own. Allowing an arrested man to drive his own car is not recommended procedure, but impounding the Electra would have meant losing contact with it, losing continuity of evidence. Molony looked as if he'd been on a week-long tear – rumpled, dishevelled, sweat-stained – but he didn't have the uneasy air of most people caught with their fingers in the till; he was courteous and cooperative. McDonald told him they'd do him a favour and let him drive his car up to 13 Division. Molony cleared debris from the passenger seat and McDonald climbed in. He was a young constable, mid-twenties, no older than Molony, and he seemed ill at ease.

"Would you mind explaining what this is all about?"

McDonald didn't want to say anything that might jeopardize the investigation. "We'll explain at the station."

"Theft. Theft of what?"

"Well, sir, those securities."

"Where we going?"

"Turn here, sir. Eglinton and Allen Expressway."

"Do you know much about bonds?"

"Not really, sir."

"To buy them you don't put up the face value. They're highly leveraged. There's so little movement in the bond market that you can buy a $100,000 bearer bond for $5,000."

"Is that so?" said McDonald.

"We'll straighten this out," said Molony, but now he had to resist the conclusion part of him was trying to draw. Something was seeping in anyway. They'd stopped him for speeding but no further mention had been made of speeding. And their eyes had popped out at the sight of the money. And the cruiser was no ordinary one, not with "S" for "Supervisor" in its stencilled number . . .

At 13 Division, a squat, cement-block building, Molony was booked and taken up to the Criminal Intelligence Bureau. Police find it useful to allow suspects to contemplate their misdeeds, and Molony was isolated in a drab interrogation room. Coming off a night of frenzy, not having slept well in a year and a half or at all in twenty-four hours, he found idleness unendurable. He was going to be late and spoil his work record – he knocked on the door and said he had to phone the bank. Somebody told him they'd look after that. Brenda would worry because he always called when he got back – he knocked on the door and said he had to call his girlfriend. Somebody said they'd check on that. He asked how long he was going to be held. Somebody said it might be a while. He'd been told to empty his pockets. At least it was something to do. Among the contents were more receipts and deposit slips from Caesars. He thought of eating them but imagined (wrongly) the room was under closed-circuit surveillance.

Finally, two sergeants from the fraud squad came in. One of them, agitated, all business, said, "All right, Brian, we want some answers." The other asked if he'd like coffee or something to eat. They seemed to know exactly how much he had just lost at Caesars but otherwise, he sensed, they were groping.

"Brian, it's over. We know what you've been up to. We just don't know how much is involved."

Molony, so tired he seemed sedated, looked around the room. Metal table, metal chairs, no windows, bare walls. He studied the two men, took them in for the first time. Bob Barbour was a solidly built man of forty. He wore a light grey suit. He'd spent five years on the fraud squad and had earned a reputation as an astute investigator. His partner, Bob Greig, was a big, handsome Scottish fellow with a permanent hangdog expression. He was dressed in navy blazer, striped shirt, maroon tie, and grey slacks. They knew what he'd been up to? They were fishing. No one knew what he'd been up to. Nobody knew but Molony himself, and their astonishment would be as great as his relief.

"Maybe you better sit down."

9

COLD TURKEY

"Anna, Anna, you must understand that I am not just an unscrupulous creature – I am a man devoured by the passion for gambling."

– Dostoevsky, in a letter to his wife, 1871

After an hour of answering questions, Molony asked to use the phone. He called David Greenspan, a lawyer and branch customer. His secretary said he was out – anything she could do? Molony said he needed the services of Eddie Greenspan, the criminal lawyer. He knew the two men were unrelated but thought they might be acquainted. Five minutes later Eddie Greenspan phoned the station. Molony said he was an assistant manager at the CIBC branch at Bay and Richmond – Greenspan's bank, as it happened, across the street from his offices – and that he'd been charged with theft over $200.

Criminal lawyers get a feel for these things. Bank fraud. Assistant manager. Greenspan imagined an embezzlement in the range of twenty thousand. They'd let Molony out on his own recognizance. He could drop by the office in a day or two.

"What's involved?" said Greenspan.

"Nine," said Molony.

"Thousand?"

"No."

"Hundred thousand?"

"No no, million."

"Nine million dollars?" said Greenspan, flabbergasted. He couldn't help laughing. It was the way Molony had said it – "No no, million" – as if baffled anyone could be so wrong.

Greenspan himself was baffled. How was it possible? It must have been a single, stupendous grab rather than a typical employee fraud. Nine million dollars? No bank is that vulnerable. He advised Molony not to make a statement.

"I think I already have."

Informed by police that a CIBC employee had been picked up with $30,000 cash and securities receipts involving $5-million, the bank dispatched two security people to 13 Division. While Greig and Barbour questioned Molony, Don Adams and Margie Peters waited outside the interrogation room. Occasionally one of the fraud sergeants stepped out to ask a question.

Don Adams drove down to Bay and Richmond. He introduced himself to Harry Buckle and said he wanted a word with him. Buckle showed him into the manager's office.

"Is Molony here this morning?"

"Not yet," said Buckle, "but I expect he'll be in before long."

"This is a confidential inquiry, and you're not to jump to any quick conclusions, but Molony was stopped coming from the airport with $30,000 on him. Can you think of any reason why he'd have that much cash?"

Buckle was perplexed. "Well, he may have been out to see a customer who gave him a deposit. But I can't think which customer it might be."

"There was also evidence that he'd been dealing with Richardson

Securities in huge volume. He told the police they were going to find a shortage. Would you mind reviewing Molony's loans?"

"Of course," said Buckle. He reviewed the computer printout for post 2 and told Adams he saw nothing unusual in Molony's loans.

"The shortage mentioned was $9-million," said Adams. "Maybe we'd better look through his desk."

Don Adams had joined the bank after a career with the Metro Toronto Police. His slimness, English accent, and intellectual features made him look like the calligrapher he was in his free time. He had pieced together a great many frauds and it wasn't long before he turned up indications of Molony's deception. Harry Buckle was flummoxed.

How could there have been such a breakdown in the system? Why hadn't he been informed of the irregularities that were showing up – the documentation for loans he knew nothing about, the notes to hold all mail, the authorized credits that didn't exist. These things should have been reported to him. While in the audit department he himself had turned up several defalcations, including a fraud at Kipling and Queensway of half a million dollars, an enormous sum in those days. Everyone in the bank had chances to steal and not everyone could resist. But Molony? In the amounts being suggested? Buckle was so shaken he could scarcely read the day's mail. One letter, from head office, congratulated him on the performance of his branch.

Or, rather, what had been his branch. He was finished at Bay and Richmond, of that he was certain. If God Himself had been manager, Russell Harrison would have seen to it that He was demoted.

At her branch of the bank, Brenda was growing concerned. Even if he went straight from the airport to work, Brian always called when he got back to Toronto. She phoned Louise, who phoned Phil, who phoned Atlantic City. Caesars still had Molony registered as a guest. Phil told Brenda that Brian had probably fallen asleep. Brian, asleep? Her concern turned to worry. It was almost noon when he finally called.

"Where are you?"

"At the police station. I've been arrested."

She tried to tell herself he was joking, but there was nothing in his voice to help her.

"I've been charged with theft over $200."

"You didn't take money, did you?"

"Everything will be all right. I'll call again as soon as I can. Brenda, don't tell my parents. Phone Annemarie and ask her to tell them. She should do it before the paper comes out. They say I have to get off the phone now."

Molony had told the police he had more money at home. They had to move him to 52 Division, which had cells, to spend the night before his court appearance, and decided they'd let him drive his car home. At the wheel of the Electra, it began to sink in. How would his poor mother take the news? She'd be devastated; so would his father. How could he have brought such shame on them? He must have been out of his mind. What would his brothers and sisters think, his colleagues at the branch, his –

"Watch out!" said Barbour. The car had wandered into the oncoming lane. "I know you've got problems, but I've got a wife and child at home. Let's stay on our side of the road."

At the highrise Brenda's car was in the lot. Why was she home? Why had she not parked underground? Brian realized how distraught she must have been. He let Greig and Barbour into the apartment and found her waiting, puffy-eyed and pale. She kissed him.

"How did you get off work?"

"I just left," she said.

Molony showed Greig and Barbour the money, $7,000 U.S. They began searching through papers, looking in closets, going through Molony's file box. When they started opening Brenda's drawers, Molony said, "That's her stuff. There's nothing there." Changing clothes, he found a Canadian twenty and a pocketful of change, which he handed over. He found some crumpled ones and twos, and turned them over. Brenda told him his mother had been trying to reach him. He repeated that she was not to tell his parents, he wanted Annemarie to break the news. Quite apart from the arrest, they'd be shocked to discover he and Brenda lived together.

"Time to go," said Barbour.

"I'll call you as soon as I can."

"Wait a minute," said Greig. Each of his fingertips bore a Band-Aid, a legacy of his days in uniform. Thwarting an arson attempt, he had suffered chemical burns. The damage to his fingertips got worse each year. The Band-Aids gave him the look of a chronic nailbiter and hindered him as he counted out five dollars. He handed the money back to Molony.

"You're going to need something for jail."

In the little room with the picture of a window on the wall, Ron Andrews listened to an incoming call on Colizzi's line. Nick Beck. Sit wires eight hours a day and you hear the panic behind everyday voices. Beck, hyper at the best of times, was almost frantic. Colizzi was even more phlegmatic than usual. Could the rumours have been true? How much had Molony already said? How much would he be persuaded to say? What were they going to do?

After getting off the line, Colizzi made plans to go to Las Vegas. He called a Chinese acquaintance and arranged to meet for a drink that night. He also got a collect call from an inmate at one of the prisons near Kingston, a man who made a living with a tire iron. Colizzi asked him when he was getting out, and the inmate said he had a three-day pass coming up that weekend. Colizzi said, "Call me when you can. I may have something."

Colizzi had recently moved, paying cash for a house in the Annex area of the city. The police obtained a search warrant and arrived that evening as he was about to go out. Members of the anti-gambling unit conducted a search and found, among other things, playing cards, dice, baize cloth, a matchbook from Caesars Atlantic City, and a new bullet-proof vest. In a livingroom expensively furnished with leather chairs and sofas, Greig and Barbour questioned Colizzi.

"Do you know a man named Brian Molony?"

"Yes."

"Is he a friend of yours?"

"Yes."

"Do you do business with him?"

"No."

"How do you know Brian Molony?"

Colizzi shrugged. "I know him from the races, you know. I'm a bookie."

"What would you say if I told you Brian Molony stole ten million dollars from the bank?"

"You shock me."

"Did you ever sign any bank drafts presented to you by Molony?"

"I signed a few. They were blank. I thought I was doing him a favour."

"Did you get any of the money?"

"No."

"Why did you sign these documents when you didn't receive any benefit?"

"I don't know," said Colizzi. "It's crazy. I don't believe it myself."

Greig told him he was under arrest for possession of property obtained by crime. He advised Colizzi of his right to counsel and asked if he understood.

"Yeah, yeah," said Colizzi. He nodded at the Morality officers searching the place. "They already told me."

At Bay and Richmond the employees were not officially informed what had happened. They were only told not to say anything about anything to anyone. They got their information from customers, or contacts in the security department. Some heard it on the radio. Because Jeremy Brown, the radio commentator, was a branch customer, many of them listened to CKFM. When they heard that Brian had been arrested they thought at first it must have been a practical joke Brown had cooked up.

The news was met with stunned disbelief. Brian? The treasurer of the bank hockey team, who badgered you if you were a day late with the $28 dues? Brian, whose suits and shoes looked like something from a thrift shop? Brian, who was always the last to pay for a round when they went to the pub? Does that sound like a guy with millions of dollars?

Such a shame, if true, such a waste of talent. Is he all right? Is he in jail? Poor guy. The bank will throw the book at him. I wonder if Sandy's heard yet. Hi, Sandy? I know. Can you believe it? How could he have done it? How could it have been going on so long? Hope he's got something to fall back on. He's too smart not to have stashed some of it away. I know, the casino in Atlantic City. Isn't that clever? What better place? You could say every cent was gone and they'd have no way to trace it. I'd love to know the number of his Swiss bank account. There's talk of suspensions? Who? Are you sure? No, I didn't. Listen, I have to hang up. Talk to you later.

Was Sandy right? Would there be more arrests? Was the girl at the next desk making plans to fly to Brazil? The next desk? – good God, Brian was always sticking things under my nose. Is my signature on bogus documentation? Such a decent guy, bringing us pizza the night we stayed late balancing the books. I can't believe he'd do it. I can't believe he'd use us. The nerve! The ruthless bastard! Betraying people whose jobs depend on mutual trust. What about Steve? They worked so closely it seemed impossible Brian could have done anything like this without Steve's knowledge.

Meanwhile, the branch was full of strange faces and grave concern. Besides the bank's own people, there were members of the Metro Police fraud squad. The police had done the bank a great favour – who knows how long Molony would have carried on undetected? – but Greig and Barbour found themselves treated with chilly disdain. You'd have thought they'd stolen the money. Most employee wrongdoing is discovered by the bank itself, which made Molony's fraud doubly embarrassing. Thank you very much, was the bank's attitude, we're quite capable of handling our internal affairs. If you're so bloody capable, was the fraud squad's attitude, how the hell did someone manage to steal ten million dollars from a single branch? And when do you think you would have caught him? And once you did, would you have turned him over to us or hushed the whole thing up to save face?

It was Bob Barbour who saw that the most recent fraud had been perpetrated the day before and wondered aloud whether there might be a way to freeze the funds. Don Adams noticed, reviewing the first draft to California Clearing Corporation, that it had been negotiated at the Bank of Montreal across the street. The security people at all the banks work closely together. Adams called a friend in the Bank of Montreal's security department and asked about the previous day's transaction. The friend told him the $1.42-million was still on deposit at the Manulife branch but that Caesars had requested immediate remittance. Because the money was in U.S. funds, the draft was drawn on Irving Trust in New York. The CIBC instructed Irving Trust to stop payment, saying there was doubt as to the authenticity of the signatures. Not true, but it seemed the best way of buying time.

The race was on. The CIBC's lawyers, Blake Cassels, discovered that California Clearing Corporation had never bothered to obtain a licence to conduct business in Ontario. Don Adams swore out an affidavit, stating: "I verily believe that if an injunction is not granted to restrain disposition of the funds . . . the fraud perpetrated by Mr. Molony upon the Bank will be furthered by withdrawal of these funds from this Province." Affidavit in hand, a lawyer from Blake Cassels hurried to Osgoode Hall. Mr. Justice J. Catzman granted an interim injunction restraining California Clearing Corporation, the Bank of Montreal, and Desert Palace Inc. from disposing of any funds in the FX 276 account.

Having frozen the $1.42-million, the bank set about determining exactly how – and how badly – it had been stung. A CIBC spokesman, asked how millions could go missing without anyone noticing, replied, "That's a question a lot of people around here are asking."

Molony's sister Annemarie, though utterly stunned after speaking to Brenda, made sure the doctor across the street was available to sedate her parents before she told them Brian had been arrested. Mrs. Molony was inconsolable. Dr. Molony prayed.

Doug and Nicole saw the news on Sarnia television and burst into tears, which set off their daughter.

Jeremy Brown was preparing his morning commentary at CKFM when he heard the news on the studio monitor. He began trembling and was barely able to go on air.

Louise got a call from a friend at Bay and Richmond. She, in turn, called Phil. After they'd got over their initial shock, Louise said, "I told you it was strange he didn't take any holidays." Phil recalled someone having said, after the auditors left Bay and Richmond, "Funny, everybody else is relieved the audit's over, but Brian doesn't seem relieved."

Eli Koharski heard the news on his car radio. He almost collided with a bus. He had to pull off and take a taxi home.

When Sherry Brydson learned of the fraud, she wondered if it had something to do with Molony's diet – all that fast food and Coca-Cola.

Stu Butts told Brydson on the phone, "I don't know what this is all about, but I'm going to help Brian any way I can. I'm going down to put up bail."

"I believe I first heard the news from my wife," recalled Barney Rooney, Molony's history teacher for four years at Regina Mundi in London, Ontario, and now the principal of the school. "She read it in the paper – she said, 'Is that our Brian?' – and of course the next day it was all over the school. My first reaction was: what he chooses to do, he'll do well. Look at the others in the Molony pack. In their chosen fields they all seem to be doing well. What was the final sum involved at the bank? Brian holds the championship, does he not? The second reaction, of course, was a feeling of deep regret. Why? How the hell did it come to this? It's like finding that someone you expected to become a great surgeon has become Jack the Ripper. The skills required in both cases are roughly similar – it's all in how you put them to use.

"I believe Brian was inflicted with me right the way through high school, though I'd have to look that up. So I got to know him reasonably well, as one Irishman ought to know another. I took a special interest in him, since his dad was from Dublin. I met Dr. Molony at a couple of dinners, and certainly enjoyed the banter that went along with it. A very capable, very witty man. A man who understood Gaelic football and hurling. I met him with the prejudice of our both being Irish. I'm a County Down man myself, but my wife's people are westerners – her uncle went to the College of Surgeons – and a lot of my classmates went down to Dublin, National University, and a lot of my friends went to Maynooth. It's a very small society, and in a sense we're all exiles.

"Brian was one of the wittiest, cleverest students we ever had. You'll find his name on plaques in the hall. The whole pack of Molonys you remember. Their outstanding characteristic was their ability as wordsmiths. There was no point just saying it – you had to say it elegantly. And I might add that they were all gamblers. I don't mean the interest in horses – I'd take that as the natural interest of people in a family that's been handicapping them for generations and knows them inside out. And I don't necessarily mean putting down money. I mean finding pleasure in the excitement that comes from taking a risk. To me that's absolutely normal. If you have two ways of coming down a slope, you choose the one that's more . . . amusing, perhaps? I always thought of students in terms of automobiles or horses. The ability to move is also the potential to crash. An old horse that will carry you over every jump deliberately and finish last is never going to throw you. One that has a chance of winning because it moves like blue hell will take you over in glorious danger. Brian was one to choose the horse that had a chance of winning.

"In my own school days I had a couple of classmates who were gamblers, and their notable trait was their total inability to get out while they were ahead. I don't know what the psychological effect would be of gambling with someone else's money, but perhaps you could more easily rationalize your motivation – you're always playing to win the money back. Brian's gambling must have become an emotional response to the situation in which he found himself, rather than an intellectual one. He had a good intellect, and intellect would tell you to get the hell out.

"When he was here at the school, he was not a particularly pious boy. Hell no. Not many are at that age. They'd rather lie in bed than go to Mass in the morning – a trait, I must say, I haven't lost myself. To a sixteen-year-old, the things that Holy Mother Church does right, she does very well. But the stupidities in which she's engaged are very, very evident. None in that group were famous for being theological or philosophical. On the other hand, I don't think Brian saw himself as the ultimate authority, in the sense of setting his own rules and to hell with everyone else's.

"If we venture into the moral field, we must ask whether what he did was a sin. Strange as it may seem, I honestly don't believe the man would sin. Let's consider it a moment. Was it a serious matter? Certainly. Did he have full knowledge? Again, yes. Did he have full control and free consent? Here is where uncertainty creeps in. I very much doubt that he did. And if I'm right about that, it would let him off the moral hook.

"The other thing is to view him in the larger context. You're taught from an early age to do your best, to overreach yourself, to keep at it. He was making use of skills and attributes he saw himself as possessing. His nickname at the school was 'Lucky Lurch,' which came from his uncanny ability to score goals in hockey in the absence of any apparent knowledge or athletic skill. It was only a house league, but he was playing against boys from northern Ontario and all over, marvellous players. He wasn't on their level, but you could practically guarantee that Lucky Lurch would score more goals than any of them. I was a gamesman in my time, and I'd say he had the ability we most admire in our athletes – the ability to see it all as a chess game and make the right moves ahead of the moment. I wouldn't be surprised if, in his gambling, he saw himself as destined to recover his losses. In which case his actions would have been those of a desperate but moral man.

"When this sort of thing happens there's a tendency to look for cause and effect in the measurables. When all the measurables are toted up, we come back to choice. In this day and age, our judgements about what's good and what's bad usually have to do with efficiency, with what works. I'd imagine that he chose to continue doing what he was doing because, within his experience, it worked. The impression is that he was functioning as an outlaw, very much on his own. I wonder, was he? Or did he see himself as a member of the norm? Every day he saw people taking risks, investing other people's money – the Irish euphemism for 'gambling' is 'investment.' This financial manipulation made up his day-to-day professional life, and I'm sure it ranged from legitimate, to semi-legitimate, to doubtful. When he was here at the school, Brian was extremely inventive when it came to such things as explaining a midnight raid on the kitchen. Given his facility at structuring models that fit the facts as he saw them, I wonder if he wouldn't have seen himself as being not much further out on the limb than the people he was among. What's the difference between a terrorist and a commando? It's all in the point of view. When we talk about Brian, we're talking about someone who made a rather spectacular mistake. But perhaps we're also talking about a child of the age."

At 52 Division, Molony had to hand over his belt, shoes, and glasses before he was locked in a cell. The bed was a steel frame, no blanket, no pillow. No matter which way he sat or lay, he felt stabbing pain in his kidneys. Time slowed to a standstill, restarted by fragmented sounds and memories. The frenzy of the classroom hamster, accustomed to running full-out on the treadmill, when a pencil was jammed in the wheel. The shatterproof toilet he couldn't figure out how to flush. Asking for something to read and being told, "What do you think this is, a hotel?" The bone-jarring slam of cell doors. Coffee and a tired hamburger slathered with brown gunk – the guard's expression when he said, "Thanks, but I don't drink coffee and I'm a plain hamburger man." Being handcuffed to a teenager with wild eyes and taken by paddy wagon to headquarters. Posing for mug shots. Trying to relax his hand sufficiently that fingerprints could be taken. The prisoner who yelled for two hours at the top of his lungs, banging on his cell door, "I've got my rights under the Charter!" The not knowing. Being hustled out at 5 a.m., the squalor and anxiety of the van full of prisoners from the different stations, arriving at the Don Jail handcuffed to a stranger. All the tattoos. The odd intimacy – everyone seemed to know everyone else. The law student from Greenspan's office: "We won't be able to do it today. Crown's opposing bail." Molony had understood that in exchange for explaining the frauds he'd be granted bail immediately; he found himself pondering how he could end his life. The prisoners at the Don who cheered and whistled when they found out who he was. Stu Butts, having got himself in by saying he was a lawyer, saying, "Nobody thinks any less of you because of this, Brian. Your mother said to say she loves you. The flesh is weaker than the spirit." Other prisoners telling him what was going to happen. You'll be out Thursday, Eddie Greenspan will get you bail. Experts, though they'd failed to make bail themselves. The prisoner who said confidently, "You'll get six and be out in two." The long-haired kid who said, "Don't say nothing to nobody in here." The rock music that blared for five hours in the afternoon. The skinny addict who, when Molony pushed aside a tin plate of slop, said, "What's the matter, it isn't caviar?" The girl from Greenspan's office asking, "If your family posts bail, will you stay in the country?" The incredible hurt. The certainty that self-destruction was the only honourable way out. Shoes and belt. Back in the van for the bail hearing. The fight in the holding area in the bowels of Old City Hall, the vivid colour of a black man's blood, the huge pool that formed on the floor. The guards who pretended nothing was happening. Stepping out of dingy darkness into the bright courtroom, like walking onstage. Being stared at by everyone except his mother, in dark glasses, head bowed. Being told he'd made bail, waiting, waiting, then getting a message that an appraisal had to be done on his parents' house. Reading in *The Toronto Sun* on Friday morning that he'd been released on $250,000 bail. Waiting. Friday noon and still nothing, good Lord, there's been a mistake, I'll be here all weekend, I'll be here forever.

Finally, in the afternoon, the walk down a long corridor, the overweight guard unlocking each door in turn. The visiting area. Being told to stand in front of a peephole. Suddenly, through the slot, his mother's eyes. He wished she'd left her dark glasses on.

"Are you all right, Brian?"

"I'm fine."

"This the guy you're putting up bail for? Come this way, lady, you need to sign the forms."

Molony was taken to a holding area. The exit gave onto the drive leading from the basement level of the jail. The moment of emergence – light, air, trees, sky. It might have been months, years. Brendan and Annemarie had pulled up to the door. As Brian climbed in, reporters and photographers hurried over; Brendan slammed into reverse and sped backwards up the ramp, scattering them.

"I might have been safer inside."

At a take-out place his mother, Brenda, and Stuart Butts were waiting. They had Kentucky Fried Chicken in case Brian was hungry. He sat in back between Brenda and his mother. The tension and distress in the car. The pungent smell of his clothes, which he'd worn for three days and nights. Brenda squeezed his hand.

"We're in this together," she whispered.

Annemarie, in front, turned and said, "Speaking for the whole family, Brian, we want you to know we're all behind you."

The call to the post came over the radio. "Turn it up," said Mrs. Molony, her voice shaky and frail.

The first at Greenwood was an $8,000 claiming race for maiden three- and four-year-olds. One of Dr. Molony's horses had been entered. "The winner of the first race was Annie Adan, a bay mare by Two Gun Dan out of Snow Feather." Dr. Molony was down in Louisville. They had all agreed there was nothing he could do while Brian was in jail, so he'd decided not to cancel his trip to Kentucky with his visiting son-in-law. He needed the time away, to collect himself and try to make sense of what had happened. Stu Butts found the attentive silence in the car almost surreal. "Annie Adan paid $22.40, $10.00, and $6.20."

Leaving behind the dismal constriction, Brian had expected to feel relief. Instead he felt the tremendous weight of the unsaid.

Everyone spoke more softly and soberly than usual. They asked if he was all right, as if he'd been in an accident. No one mentioned the fraud. He owed them an explanation but did not know how to explain. In a strange way the whole thing seemed as bewildering to him as it must have to them. In the shower at the house he stood under scalding water for what seemed hours. Annemarie knocked. "Pass me your clothes, Brian. I'll throw them in the wash." She pressed fifty dollars in his hand, apologizing it was all she had. He went downstairs and found his four-year-old nephew in front of the TV.

"What are you watching?"

"Cartoons."

"Can I watch with you?"

"Sure."

Brian sat beside him; after a while Garrett climbed onto his lap. Together they watched humanoids zoom between fantastic worlds, propelled by rocket packs on their belts.

Brian's mother told him he was welcome to stay at the house, but Inglewood, weighted with grief, was the last place he wanted to be. On the way to the apartment Brenda told him her parents had taken the news well. For them, too, it had been a double whammy. They hadn't known she lived with Brian. They'd offered money or whatever might help. Her manager had told her downtown wanted to speak to her but not to return until she was ready. Phil had dropped by; he and Louise wanted to put up their house to raise bail, but Louise had asked her manager and he'd said no. Sue had come over to lend support, Stu had put up part of the bail, Doug had called from Sarnia to say he'd drive up if it would do any good. None of them knew what had happened to the money, only that Brian had admitted stealing it. They were acting on faith and friendship. He had never been in such dire straits and yet felt extraordinarily fortunate.

They were barely in the door when Eddie Greenspan's office called. Brian was told not to discuss the case with anyone, even Brenda; because they weren't married, she could be subpoenaed to testify against him. Brian was relieved, and when he and Brenda made love it was unlike anything they'd shared. Now that the whole iceberg was visible, everything was different between them. The intimacy of revelation was almost painful. Afterwards Brian felt hungry for the first time in a week. They didn't want anyone coming to the door – Brenda was terrified of the press – so they asked her cousin, two highrises away, if she'd pick up some Swiss Chalet chicken. Brian slept more soundly than he had in months, years.

In the morning he told Brenda he needed to do something physical, hit golf balls. She called Phil and Louise, who picked them up. The driving range was twenty miles away and the trip seemed to take forever. The car was unnaturally quiet. Phil and Louise were afraid to say the wrong thing. Brian broke the silence.

"If we reach the border, I can't go any further."

Everyone laughed uproariously. Then it was quiet again except for the hiss of the tires.

"I don't know how you can joke," said Louise.

"Now it's from relief."

"I just don't know what to say. I thought I knew you."

"Louise," said Phil.

"No," said Louise. "I want to know."

"I wish I knew myself," said Brian.

At the driving range they got buckets of balls. Phil horsed around but Brian took it seriously, teeing up the ball, addressing it soberly, concentrating on the mechanics of his swing. The ball jumped off his driver before slicing to the right. He studied its flight, teed up another, adjusted his stance.

He wanted to hit one exactly right. He wanted to hit one so hard it screamed off, farther and farther, and just kept going.

When Brenda returned to work, the Monday after Brian's arrest, she was told head office wanted to see her. She took the subway to Commerce Court and met with Mel Simmons, the chief of security, and Brian Jilek, an inspector. They wondered if she knew why Brian had taken the money. They wanted to know how often he went away, and whether she knew where he'd been going. They asked what he'd majored in at university. They wanted to know whether she knew what he'd been up to, and why she thought he took the money. And whether she'd ever seen him bet, and where his credit cards were, and whether he'd help with an audit, and how much he gave her to look after the apartment. When she told them, they laughed and told her he was a cheapskate. They wanted to know if he'd been getting strange calls at home and how often he'd gone on trips and whether he'd cooperate with their investigation and whether she'd known all along and how it was possible not to have known and whether she understood the repercussions this would have and whether he would help with an audit and why she thought he took the money, and when they finally let her go she barely made it to the elevators before the tears came. She could feel them behind her back, staring and whispering.

At her own branch she felt a little better. Then they started phoning. They wanted his personal and business Visa cards and his help with an audit. They thought she'd like to know that thirteen people had been suspended, including the manager, the senior assistant manager, the credit officer, a foreign-exchange clerk, the audit inspector, and the assistant general manager. And that Bert

Mills, the vice-president, was drawing a lot of heat, and his wife had just had a pacemaker implanted. They wanted Brenda to know that these people just might get their jobs back faster if Brian helped with the investigation and that, frankly, nobody believed she didn't know what he'd been doing, and after a week of trying to answer their questions and ignore their knowing smirks she found herself sobbing hysterically. One of the girls at her branch took her to the emergency department at Women's College Hospital, where they gave her sleeping pills and sent her home. She slept from nine at night until five the next afternoon, but when she got up she was even more exhausted. Brian had never seen her this way. He worried about her.

He also worried about his parents. He'd had a long talk with his father; this was simply beyond Dr. Molony's understanding. "I don't know what to do," he told his son as they sat together in the livingroom at Inglewood, not bothering to switch on a lamp as daylight seeped from the room. "I don't know what I should do. I don't know what I can do. I simply don't know. If you need anything, Brian, please ask."

"Thank you."

"Take care of your health. This is no time to start drinking. You'll need your wits about you."

"Yes."

"Sieg called, to say you could stay out at the farm."

Brian wanted to keep busy, not sit around. He looked for a job in the want ads, made calls, put the word out. Everyone asked why he'd left the bank, of course, and when he told them they nodded: "We appreciate your candour." His irritability grated against Brenda's distress; they started getting short with each other. He tried not to resent the ten dollars she left on the kitchen table each morning but hated not being the breadwinner, the humbling lack of control. He started drinking rum-and-Cokes; she was getting dark circles under her eyes. By the terms of his bail he couldn't leave the city, but when friends offered their cottage up north he urged her to go.

After a week's rest Brenda seemed better, but then the phone started ringing again. Her mother told her the bank had called asking where Brian's business Visa card was. Brenda was so upset she fired a pot at the kitchen wall. Brian had a demand loan from the bank for $488, and the bank towed off his car in the middle of the night. He kept looking for work; finally, at a head-hunting firm, he was called back for a second interview. When they asked him in again, he thought they were going to offer him a job. The president said, "Just one question. We do a couple of hundred thousand dollars' worth of business with the CIBC each year. If we hire you, will that business be affected?" "I'm sure it will," said Brian, and the offer never came. Finally, stone broke, too proud to ask his parents for money, he applied for unemployment insurance. Why not? Wasn't this exactly what the program was for? Hadn't he contributed for years? He began receiving $280 a week in benefits. Word got around at Bay and Richmond; everybody thought it hilarious. The $10-million man was collecting unemployment.

Walt Devlin was reading the Sunday papers over breakfast in Washington, D.C., when a headline caught his eye. He put on his reading glasses. The article, by H. G. Bissinger, said that "a mild-mannered assistant bank manager" in Toronto had been charged with defrauding his employer of more than $10-million, most of which he'd lost at Caesars in Atlantic City. Devlin went through the piece with care. He was looking for suggestions that the banker had enhanced his material life – cars, jewellery, expensive trips. Had he found such indications he would have thought no more about it. Instead, the article referred to Molony's unassuming appearance, his privileged background as the son of a respected surgeon, and the one-bedroom highrise apartment he shared with his girlfriend. Molony was out on $250,000 bail and was being represented by "perhaps the finest defence lawyer in all of Canada."

Next morning Devlin called Toronto information and got Eddie Greenspan's number. He talked his way past the firm's secretary and Greenspan's own secretary. When Greenspan came on, Devlin identified himself as executive director of the council on compulsive gambling in Washington. Had Greenspan started debriefing his client about the case?

"Why do you ask?" said Greenspan.

"I want you to understand I'm not a crank. I'm not out to commercialize this thing. I want to help. Are you aware there's a medical diagnosis of a pathological disorder of impulse control?"

Beware people who see $10-million in the newspaper and want to help. Beware anyone who says, "I want you to understand I'm not a crank." This was not the first call Greenspan had received about Brian Molony. Besides the crown and the police and the bank's lawyers and the bonding company's lawyers and the casino's lawyers there were reporters wanting interviews, a publisher putting out feelers, someone inquiring about film rights. Greenspan lit one of the sixty Belmont cigarettes he smokes each day.

"No," he said. "I didn't know there was such a diagnosis."

"I've never met Brian Molony, but I'm going to tell you about him."

"Just a minute," said Greenspan. His secretary was gesturing that he was late for a meeting – he indicated he'd only be a moment. "Sorry, you were going to tell me about Brian."

"First of all, everybody's going to think he's got something put away. He doesn't. There's no money. Nothing buried in a tin can in his backyard. No account in Switzerland. Whatever the final number happens to be, he lost it all. He's not going to be able to pay you unless the money comes from family or friends."

"Is that so?" said Greenspan. Molony had told him all the money was gone.

"I don't know if you're this far along, but when you look into the embezzlements you'll find he went in hand over fist. This is no Robert Vesco, crafting an elegant scheme. He grabbed. Once he started having to cover up, that's when you'll find the artifice."

Greenspan's own understanding suggested Devlin was right.

"You'll find he started small. You'll find the embezzlements get bigger as he gets more desperate. The size grows wildly toward the end."

Greenspan motioned to his secretary that he was going to be a few minutes after all. He reached for pencil and paper. "Anything else you can you tell me about Brian?"

"He's been under incredible strain. While the frauds were going on, he lived in a pressure cooker. Each time he dips in, the heat gets turned up another notch. When it ends so abruptly, when your life is altered so dramatically, it does things to your head. Throw in this guy's young age, his staid background, the banking environment, the huge sums involved, the notoriety he's facing – he's struggling with some big issues. I'm worried about his state of mind. He could be suicidal."

There was something irritating about Devlin's cockiness, but Greenspan was impressed. He asked for some personal background and learned that Devlin himself had come to grief gambling. He'd been abandoned by his father when he was seventeen days old and raised by his mother and, eventually, his stepfather in Newark, New Jersey. They lived in an eight-family, cold-water tenement house. An inordinately tall kid and gifted athlete, Walt had used basketball as his ticket out. After a career at George Washington University he was a first-round NBA pick and went on to play four seasons as a guard with the Pistons and the Lakers. When his pro career ended he was disillusioned to realize the adulation had been aimed not at him but at his uniform. He was happily married to a nightclub singer, though, and they had a lovely daughter.

Devlin became a partner in a bar and restaurant in Newport Beach, California, and bought a house on Balboa Island, where the neighbours included film stars. Life was rich and rewarding. When a friend ran into marriage difficulties, Devlin invited him to move in until he got back on his feet. Over several months, Devlin's wife fell in love with the man. One day she announced she was leaving and taking their daughter with her. Devlin, distraught, phoned his stepfather in Newark. A few hours later his stepfather died of a heart attack.

Three of the four most important people in his life had been taken away. Not only was Devlin unable to keep his family together, he had killed his stepfather. He ended up in Las Vegas. The noise, the stimulation, the constant presence of others, the sensation of money at risk – it had an analgesic effect. As long as he was gambling he was immune to his problems. When he stopped, life seemed unbearably painful.

Thus began a seventeen-year odyssey in which Devlin alienated everyone who had known him. He lost every dollar he had, then every dollar he could borrow, con, or steal. He lived in dozens of cities, bailing out when the bad cheques caught up to him. For a year he went off each morning, spent the day at the racetrack, and returned to a woman who believed he worked as a building contractor. He was shot at and stabbed, arrested six times, sentenced to penitentiary. Twice he came within an inch of suicide.

Devlin wanted to stop gambling but couldn't. He couldn't understand why he couldn't stop, couldn't understand why he couldn't understand. He concluded he was crazy and signed himself into Western State Hospital, a psychiatric facility in Staunton, Virginia, for observation. It was three months before a doctor saw him; by then it was too late. When he told the staff he wasn't crazy, they solemnly agreed. When he yelled and raged they put him on Thorazine. When he curled up in the corner he was deemed sicker than ever. Eventually he got out by seducing a woman supervisor who helped get him discharged in the belief that he loved her.

Devlin's search for self-enlightenment eventually led him to Dr. Robert Custer, a gentle, sad-eyed Washington psychiatrist whom he had read about in *Reader's Digest.* Custer worked for the Veterans Administration and specialized in the treatment of alcoholism. Some drunks were also compulsive gamblers, and he began to see that gambling, too, could be a devastating addiction. Devlin approached him in 1974; Custer apologized that he could treat only veterans. Five years later Devlin found himself managing a new restaurant in Atlantic City. He had just stolen the first week's receipts – $17,000 – and blown it in the casino at Resorts. His worldly possessions consisted of T-shirt, Levis, and sneakers. He'd ripped off everyone he knew, including his sister, brother, and mother. He showed up at Custer's office and said, "Whether I'm a veteran or not, you're taking me on. You've got to. If you won't, I'm going straight from this office to the Calvert Street bridge."

Custer was a godsend. After seventeen years of degeneracy, self-contempt, and incomprehension, Devlin was told, "You're not a common thief, you're ill. You're not hopeless, you're treatable. You're not unique, you're like scores of people I've come across." For Devlin, the arduous process of recovery entailed support groups, broad reading, explorations of formal religion, and therapy with Custer. He realized he could not have helped himself unaided and decided his time was best spent helping others in the same position. One way he found them was to monitor the papers and look into cases in which seemingly accomplished, responsible people had stolen money. A surprising number, he discovered, were feeding a gambling habit.

On the phone from Washington, Devlin told Greenspan he thought he could help him make sense of Brian Molony. He offered to come to Toronto at his own expense. Terrific, said Greenspan, look forward to meeting you.

Once he was out on bail, Molony realized he couldn't afford Eddie Greenspan. He explained his financial situation and asked Greenspan to recommend another lawyer. Greenspan said, "We're not going to talk about fees today. We're not going to talk about them next week. We're not going to talk about fees until you're back on your feet – whenever that is." Friends told Molony to be careful, Greenspan obviously intended to use the case to heighten his own public profile. Why else would a lawyer with a reputation for billing handsomely be so unconcerned about getting paid?

Greenspan found himself responding to his client in a forceful way he himself did not at first understand. He had grown up in Niagara Falls, Ontario, a raw town behind the wax and neon. Some of his childhood friends ran afoul of the law. Greenspan's father spent a year at law school, intending to become a lawyer, but returned to the family scrap business when his own father's health failed. He himself died of a heart attack when Eddie was thirteen. To make ends meet, Greenspan's mother took a job as a secretary at the public school.

In 1962 Eddie graduated from Niagara Falls Collegiate Institute and was accepted in the general arts program at the University of

Toronto. He got a student loan and worked the summer demonstrating and selling kitchen knives in the Pure Foods Building at the Canadian National Exhibition. One of his late father's best friends had been a racetrack denizen named George. One day, out of the blue, Uncle George showed up in Toronto. The man knew Eddie disliked him but wanted to talk. He'd been a schmuck, he was sorry, he hoped Eddie could forgive him. He was straightening out his life. He'd landed a good job, things were going well, but he needed help over the hump. He couldn't go to anyone else and wondered if Eddie could let him have a thousand dollars for a week. A thousand was almost exactly what Greenspan had banked for the school year. He wrote a cheque. Uncle George had a job at a plumbing supply store, and Eddie drove him to work in his beat-up Rambler. The man climbed the steps, turned to wave, and went inside.

A week passed, two weeks, three. Eddie couldn't understand why Uncle George hadn't phoned. He didn't want to pester him but he needed the money. In desperation he looked up the number of the plumbing supply company. They'd never heard of the man. The loss of money was catastrophic; even worse was the emotional blow. His father's close friend had taken him for every cent he had. How could anyone do such a thing? Hurt, confused, and humiliated, Greenspan had to ask his mother for help. Between his mother and his aunt, they scraped up enough to see him through.

As a U of T student, Greenspan did a little gambling himself – cards, hockey games, the racetrack. Like junk food and late nights, gambling was a part of being away from home for the first time. Greenspan settled down, met his future wife, and entered Osgoode Hall Law School. Inspired by G. Arthur Martin, a renowned criminal lawyer and appeal judge, he threw himself into his work and graduated near the top of his class. For his year of articles he joined the provincial attorney general's department in Welland. He worked for an old friend of his father's, Don Scott, who sent him around to the different courts in the area.

One Friday, as Greenspan was preparing for a Monday appearance in Niagara Falls, Scott told him he wanted him to go to Fort Erie instead. Greenspan asked why. "Eddie, just go to Fort Erie." From one of the other crown attorneys Greenspan learned Uncle George was on the Niagara Falls court list for Monday. He was depressed that the man was back in trouble but happy not to have to encounter him.

Greenspan went on to become a capable and celebrated criminal lawyer, gaining public acclaim before he was thirty. He and his first partner, Joe Pomerant, represented Peter Demeter, a Hungarian-born developer, in a sensational murder case. Demeter, the jury concluded, had arranged to have his wife's brains bashed in, and was sentenced to life. But Greenspan distinguished himself, brilliantly arguing against the conduct of the police investigation and the admissibility of certain wiretap evidence. He made his mark again during the appeal. Reporters found him a willing interview, gifted at untangling legal complexities; judges found him hard-working and prodigiously knowledgeable. Before long he was attracting high-profile clients of his own, making a splendid living, and worrying about his double chin on magazine covers.

His success, he felt, was due to hard work and to luck, but also to his sympathetic nature. Psychopaths were one thing, and you gave them legal representation; but most clients were ordinary people led into trouble by passion or greed. They were not unlike the kids he'd grown up with, and Greenspan empathized with them. About the only petty criminal for whom he had no feeling was Uncle George. He'd done the unforgivable and Greenspan had shut the door on him.

Then, one day, in walked an unlikely bank thief. Brian Molony struck Greenspan as principled, intelligent, and decent. Yet he'd jeopardized everything – career, family relations, liberty, even his well-being – to satisfy an extraordinary urge to gamble. Greenspan was intrigued by Molony's character, which seemed to accommodate two separate personalities, and fascinated by the fraud, among the biggest in the history of criminal law. But his involvement ran deeper. As he got to know Molony he began to catch glimpses of the demons that lurked in his own past.

A couple of weeks later, in walked Walt Devlin, a loquacious, easygoing ex-jock. Devlin's hair had turned white, but he'd kept to his playing weight, towered over you, and moved with easy self-possession. Each day he selected a different cap to coordinate with his sweats and size 13 running shoes. He had a beaming smile and a graceful way with sporting analogies. "She's lost something off her fastball," he'd say of a middle-aged woman dressed as if she were twenty, "but she'll still get you out with off-speed stuff." A charming fellow, in short, with a pitch that made you check for your wallet. More demons.

Devlin came to Toronto with Gerry Fulcher, a one-time New York policeman who was also a recovering compulsive gambler. When the two men introduced themselves to Molony, he seemed skeptical and reserved. His handshake was limp; perspiration darkened the armpits of his suit. When Eddie Greenspan finally arrived – he'd been delayed in court – he showed them into his office. Molony immediately took the far end of the sofa. For a man of 220 pounds he seemed oddly diminutive. To Devlin he appeared to be in acute pain.

Devlin explained that he had recently aided in the defence of a compulsive gambler in Maryland who had embezzled more than $1-million from a stevedoring company and lost it in Atlantic City. Devlin had arranged for psychiatric and psychological evaluations, got the man into a treatment centre, and helped orchestrate the *mens rea* (diminished capacity) defence. The man had got eighteen months in a halfway house. Devlin was optimistic that Molony's gambling problem, if properly presented in court, would lead to a similarly lenient sentence.

"I don't have a gambling problem," said Molony, wondering why he was wasting his time. Meetings with lawyers cost money. "I have a financial problem."

"If it's not a gambling problem, what was your number?"

Molony didn't understand.

"You went through more than $10-million," said Devlin. "What number were you shooting for? Twenty? Fifty?"

"I was trying to win the money back."

"Why do you think you were in the position of having to borrow it in the first place? And if you had won it back, do you think you would have stopped gambling?"

"Yes."

"You're wrong, my friend. You may not know it yet, but you're a sick puppy."

To Greenspan, Devlin and Fulcher seemed a pair of smooth-talkers who didn't understand much Canadian law. They spoke as if a temporary insanity defence would induce a judge to say, "Fine. You have a problem, Mr. Molony, you're therefore not guilty, goodbye, good luck, please don't do it again." In Canadian law there was no such thing as a temporary insanity defence. The insanity defence required that the accused suffer from a disease of the mind so debilitating as to render him incapable of appreciating the nature and quality of his actions. Hardly the case when someone had embezzled $10.2-million over nineteen months while otherwise performing his duties in exemplary fashion. Still, it was a staggering theft, and Greenspan welcomed any information that might help mitigate or explain it. On the surface nothing about Molony indicated illness or impairment, but then nothing about Devlin or Fulcher did either. Or Uncle George.

Devlin suggested that Molony undergo therapy at Johns Hopkins University, the first centre for treatment of addictive gambling. A month of treatment, plus the psychiatric and psychological evaluations, plus the cost of bringing half a dozen experts to testify at the sentencing, might run to $25,000.

"Out of the question," said Molony.

"Let's think about this," said Greenspan. He asked about ways of reducing the expense – fewer experts at the sentencing, one psychiatric evaluation instead of two, perhaps a shorter stint at the Hopkins clinic. After some negotiating, Devlin agreed it might be possible to put the whole thing together for $10,000. Molony didn't like the sound of this, but he'd come to trust Greenspan and asked his opinion.

"I think you should go, Brian." Greenspan was lighting another Belmont and remembering Uncle George. "And not just because these guys may well be the difference between a ten-year sentence and two years."

In a letter to a friend, written in Rome in 1863, the Russian novelist Dostoevsky outlined his idea for a story about a gambler. "I'll try to portray a straightforward man who, while quite acceptably educated and sophisticated, is yet a very incomplete human being. He has lost all faith and yet he does not dare to be an atheist; he rebels against all authority and yet fears it. . . . My hero is, in his way, a poet, but he is ashamed of the way his poetic feelings are expressed. . . . His need to risk something ennobles him in his own eyes."

Dostoevsky was himself ruinously drawn to the roulette wheel. The story he eventually wrote about a young man addicted to gambling was churned out in a month to avert financial disaster. Had he failed to deliver the manuscript on deadline, all his writings would have become the property of the conniving publisher Stelovsky. While writing *The Gambler*, Dostoevsky was also working feverishly on *Crime and Punishment*, contracted to another publisher. He lived daily with risk, pressure, and insolvency, and his character sketch seems – in light of what we now know about the compulsive gambling disorder – particularly astute.

Walt Devlin's therapist, Dr. Robert Custer, is the pioneer in this field; more than anyone else's, his work enables us to say who compulsive gamblers are. Five times in six, they're men. They tend to be friendly, sociable, and generous. Easily bored, they crave stimulation and excitement. They're persuasive, assertive, outwardly confident (inwardly the opposite), and highly competitive. They thrive on challenge, risk, and adventure, channelling their superior intelligence and high energy into work. If the profile seems that of the successful executive, well it might: many compulsive gamblers work in business or the professions and have a record of consistent achievement. Along with brokers, lawyers, and accountants, bankers are inordinately represented. Most come from a background of traditional family life; few encounter legal difficulties prior to the onset of the gambling compulsion.

Therapists explain the compulsive gambler much less confidently than they describe him. Speculation about the psychological foundation of the disorder extends back to Freud, who analyzed Dostoevsky's passion in an essay called "Dostoevsky and Parricide." Freud saw Dostoevsky's gambling as "a form of self-punishment" and speculated that he enjoyed debasing himself in an orgy of contrition after losing at the casino. More generally, Freud saw the gambling urge as a "repetition of the onanism compulsion." The compulsive drive to gamble was a translation of the child's compulsive drive to masturbate; the consequent losses were a form of self-punishment necessitated by the child's unconscious guilt at his wish to replace his father as his mother's mate.

Because the compulsive gambler never wins – because he cannot quit if he gets ahead – he is widely viewed as a compulsive loser. Freud's idea of self-punishment recurs in other interpretations. Edmund Bergler believes the disorder begins when the blissful self-centredness of infancy is destroyed by the parents. The compulsive gambler, he theorized, is rebelling against the people who robbed him of his omnipotence. By inflicting on himself financial loss and humiliation, he also alleviates his guilt. Ernest Simmel believed the compulsive gambler to be someone who felt deprived of parental love. This feeling creates a neurotic hunger for pleasure and gratification. The excitement of gambling and the anticipation of winning dull the hunger and promise to appease it entirely. Like all neurotic yearnings, however, it can never be satisfied; no matter how often the deprived person gambles or how much he wins, his endless hunger compels him to continue gambling. Wilhelm Stekel saw the compulsive gambler as someone frightened by adult responsibility and incapable of dealing with it; he flees by regressing into child-like fantasy and play. Ralph Greenson suggested that gambling was oral, anal, Oedipal, masochistic, and latently homosexual – take your pick.

Robert Custer's view is more empirically based than most; he has treated or evaluated more than 1,000 compulsive gamblers. Rejection, he believes, is the most painful human experience, and the low self-esteem of compulsive gamblers is often the result of rejection in childhood. A child reacts to rejection in one of three ways: he develops anxiety, sometimes to the point of phobia; he becomes withdrawn and isolated; or he becomes angry. The anger may be denied and suppressed, but sooner or later it seeks expression.

Custer believes compulsive gambling is usually the expression of this buried anger.

In evaluating Molony, Custer felt he saw someone who had struggled for his father's acceptance. The father's lifelong devotion to work had brought financial success and a respected career. The son learned to equate success with diligent application and financial achievement. He strove to succeed on the father's terms and was succeeding brilliantly. Yet the father's acceptance remained out of reach. It was not deliberately withheld; the father's emotional repertoire simply did not encompass the bestowing of affection on his children. He was busy with work; nurturing of the children was left to the mother and the housekeeper.

Stimulating as all the various explanations of compulsive gambling may be, they have in common a failure to explain why the root cause manifests itself in a gambling compulsion rather than in alcoholism, kleptomania, or any other expression of psychological ill health. They also fail to explain why, in a family such as the Molonys, one son would fall victim and six others not. Custer is convinced the brain chemistry of compulsive gamblers differs from that of non-gamblers. Molony was not the first person to describe to him the volcanic, almost orgasmic sensation that sometimes rose up from the back of his neck and spread through his head, glazing his eyes and turning the casino into a slow-motion enchantment. Custer wonders whether endorphins come into play, as they do when marathoners experience "runner's high."

Other signs steer Custer to the biochemical hypothesis. The stamina of compulsive gamblers defies explanation. A gambler Custer treated once played poker for five days and nights without missing a hand, eating at the table and going to the washroom when he'd folded early. Molony went sleepless to work without any letdown in performance and often spent two and three weeks without more than a couple of hours' sleep here and there. Custer himself enjoys the racetrack, where he bumped into a compulsive gambler he knew well. Not three feet away, the man failed to return his greeting. Custer would have sworn the man was gone on alcohol or drugs if he hadn't known the man never used alcohol or drugs. Perhaps the most telling sign of all, however, is that many gamblers who quit cold turkey exhibit withdrawal symptoms remarkably similar to those of alcoholics and drug addicts – chills, tremor, headache, insomnia, abdominal pain. If they resume gambling, the withdrawal symptoms disappear.

So far Custer's biochemical hypothesis remains unsupported. A study under way at the National Institute of Mental Health in Bethesda, Maryland, may change that. Compulsive gamblers without other addictions – those who were also substance abusers were weeded out – were put through several days of tests that included a spinal tap. The spinal fluid is being tested for, among other things, serotonin, dopamine, and norepinephrine. People who suffer from other obsessive compulsive disorders, such as repeated hand-washing, have been found to have unusually high levels of serotonin; Custer thinks compulsive gamblers will exhibit a similarly high level. If so, the study will have yielded the first hard evidence of a biochemical contribution to the disorder. The implications of such a discovery could be considerable. Foremost, perhaps, would be the development of a test to identify people at risk. Any number of institutions might use such a test to screen prospective employees – banks, for example, and casinos.

Perhaps because the causes of compulsive gambling remain elusive and the explanations speculative, the treatment has been hit and miss. Aversion therapy has been used with some success, but critics argue that pairing electric shock or regurgitative drugs with undesirable behaviour merely suppresses the behaviour rather than confronting its causes, and that the underlying pathology will find some other form of expression. Intensive therapy seems the most effective treatment. Even so, the success rate is dismally low.

In June, two months after his arrest, Molony obtained a variation in the terms of his bail – the surety was raised to $325,000 and he had to report regularly to the Metro Toronto Police fraud squad by phone – and flew to Ohio. Clearing U.S. customs, he was asked his destination.

"Johns Hopkins University."

"Go ahead, doctor," said the customs officer.

In a Cleveland hotel room, Molony was evaluated by Dr. Julian Taber, an amiable, portly psychologist. Taber had grown interested in behaviour modification while working at the Veterans Administration Hospital in Brecksville, Ohio, near Cleveland. Like Custer, he found that some alcoholics were also compulsive gamblers. He became fascinated by compulsive gambling and eventually became coordinator of the Gambling Treatment Program at Brecksville.

Taber interviewed Molony at length and administered the usual battery of tests, including the Minnesota Multiphasic Personality Inventory, the California Psychological Inventory, the Weschsler Memory Scale, The Shipley Institute for Living Scale, the Survey of Compulsive Gambling Questionnaire, and the Trail Making Test. Draw a line under the one word that comes closest in meaning to the word in capital letters. SMIRCHED: stolen, pointed, remade, spoiled. Compared to most people your age, how would you rate your present state of mind? (Molony checked "about as happy as most.") Assuming the thrill you got from gambling rated 100 on a scale of 1–100, what numerical value would you give to the biggest thrill you've gotten since you stopped gambling? (Molony answered "20.") After gambling, did you ever feel like you'd been in a trance? (Molony checked "frequently.")

The Gough Adjective Check List contained three hundred adjectives. Molony was asked to check off those he thought applied to himself. He checked "adaptable" and "adventurous," bypassing "aloof" and "arrogant." "Civilized" and "considerate," but not "conventional" or "deceitful." "Helpful" and "insightful," but not "inhibited" or "intolerant." He checked "practical" and "realistic," skipped "selfish" and "sly." As Taber pointed out in his report, Molony's self-description was sometimes conflicting. He saw himself as both assertive and shy, easygoing as well as demanding, simultaneously wary and trusting.

The next day Molony flew to Philadelphia, where he was met by Gerry Fulcher. Molony had flown many times to Philadelphia, of course, and said to Fulcher, "Just like old times." On the drive to Baltimore they stopped at Howard Johnson's. Returning from the washroom, Molony told Fulcher he'd thought of slipping out the window. A joke, but he seemed to Fulcher plainly anxious about what lay ahead.

Mount Wilson is a hilly Baltimore suburb; stands of pine and oak, once abundant, are giving way to housing developments. In 1978 the Maryland state legislature had passed a bill authorizing treatment of compulsive gamblers. Four different agencies submitted proposals; Johns Hopkins University was awarded the grant. The treatment facility was on the grounds of an old Maryland state hospital. The grant money was used to restore and staff a two-storey colonial house that had been the home of a surgeon at the hospital; Hopkins turned it into an out-patient treatment centre. The original grant covered only residents of Maryland, but soon after the centre opened, in 1979, people from all over the country were calling for help, and an in-patient program was established. Molony was the first patient from outside the U.S.

The third floor of the house had been turned into a dormitory. Molony found he would share the space with three other compulsive gamblers – an auto worker from Michigan, a butcher from North Dakota, and a stockbroker from Iowa. Immediately they had to come to terms with each other. Who would sleep where? Use the bathroom first? Take which dresser drawers? Their comfort would depend on mutual reliance and cooperation, and on mastering the skills of daily living. The staff consisted of a house manager, two peer counsellors (themselves recovering compulsive gamblers), and two professional therapists. Molony was given a schedule, telling him where he was expected to be for each session, and who would be in charge. Apparently there would be some sort of therapy all day, every day.

The first night Molony said very little, listening to the others tell gambling stories. Much of what they said hit home – he'd had similar near-misses, dealings with bookmakers, heartbreaking, last-second losses. But he was appalled by their bravado and one-upmanship ("That's nothing, let me tell you about the time I had fifty thousand on the Cowboys"), their almost swaggering way of recounting their experiences. He lay in the dark, half curious about what lay ahead, half afraid. He'd thought long and hard before accepting Brenda's money to pay for this treatment; he wondered if he'd made a mistake. Jail had been trying enough. This was starting to look like it might be the longest two weeks of his life.

"I remember Brian as being somewhat aloof," recalled Joanna Franklin, an addictions counsellor at the Johns Hopkins clinic. "He was rather isolated from the group he was with. Just about everybody goes through that at the start. It's very strange, a little scary, and you need time to come to the realization that you not only have to wear this bloody label for the rest of your days, you also have to do something about it. It's not a pleasant thought. Usually when they hear each other's stories – 'That happened to you? Really? That happened to me, too' – they begin to bond. I don't recall seeing Brian do that. I don't think he wanted to identify with these people. Even though some of what he heard may have clicked inside – 'I felt that way, too' – I don't think he allowed himself to experience it in the therapy sense of sharing and catharsis and all that neat stuff.

"Brian was an incredible intellectualizer. It's a common defence, and he was very good at it, a very bright man. Our team would talk about him – 'God, this guy has got a case of the head' – meaning he was stuck in his head like nobody we had seen in a long time. He was particularly difficult in that respect. My feeling was that he was as introspective as the others, just not as disclosing. I don't see how he could help but ponder some of the things being suggested, even if he didn't share a lot of his views. He wasn't one to say, 'I've thought about what you said yesterday, and this is how I think it relates to me.' I don't believe he reached that level of trust while he was with us. He was willing to take in what he thought might be useful to him, and I'm sure he took in more than he realized, but it was not a two-way kind of exchange, as it usually becomes. You eventually click with them. Some of the defences come down and there's an exchange, the emotional kind of exchange that therapy is about, sharing on that level.

"Four or five hundred compulsive gamblers have now gone through this program, and I don't remember anyone other than Brian bringing a briefcase to the sessions. He'd come down in the morning for breakfast with his briefcase. I think some of that symbolism represents how he felt. I'm here, this is something I have to do, I'll work at it. He was determined to do it to the best of his ability, without having the hang of how you do therapy. You certainly don't do it with a briefcase.

"I think we may have been seeing Brian doing what his dad did. Work very hard at what you do best. Brian worked very hard at his job and he worked very, very hard at his gambling. The work ethic seemed deeply rooted in the family. If at first you don't succeed, back you go, shoulder to the wheel. This do-do-do stuff works wonderfully well in the professional setting, but it doesn't work with gambling. If at first you don't win, bet again? You're going against the laws of probability, and you can't change those laws. But that's not allowed to sink in. If I work hard enough and long enough with my brights – and I know I'm smart – I'll beat this. Now we're into magical thinking, the distortions people take across the line that separates the social gambler from the compulsive gambler.

"To build a picture of who this was we were seeing, I'd start from the family history. I believe Brian is very much a product of how he was raised. I don't mean his parents exclusively, but everything around him – siblings, friends, community environment, school experiences. When you treat those things as puzzle pieces, you begin to get a picture of someone who had a sense of responsibility within the family structure, responsibility to his parents and to his own sense of what a good boy should be. He had a very strict, internalized set of morals and ethics – if anything, a little too strict. Many years later, when he found himself violating his own ethical concerns, I believe he got very depressed. That begins the cycle. The violation causes pain. To get away from the pain, you gamble, which causes more pain, which you need to get away from. And so on.

"After the earliest stages, winning money disappears as the focus. Gambling becomes almost entirely an emotional experience.

It triggers the competitiveness compulsive gamblers have in common. I refuse to be beaten by the cards, the horses, the casino, whatever it happens to be. As if willpower and tenacity will see them through, as they did in business settings. I'm down ten, I won't be beaten, next time I'll bring twenty. Now we're into the chase, the beginning of the end. It's a hopeless cycle because I can't stop, can't save the money without losing my sense of who I am – a person who succeeds, who sees things through. I couldn't handle losing that, my self-esteem is already low. I'm in for the duration. That's the only way I'm going to find the quality in myself that I value and I want everyone else to value.

"When I met Brian's father he seemed very one-two-three. Not cold, but undemonstrative in terms of affection and emotions. In that family I'd imagine that emotional concerns were rarely discussed, and when they were it would probably be around a critical issue – disappointment, pain, embarrassment. There would be more to hide than to put on the table and say, 'Let's look at this.' I'd get the message I had hurt my parents by doing this or that, but it wouldn't be communicated directly. I've been bad, that was bad of me, I'm going to have to make it up and also carry the guilt. I didn't mean to do it, I care about my family very much. I must be a wormy person to have done that to such good people.

"Brian was typical in coming from a large family with an absent father – be it by death, divorce, or workaholism – and having a lot of emotional needs that were not fulfilled at an early age. I assure myself I'm okay, but I don't really believe that, and if you get to know me well enough you'll see that too. I can't let that happen, I have to remain at a distance from you. I need your acceptance, your love and care and attention, and I'm going to do what it takes to get those things. But I'm going to stay at a safe distance because you also represent a lot of potential pain. Gamblers have a notoriously poor tolerance for rejection. I'm going to give you enough to keep you around, but I can't afford to let you get too close. I'll do as little emotional investing as possible, which is what we saw when he was in treatment.

"Brian did not emotionally invest, but he couldn't afford to. At that time, having a sense of what he was facing, he needed all his emotional resources just to stay intact. To keep functioning. It's like asking me to invest in the stock market. I'd love to, I trust your judgement, there's profit to be made, but I have to use my money to keep myself fed and clothed. I can't afford to lose, I absolutely can't take the chance. Brian had an incredible drive to keep functioning, to be the competent guy with the briefcase. He didn't have a lot left over to do other things with.

"Our handicap at the time he was here was that we only had two weeks with him. Now it's an average of four to six weeks, and people might stay longer. Two weeks was just long enough to identify concerns and address crisis issues and make recommendations. When Brian left I think he intellectually grasped what we were talking about but, in the emotional sense, was just beginning to. When someone leaves, there's something clinicians exchange that doesn't go on the record – 'Has this guy got a shot or not?' I believed Brian had a very good shot because he was scared shitless of what was going on and he used his fear as a motivator. I had a sense that when the realization of what he'd done really sunk in he would hold on to his skills and abilities to see him through. His abilities lend themselves to many productive things, but those same abilities handicap him in the sense that he doesn't have to change. Doesn't have to focus on himself. Doesn't have to address, in long-term therapy, what may be deep down inside.

"When Brian left at the end of his treatment, I felt he was someone who would stay in a position where he could maintain equilibrium, the safe place emotionally. The ironic part, which I don't think he really appreciated while he was here, is that the last time he chose the safe place – in terms of who I think I am and what I need to do to continue being who I think I am – he ended up doing some of the most dangerous and self-destructive things anybody could do."

10
SETTLING ACCOUNTS

"The gambling of business looks with austere disfavour upon the business of gambling."

– Ambrose Bierce

Most people who read about Molony – in the *Wall Street Journal* or *National Enquirer*, *The New York Times* or *News of the World*, *The Baltimore Sun* or *The Toronto Sun* – assumed his fraud had been perpetrated by sophisticated use of a computer. They'd heard about another bank employee who diverted fractions of cents and wound up half a million dollars richer, or the teller who turned her boyfriend's $300 deposit into $300,000, or the Los Angeles computer analyst who stumbled on the code word and dispatched millions of dollars to himself in Switzerland. How else could an assistant manager with lending authority of $35,000, in a branch with lending authority of $100,000, have committed ninety-three separate frauds, in amounts as high as $1.8-million? Who but a computer expert could have stolen almost $17-million over nineteen months, strategically repaying $7-million to avoid detection, leaving the bank – on the day of his arrest – $10.2-million poorer? Molony must have been a technological whiz, like the eighth-grade students in Manhattan who, using a school computer and a telephone, penetrated the data banks of twenty-one corporations.

In fact, Molony's frauds had little to do with banking technology. Customers may be subject to the tyranny of the computer – "Sorry, I can't update your passbook, the computer's down" – but employees still rely on scribbled notes. As Walter Stewart pointed out in his book about the Canadian banks, *Towers of Gold, Feet of Clay*, "Eighty per cent of all banking transactions are still paper-based, only twenty per cent consist of electron talking to electron." Pieces of paper set money in motion; one reason the frauds went undetected is that so many pieces of paper are in motion in a bank that no one has time to look carefully at them all. On a typical day Harry Buckle approved more than a hundred notes. Easy enough to imagine him glancing at each in turn, initialling the corner, his mind wandering. Easy enough, in the Wednesday deluge, to forget the Tuesday entries that had said, "Dummy note to follow."

After an exhaustive investigation, the bank characterized the defalcation as "brilliant." The frauds were actually impulsive; perhaps if they had been more carefully planned they would have been more easily detected. It's tempting, in retrospect, to see the ninety-three transactions as part of a master scheme. But Molony viewed each fraud as the last – the big win, just around the corner, would bring salvation. The size of the embezzlement and its improbably long duration owed more to faulty safeguards and unusual circumstances than to Molony's brilliance.

A former CIBC employee wrote to Eddie Greenspan: "After working for the Midland Bank [in England] for several years, I was horrified by the systems with which the CIBC controlled their credit operations. On the 5th and 20th of each month, a liability return was sent to head office. Any manager who wanted to be dishonest knew when the returns were due. In England it was done on a surprise basis, and not all branches on the same date. I feel the bank should be partly responsible for the missing funds . . ." That procedure was changed, coincidentally, midway through the Molony frauds; the liability return became a monthly control that could be sprung on any date. Like the branch audit that failed to turn up a shortfall of more than $2-million, however, the liability return was evidence of the failure of the bank's systems.

The Molony case brought to light many failures. Sherry Brydson's signed promissory notes, for instance, should have been numbered and properly recorded. The assistant manager administration should have routinely perused staff accounts and remarked on Molony's first purchases of U.S. cash at Deak Perera and Friedberg & Co. When Molony used U.S.-dollar drafts, the purported purchaser's signature should have been required. It was right there in BMO XIII-7-4.01: "A requisition for a draft should be taken on the requisition part of the multipart foreign draft form, or on Form 27, and be signed by the purchaser . . ."

When a corporate account was opened, the customer signed a standard agreement with the bank that included a list of signing authorities and specimen signatures. When Molony created the fictitious 499726 Ontario Ltd., the bank had no such agreement and no list of signing authorities. The person responsible for ensuring that the agreement had been executed was Molony himself. He showed the numbered company as having an authorized credit of $3-million. Because the credit exceeded the $100,000 branch limit, a loan writeup that included the head-office authorization should have been filed in the manager's office. Harry Buckle evidently never confirmed the authorization. Given a supposed limit of $3-million, how was Molony able to advance himself more than $4-million through the numbered company's account? Loan advances in excess of $3-million ought to have prompted inquiries when they showed up on the daily transaction journal.

Each day the branch received a transaction journal reflecting the loan activity at Bay and Richmond. The journal was a computer printout, generated by the data centre beneath Commerce Court, listing every loan advance made the previous day. Attached to the journal were the promissory notes, one for each loan. The journal and the notes were routed through the branch. As manager of post 2, Molony received the journal along with the notes for loans at his post. According to bank procedure, in other words, the person responsible for ensuring that the loans made by post 2 were properly recorded and documented was the manager of post 2. Molony simply initialled the notes, indicating that they corresponded with the journal entries; the journal was then passed to the manager of the next post, who initialled his own notes. After all the assistant managers had initialled their notes, the journal and the notes were passed to the manager. He, too, initialled each promissory note. If anything seemed amiss, he could refer to the transaction journal, or to the loan sheets filed in his office. He was supposed to have a write-up for every loan made by his branch.

The extensive use of dummy notes helped make possible some of the frauds. A branch should lend only to the presigned promissory notes on hand. For anything above that, the customer should have paid overdraft charges at a higher interest rate. Dummy notes sometimes had to be used in a pinch, when a customer was in urgent need of funds and the branch had no more of his signed notes; but their routine use ought to have been discouraged. When a loan was recorded in the bank's discount department as having been advanced against a dummy note, the post manager was responsible for ensuring that the dummy note was replaced by a signed promissory note. By the bank's system, then, Molony was again supposed to have monitored his own loans. A manager on his toes would have followed up the dummy notes, checking with the discount department to ensure that they had been replaced by signed demand notes. Increasingly in recent years the CIBC has adopted the U.S. procedure of using overdraft borrowing to cover a customer's operating loans, and the use of dummy notes has dwindled.

Once a year every CIBC employee with a holiday entitlement of more than two weeks was supposed to have taken at least two weeks consecutively. The assistant manager administration was responsible for looking through the records and preparing a letter for the manager. By February 28, the manager was supposed to have confirmed in writing to head office that every staff member had taken holidays the previous year in accordance with PAM, the personnel administration manual. Molony did not do so in the last year of the fraud; apparently no one at the branch was aware of the violation. It's a banking cliché to beware the employee who avoids holidays, and a manager on his toes might have had his curiosity pricked.

No one in the bank was much surprised that the CIBC's own audit failed to uncover more than $2-million in bad loans. An inspector grades each loan as a good, average, or bad risk, and verifies the terms, conditions, and security. He's looking not so much for irregularities as for documentary confirmation that this loan – like the huge majority of loans – is legitimate and sound. If the documentation shows that the company is doing well, or that the loan is fully secured, or that the borrower has substantial net worth, the inspector tends to purple-pencil it routinely. He's more interested in whether the paperwork is in place than in whether the information it contains is accurate. The audit should also have scrutinized employee accounts and noted the unusual activity when Molony first bought U.S. cash.

Had the two branches not been merged six months after the

fraud began, Molony would probably have been tripped up sooner. The merger brought confusion, as well as changes to the physical plan of the branch. The changes aided Molony. The securities department was moved from the ground floor to the basement; when Molony sold bearer bonds from Richardson's to the securities department of his branch, purportedly on instruction from a customer, he was unseen by people in other departments unless they too happened to be downstairs. At the same time, Molony's office was moved from the ground floor up to the mezzanine level, out of sight of the discount department and the foreign-exchange department. When he picked up cash parcels, pretending that Roger Oskaner was waiting in his office, the head teller would have had to follow him, at least to the foot of the stairs, to see that his office was empty.

The merger also meant the replacement of Alex Osborne by Harry Buckle, and Molony would not likely have survived so long with Osborne at the helm. Buckle was a manager from the old school. He had little contact with junior employees, preferring to let his senior people communicate with them. His management style meant he had less feel for day-to-day operations than a hands-on manager would have had. He was riding out his last year before retirement, no longer motivated by the prospect of promotion. Who, in that position, would have been as rigorous a monitor of branch affairs as someone whose performance would speed his way up the ladder?

Molony's success at defrauding the bank may also have owed something to his timing in the larger setting. In 1964 a royal commission into Canadian banking called for "a more open and competitive banking system." The 1967 Bank Act, "A Blueprint for Competition," was meant to promote that competition, but it had the opposite effect. Canadian banks had previously been limited in the interest rate they could charge, and the limit – 6 per cent – made it uneconomical for them to make consumer loans. Canadians who needed money for a car or a vacation generally went to a finance company. When the 6 per cent limit was lifted, the banks began underpricing the finance companies and soon dominated the consumer-loan market. Between 1967, when the banks moved into personal loans, and 1982, when Molony was arrested, the consumer-credit market grew by a factor of five; the banks' market share increased from about a third to more than three-quarters. The Bank Act revisions had a similar effect on the mortgage market. In the decade after those revisions, the banks' residential mortgage portfolio grew from less than $1-billion to more than $18-billion. When Molony started at Bay and Richmond, in 1978, the bank's total assets were about $37-billion. When he was arrested, four years later, total assets stood at $68-billion.

The 1970s and early 1980s were years of great activity and growth, in other words, and the CIBC – though not performing as spectacularly as some of the other banks – was making money hand over fist. During Molony's time at Bay and Richmond, the branch limit was raised from $40,000 to $50,000, then $100,000. Business was booming, Bay and Richmond was a busy branch – all the more so after the merger – and Molony's was the busiest post. Everybody was up to their ears in work.

Which brings us to the single most important explanation of why Molony went undetected while losing, on average, $18,280 of the bank's money every day, seven days a week, for more than a year and a half. As a bank employee, you're trained to be careful and skeptical: never sign anything you don't understand, never initial incomplete documentation, alert your superior to anything dubious. In practice, though, you have no choice but to trust your colleagues. For all the built-in security measures – by-the-book procedures, double signatures, frequent balancing – you rely on mutual trust. When someone hands you a scribbled note and says, "I need a draft, I'll give you the documentation later," you assume he's acting with integrity. You must. If you did everything as scrupulously as you were supposed to, you'd never get the day's work done.

Everyone who knew him well agreed Brian had changed during his two weeks in Baltimore. The treatment program had evidently given him some answers and some useful tools. He was willing to talk about himself and what had happened. Eddie Greenspan found him no longer skeptical of a defence based on what Walt Devlin called "a disorder of impulse control." Brenda found him less driven and more communicative. Molony, of course, had a psychological need to embrace any medical explanation of what he'd done, and his newfound understanding might have been suspect if he'd used it to diminish his own responsibility. But his interest in compulsive gambling wasn't so much a convenient enlightenment – "Great, I was sick, it wasn't really my fault" – as an intellectual curiosity about the addiction. He was haunted by his actions, and by the knowledge that the repercussions were being felt in many other lives.

In the fall, six months after Brian's arrest, Dr. Molony took his wife to Ireland to see family and friends, visit horse farms, and play golf. Mrs. Molony began having trouble with her back. It interfered with her swing, then began to bother her so much she could barely move. She refused to go to hospital in Dublin, telling her husband she preferred to wait until they got back to Toronto. She had to use a wheelchair. The day they returned Brian dropped by the house and found her in bed, suffering terribly. Next day she went to hospital for tests, which revealed cancer in her spine.

An operation was performed on Dr. Molony's birthday. His children took him to dinner, a grim celebration indeed. He had spoken to the operating surgeon. "Sometimes," he informed his children gently, "I wish I weren't a doctor." Mrs. Molony's kidney proved extensively malignant and had to be removed. She was admitted to Princess Margaret Hospital for radiation. She was able to go home for Christmas, then had to be readmitted. A portion of her spine was removed and metal rods inserted for support.

The family was devastated. They all adored her. What other mother of nine never failed to serve a hot meal at midday? Oh, Katie, a budding feminist, teased her sometimes for catering to Dr. Molony, preparing a second dinner when he got home each night. And they all ribbed her about her stock-market forays, though she made shrewder investments than any of them. But in her quiet, gentle way she anchored the family. They went off on their adventures and brought home their pals and girlfriends, knowing she'd always be there to cook their meals and iron their shirts. She had the patience of a saint and never uttered a murmur of complaint.

Only once before had she ever been seriously ill. She had joined her husband in Toronto in 1953, coming from Ireland with her first three children and Maud McCabe, the housekeeper she had hired in Dublin. A year later, about to give birth to her fourth, she was found to have a melanoma on her arm. When the doctors removed it they discovered the cancer went deep into the muscle, right up to her neck. They had to operate, a radical procedure that left her utterly depleted. Giving birth took the last of her strength. When they sent her home she was a frightening sight. Brian Patrick Molony was a healthy 8 pounds, 7 ounces. For many weeks it looked as if his mother would not pull through. Gradually she recuperated, though, and ever since had been in fine health. Once a year, regular as clockwork, she came down with a mysterious flu that made her shiver and moan and scared the daylights out of them. But after a day or two in bed she was good as new, cheerful and uncomplaining.

The realization that she was terminally ill stunned the family. Brian's problems shrank to insignificance. He had found work with a computer software company. The office was a good forty minutes from the hospital but he visited each day, sometimes more than once. He organized a schedule to ensure at least one family member was with Mrs. Molony at all times. She missed her music, so he brought her a tapedeck and the Irish folk songs and Roger Whittaker ballads she enjoyed. He had never spent so many hours with her; it was a time of great intimacy. They talked about his work, the stock market, the weather, the wonderful nurses at Princess Margaret. They talked about everything except her illness and his crime. She didn't want to burden him with her problems, and he felt it would have been inappropriate to raise his troubles when she was gravely ill. Besides, he hadn't forgotten the sight of her eyes through the peephole. He knew the depth of her shame.

Meanwhile, the cancer was spreading. One day, when the nurses turned her over, her arm fractured near the shoulder. She told her children she'd slipped in the bathroom. They had enough to worry about without worrying about her. When she felt well she liked to read the paper, but had trouble managing with only one arm. Brian hit on the solution. He sliced the newspaper in half so she could read a page, turn it over, and discard it.

Brian had had no experience of death. No one in the immediate family had died or been grievously ill. It was ghastly, a roller coaster of pain and relief. One day he'd find his mother sitting up and laughing at the antics of visitors, something of the beauty and fullness restored to her face; next morning she'd be in such intense pain she could barely utter a greeting, her face a mask. The doctors said she was terminal, but they'd said that about plenty of other patients who had recovered. Brian's brother Brendan was planning to marry and she had every intention of celebrating the occasion. There were bank accounts that required her signature, though, and the house was in her name, so Brian asked Stu Butts to draw up a power of attorney. Not that he'd given up hope – on the contrary. She was included in the prayers of a great many people; Brian himself had resumed going to Mass; there was always the chance of a miracle. Who believed in miracles more keenly than a loving son who still half believed, a year after his arrest, that if he hadn't been caught he would have won back the $10-million and repaid the bank?

At the time of the arrest, and with each court appearance, much was made in the pulp press of Molony's Jekyll-and-Hyde nature. An English tabloid referred in its headline to his "double life." A story in the *National Enquirer* bore the headline "Brown-Bagger by Day, Wild High-Roller by Night." Mention was made elsewhere of his "split personality" and "schizophrenic" character. This psychological speculation was buttressed by references to the symbols of his two lives. The staid probity of the bank worked nicely against the glamorous excitement of the casino.

The two institutions are not so unalike as image might suggest. Both are powerful lobbyists in their constituencies, conducting their affairs with sanctimonious arrogance. Both represent corporate enterprise refined to its sublime limit. There is no product to intrude in the making of money: the product is money. Both are highly structured bureaucracies that require employees to act along prescribed lines. Both emphasize security and reflect the assumption of employee dishonesty. Both are dominated by men and deeply sexist. Both demand loyalty and adherence to the corporate line. Neither can tolerate the exercise of individual conscience. The casino executive will welcome a heroin dealer, provided he has cash, as the banker welcomes a businessman who has plundered his company, in hopes of landing his account.

Like the employees at Bay and Richmond, the employees at Caesars in Atlantic City were never informed what had happened, only that they were not to discuss Molony with anyone. People in the craps pit were called in, one at a time, and told violation of this edict would lead to automatic termination. In each case the company seemed less interested in correcting the flaws that had permitted abuse than in getting the corporate story straight and isolating scapegoats. Though the CIBC is traded on the Toronto Stock Exchange and Caesars New Jersey on the American Exchange – though both are public companies – neither has ever explained the affair to shareholders.

The CIBC found it hard to believe Molony had acted alone; anyone who'd had anything to do with him was suspect. At Richardson Securities, Jim Surgey found himself having to answer the same questions again and again; he had the feeling the bank would have loved to have discovered collusion. When a New York lawyer for Lloyd's of London, the CIBC's bonding company, raised the possibility of filing suit against Richardson's, however, he was discouraged. Apparently he was unaware that Richardson Securities was a prominent CIBC customer, and that George T. Richardson sat on the bank's board of directors.

On the morning of the arrest, a phone message was found on Molony's desk from a Mr. Greenspan. The bank assumed Molony had contacted Eddie Greenspan before being caught and treated Greenspan with contempt. He was told that if he accepted money from Molony he'd be accepting stolen funds. He happened to be a customer and found his affairs carefully scrutinized. Normal courtesies were no longer extended. The bank wouldn't allow his bookkeeper to cash his endorsed paycheque; he himself had to stand in line. The treatment was so irritating he almost pulled his account from the branch.

When the bank investigators examined the frauds, they found that the Sherry Brydson loan account had been extensively manipulated. Had she been in on the scam? There was reason to think so. Elm Street Holdings, the final fraudulent account, was a clear reference to the Elmwood Club. And Brydson's lawyer, Stu Butts, was a personal friend of Molony's. The morning he heard the news he had gone down to the branch to raise bail money, an act of friendship that raised more than a few eyebrows. And when the inspectors looked at Brydson's flow charts, they discovered a corporate organization – a welter of companies, many inactive – that seemed contrived for purposes of fraud. Brydson was brusquely questioned, and for many weeks her controller was harassed virtually every day. The new assistant manager at Bay and Richmond, Bill Gray, dragged her out of meetings to say the Westerkirk account was a few hundred dollars overdrawn. If the money weren't deposited by day's end, the bank would be forced to take drastic action. Brydson's signature on cheques was questioned. She had no doubt that she was under suspicion, and that her loan would have been called had she not been a member of the Thomson family.

In the bank itself, responsibility had to be laid at someone's feet. The inspector who had been in charge of the audit was demoted. A regional vice-president was sent to Sault Ste. Marie, Ontario, banking purgatory. Three of the Bay and Richmond employees who had been temporarily suspended – Johanne Prescott, Karen McCaffrey, and Jackie Ho – were demoted a grade or two and forced to take salary cuts of up to $3,000. At other branches of the

CIBC, word went around that salary increases were being reduced or withheld because of the fraud. Never mind the billions in bad loans the CIBC had made to bankrupt countries and companies. Never mind that it would recover all but the $250,000 deductible portion of its policy with Lloyd's of London. The CIBC was happy to have employees believe they were suffering because of what Molony had done.

Alex Osborne had been at Bay and Richmond during the first six months of Molony's fraud. The bank's internal report recommended his dismissal, but the recommendation was overruled and he took a salary cut instead. Before long he was promoted to assistant general manager for the Ontario region, then transferred to Vancouver to manage the main branch there. That, too, was a promotion, but Osborne didn't necessarily see it as such. Commerce Court is where he had hoped to end up; Vancouver was about as far from Commerce Court as you could get.

Harry Buckle had been at Bay and Richmond more than a year when the fraud was revealed. As manager, he was responsible for all aspects of branch operation. The bank was contemplating further legal action against the casino; if the action ever came to trial, Buckle would undoubtedly be subpoenaed. It was in the bank's interest not to antagonize him. He was given a choice between demotion or early retirement. The CIBC pension was based on an employee's last five years rather than his best five; a demotion, with pay cut, would have meant a lower pension. Early retirement was the sensible choice. By not penalizing Buckle financially, by providing a graceful exit, and by keeping his name out of the newspapers, the bank treated him as well as he could have hoped.

Molony's credit officer, Steve Richardson, was treated rather differently. His job was to fetch files, ensure documents bore initials, make the phone calls Molony didn't wish to make. He was expected to act with little independence and had never been encouraged to think his responsibilities included making judgements about what his superior was doing. He'd held a training position; he was a minion, and a good one. Customers thought highly of him and fellow employees liked him. Richardson expected he'd be promoted to replace Molony. When told instead that he was being fired, he couldn't believe his ears.

"No, I'm not," he said.

"Yes," said Gord Ormston, the vice-president doling out the medicine. "You are."

Having confessed to the fraud, Molony gave no thought to a plea of not guilty. Even if he did recant, Lindquist Holmes, the forensic accountancy firm hired by the attorney general to assist the police investigation, would have no trouble producing reams of damning documentation. Greenspan advised Molony not to help with that investigation until it was complete. If he cooperated and overlooked a fraudulent transaction, he might appear to have been concealing the full extent of his crime.

Because of the complexity of the embezzlement, the report took eighteen months to prepare; the legal proceedings had to be set back again and again. It was the low point of Molony's life. His mother's agony was beginning to seem as interminable as the wait for his own legal reckoning. He was seeing a Toronto psychiatrist, Dr. Kilian Walsh, and attending weekly meetings of a support group. Like alcoholics and drug users, compulsive gamblers tend to fall off the wagon when they're under great pressure, and Molony's life was unending anxiety. Oh, for a day at the races!

Brenda, by now, had been transferred; she worked as an efficiency expert, assessing CIBC branches that had requested additional staff to see if they were fully utilizing their personnel. She lived in constant fear. She was afraid of publicity. She was afraid of the reporters who phoned and knocked at the door. After Brian made bail a photographer had jumped out of a stairwell, and a photo of Brian and Louise turned up in the paper. The caption described her as an "unidentified female companion," but the bank had little trouble identifying her. Louise's manager promptly had her transferred, apparently feeling that corporate loyalty ought to have negated friendship.

Brenda was also afraid she'd be called to testify. After such exposure, how would she be able to stay on at the bank? She'd have no choice but to resign. If she resigned, how would she earn a living? Each bank had its own way of doing things; skills acquired at the CIBC weren't really transferable. Brian was making decent money with the software company, but his legal bills would eat far more than he could earn. Once he went to prison she'd have to manage on her own. One night in bed he admitted that he too was frightened of what lay ahead. It was evidence of the wonderful changes in him – in the past he would never have expressed his feelings so directly – but his fear redoubled hers. As in the months before the arrest, the strain he was under blossomed in her.

They both tried to put the future out of mind. Brian more or less succeeded by thinking his way around it. Nothing he could do would change what would happen, therefore it wasn't worth dwelling on. The way to avoid dwelling on it was to keep absorbed in work. Working harder also meant making more money; down the line, the extra income would make things easier. The software company had developed a program that allowed mainframe computers to talk to laser printers. The people were technically brilliant but lacked business expertise. Molony helped establish reporting and marketing systems. By reducing expenses, negotiating with suppliers, and urging changes in pricing methods, he helped solve the cash-flow problem. In a few months a company that had been running a $100,000 deficit was in the black. The turnaround owed a great deal to Molony's grunt work. Most of the time he could be found at the office; he was doing sales projections the morning his father called.

"Your mother's gone to the Lord."

"I'll be there shortly."

"Brian, if you'd pick up Katie on your way. She's at the house."

Katie had taken off school because of her mother's illness. She was still asleep when Brian got to Inglewood. No one else was home. It hadn't occurred to Brian he'd have to break the news. Katie was the second youngest. He had a special feeling for her and wondered what to say. He woke her by touching her shoulder.

"Katie. Let's go to the hospital."

She stretched and yawned. "Why?"

"Mommy passed away."

After a while she calmed down enough to say she wanted to make her own way to the hospital. Brian said no, he'd take her. She vented her grief in the car, and when they got off the elevator she ran sobbing down the hall. Brian was numb but clear-headed. The sight of the body didn't disturb him; he had seen his mother in a coma. All the family had gathered.

"I believe in God," Dr. Molony began, "the Father Almighty, Creator of heaven and earth, and in Jesus Christ, His only Son, our Lord, Who was conceived by the Holy Spirit, born of the Virgin Mary, suffered under Pontius Pilate, was crucified, died and was buried. He descended into hell; the third day He rose again from the dead; He ascended into heaven; sits at the right hand of God, the Father Almighty; from thence he shall come to judge the living and the dead. I believe in the Holy Spirit, the holy catholic church, the communion of saints, the forgiveness of sins, the resurrection of the body, and life everlasting. Amen."

"Our Father," returned his children, "Who art in heaven, hallowed be Thy name," and they all said a rosary together, taking turns announcing the mysteries, joining together for the Our Father, the Hail Mary, and the Glory Be.

Brian accompanied his father to the funeral home, relishing the short walk. Perhaps it was relief at leaving behind the hushed air and medicinal smells. Perhaps thanks that his mother's suffering had ended. Perhaps simple pleasure in his father's company. Not often did he get a chance to be alone with his father. At the farm, sometimes, and on the golf course, years earlier, when he'd caddied; in the car, driving down to Regina Mundi, the turn signal ticking because his father couldn't hear to shut it off; at the School for the Deaf in Milton, where the swimming pool was eerily overrun, the kids splashing and playing in silence; at the races one day, when Brian was twelve or thirteen. One of Dr. Molony's horses must have been running. Brian knew something about horses and tried to tell his father which one he thought would win. Between his father's impaired hearing, though, and the din of the crowd, it was hard to make himself heard.

The mortician's dark suit and deep, concerned voice went perfectly with the ornate furniture and sombre Muzak. "Very sorry to hear about your loss," he said gravely, a young man no older than Brian. The ritual phoniness was dispiriting. "We've arranged to go to the hospital." He clicked a pen. "Now, if we could confirm some details." Dr. Molony had already selected the coffin, an unadorned model. He and Brian had only to finalize arrangements and decide on the wording of the death notice.

People were gathering at Inglewood. The house around him swelled with grief, but Brian was controlled and pragmatic. He phoned the farm to tell Sieg, then suggested they draw up a list of people to call, friends and acquaintances whom they didn't want hearing the news from someone else. He drove to the liquor store and bought supplies. Not wanting to go home, he went to Swiss Chalet and tried to eat chicken. When he did return, in late afternoon, he found everyone asleep. He too was drained but didn't want to rest; he phoned people, he kept moving. What might happen if he stopped?

The long hours at the funeral home were arduous. Hundreds of people came, patients of Dr. Molony, colleagues, church friends of Mrs. Molony, neighbours. They all knew about Brian, of course, but no one let on. He was told again and again what a fine woman his mother had been. Strange that he had adored her and admired his father and thought of them as wonderful parents without realizing how many people they had touched. How deeply one life – every life – affects others.

The Molony men held fast until the day of the funeral. Just before the casket was transported to Our Lady of Perpetual Help the family had a few minutes alone with the body. Dr. Molony couldn't keep it inside any longer; he broke down, then one son did, then another, and another. The hugged each other and said a rosary, Dr. Molony drawing strength from his faith, his children from one another. As he had after the arrest, Brian found himself at the mercy of forces beyond his understanding and his power to monitor. To feel yourself a part of something so majestic and inexorable was painful, yet complete.

Our Lady of Perpetual Help was crowded to overflowing. There seemed an extraordinary number of young people. Bishop Leonard Wall had returned from a retreat to conduct the funeral, and his words were rich and consoling. Brian was in a daze, looking right through people he knew. The bank had made known to at least one employee that it would not be responsible for any "negative consequences" that might grow out of association with Molony. Some friends from work, worried a CIBC spy would be at the church, didn't attend the service.

Brian found himself thinking of his mother. To feed such a large family, she'd shopped at a "food warehouse" where the carts were oversized. At dinner one night this gracious woman who never uttered a profanity, recalling an incident at the grocery store, exclaimed, "Those stupid baskets!" Everyone stopped eating, stunned, and then broke into laughter. "What's so funny?" she wanted to know. Tears of mirth ran down their cheeks, they laughed as hard as they'd laughed the time their mother ran out of bus tickets. Her friend Maura Grant gave her a senior citizen's ticket, saying, "Here, use this. What's the difference?" Seniors paid a reduced fare; Mrs. Molony was petrified she'd be caught in this transgression. As soon as she passed through the turnstile, though, she was offended the ticket-taker hadn't challenged her. How could he have possibly let her pass her for sixty when she was only fifty-eight?

The girls from St. Joseph's filled the air gloriously with "Ave Maria." Many people in the church were crying, and Brian found tears washing his own cheeks. What were the last words his mother had said to him? He'd not realized they would be her last, of course, and they'd slipped his mind. It seemed vital to remember them. He racked his memory but couldn't recall. The words that remained were those she'd uttered the morning after her operation. Surgery had devastated her; she was barely able to open her eyes and move her lips in greeting. He took her hand and felt a delicate, urgent pressure. She was saying something; he leaned close. "Brian," she whispered, "make sure you father gets his supper."

By freezing the final $1.42-million before it left Toronto, the bank had served the first point in a game of legal ping-pong that would last years and occupy a dozen law firms in Canada and the U.S. The bank and the casino both took the position that the money Molony gambled away was rightfully theirs. In its original injunction, the bank argued that Caesars had known Molony was gambling at a frequency, and in amounts, to create suspicion; had an obligation to inquire into his background and the source of his funds; and had the means, through the Caesars office in Toronto, to make such inquiries. The bank argued that the casino either knew Molony was employed by the CIBC, or else chose to remain wilfully blind to his employment and the source of his funds.

The casino returned serve: nobody at Caesars had any reason to believe Molony was employed by a bank or was acting in fraud, or that the money credited to California Clearing Corporation was anything other than the valid deposit of a casino patron. If the CIBC did indeed sustain a loss, the casino went on, it was brought about by the bank's own negligent failure to check out Molony properly before putting him in a position of trust, to establish procedures that would have tripped him up, and to institute an audit that would have revealed the fraud.

Soon after the arrest, the two drafts totalling $1.42-million were returned by Irving Trust in New York to the Bank of Montreal. The drafts were examined by representatives of the CIBC, who determined – surprise! – that the personnel who had signed them had indeed been authorized to do so. Pending settlement of the question of whom the money belonged to, the Bank of Montreal argued that it ought to retain possession. The CIBC agreed to honour the two drafts by issuing B of M a new draft for $1.42-million. Hence, said the casino, any loss suffered by the CIBC was the result not of anything Caesars had done but of its own decision to reimburse the Bank of Montreal.

Give the first point to the casino.

The bank retained service, however, and was just getting warmed up. Letters, orders, motions and supplemental motions, writs and amended writs, affidavits, subpoenas, and statements of claim bounced back and forth. Employees of banks and casinos were examined for discovery. Eventually Mr. Justice Archibald Craig of the Supreme Court of Ontario ruled that the CIBC's voluntary settlement with the Bank of Montreal was not a bar to its claim against Caesars, and that money paid under a mistake of fact may be recovered no matter how careless the payer may have been. Mr. Justice Craig found it "rather incredible" that a twenty-six-year-old could draw markers for more than $11-million without exciting suspicion. He concluded that Caesars "knew Molony was using Colizzi's name to effect transfers into the Bank of Montreal. In this way, both the source and recipient of funds would be recorded in Toronto as being other than the true parties. This kind of arrangement invites suspicion of fraud."

Second point to the bank.

Meanwhile, more headaches were looming for Caesars in the person of Thomas O'Brien, a red-cheeked, curly-haired lawyer in Morris County, New Jersey. O'Brien had voted against casino gambling in the 1974 referendum and again in 1976. When New Jersey's attorney general, Irwin Kimmelman, offered him the job as head of the Division of Gaming Enforcement, he was surprised. He had no particular expertise in casino gambling but was stimulated by the challenge of regulating an industry in which subtle social and moral questions had to be weighed against the economic benefits New Jersey was enjoying through its 8 per cent tax on gross gaming profits. At the start of 1983 O'Brien moved into the DGE director's office at the Hughes Justice Complex in Trenton – perhaps the most unappealing state capital in the United States.

A few weeks into the job, O'Brien got a call from a young reporter on *The Philadelphia Inquirer*. H. G. Bissinger, whose coverage of the Molony case helped him win a Nieman Fellowship at Harvard, asked about the status of the DGE investigation. O'Brien recalled reading about Molony and feeling that the case exposed many of the pitfalls of casino gambling. But the file, he told Bissinger, was inactive. Having followed the Canadian proceedings with care, Bissinger couldn't understand this lack of interest. Didn't the DGE find it strange that Caesars would fly people to Toronto to get a bookmaker to sign over stolen money? That it would help Molony funnel money through a dummy company? That it would claim to know nothing about him when casinos routinely check out high rollers?

O'Brien happened to be intrigued by compulsive gambling; his law firm had represented a number of bonding companies, and he had seen other instances in which highly regarded employees had embezzled funds to feed a gambling addiction. His own curiosity and Bissinger's tenacity prompted a full-fledged investigation. O'Brien discovered that, in the wake of the arrest, the DGE had merely reviewed Caesars' cash and credit procedures in dealing with Molony. The question at the time was not whether the casino had been at fault but whether the DGE ought to move against Molony. Clearly the case merited renewed scrutiny. O'Brien assigned the file to a deputy attorney general, Stephen Schrier, and the DGE's top investigator, Richard Handzo, telling them he wanted a thorough investigation. Talk to everybody, use whatever legal muscle you need, work with the Canadian authorities, fly up and see Molony.

Caesars, already embroiled in the Ontario Supreme Court litigation, thus found itself doubly under siege. And the Division of Gaming Enforcement was a more dangerous opponent than the CIBC. The bank merely wanted the frozen $1.42-million. The DGE made recommendations to the Casino Control Commission, and the commission had the power to levy fines, strip employee licences, even revoke the casino's operating permit. Brian Molony, who had seemed such a splendid gift horse, had turned into a pain in the neck.

Molony pleaded guilty to a charge of fraud over $200 the same day police found the body of Paul Volpe in the trunk of a car parked at Pearson International. To Dr. Molony's relief, the murder pushed his son's plea off the front page. Molony was eager to be sentenced – anything would be better than not knowing – but the next open date was three months off. The wait was agonizing. Then, as the day approached, Molony learned that Robert Custer would be unavailable. He urged Greenspan to go ahead without Custer, but Greenspan considered the testimony of the Washington psychiatrist indispensable. Dr. Molony had cancelled all his operations. Brian had to inform him, and a dozen other people who'd reorganized their schedules, that the date had been put back.

The software company had begun marketing its program abroad, and Molony had been put in charge of international sales – an ironic job for someone whose bail conditions prohibited him from travelling more than twenty-five miles from Toronto. Commissions had doubled his income, but Brenda remained anxious about finances. Just before the sentencing Dr. Molony had told Greenspan he'd look after legal fees. Greenspan turned him down: "Brian told me he's good for it." Brenda was also anxious about Brian's fate, of course, but was prepared for the worst. The night before he was to appear in court they talked about their future.

"I may not be dating in the next while, but that doesn't mean I expect you to sit home every night."

"I think you may get ten years and serve all of it, because of the power of the bank," she replied. "I'm prepared to wait."

Greenspan arranged things at York County Court so that Brian would appear before Judge William Rogers, whom he considered tough on violent criminals but sympathetic toward white-collar offenders. Rogers was a little man with a neat moustache and glasses who presided with a stern, slightly skeptical air, like a school principal who takes the strap out of his desk before asking how the fight began. I'm willing to listen, but this had better be good.

Greenspan's argument was a novel one in Canada, and he knew it would succeed only if he managed to educate the court about compulsive gambling. He rarely referred to his client without using such words as "pathological," "uncontrollable," "insatiable," "sickness," "disorder," "illness," and "compulsion." If it seemed melodramatic at the outset, it seemed less so after the testimony of each witness. Greenspan first called Dr. Robert Custer. Since 1980, Custer testified, pathological gambling had been included in the *Diagnostic and Statistical Manual* of the American Psychiatric Association. It was also classified in the *International Classification of Diseases* published by the World Health Organization. He said that four states – Maryland, Connecticut, New Jersey, and New York – had funded programs for the treatment of pathological gambling. He outlined the diagnostic criteria for pathological gambling and said it was his belief that Molony, during the time he committed the frauds, had suffered from a serious disease of the mind. Molony's compulsion, he said, was the flip side of a phobia. Just as a person with claustrophobia will do anything to avoid stepping into an elevator, the compulsive gambler will do anything to continue gambling. He testified that Molony, like other compulsive gamblers, was not after material benefit. He was seeking to alleviate psychological pain.

Julian Taber, the psychologist from Ohio, testified that he devoted his practice to the treatment of compulsive gamblers and had dealt with some 350 of them. He agreed with the substance of Custer's testimony and added there was no indication Molony suffered from an antisocial personality disorder. Molony experienced genuine remorse at the effects of his behaviour on others and posed no danger to society. Taber considered compulsive gambling not merely a serious mental illness but a sometimes lethal one. A number of gamblers he had seen since 1978 had committed suicide.

Joanna Franklin outlined the origins and nature of the treatment facility at Johns Hopkins. Dr. Kilian Walsh, the Toronto psychiatrist, suggested Molony's illness was best understood by comparing it to alcoholism. "Obviously, intelligence plays no part where the addictive process is concerned. The ability to reason in the area of the addiction is defective. In the same way that an alcoholic, against all reason, is prepared to ruin his life and the lives of those close to him to satisfy his illness, so also is the pathological gambler." Walsh testified that Molony's awareness of his disease had grown. "In his therapy sessions with me, he has made progress in terms of his ability to be aware of his feelings, to express and deal appropriately with them, particularly feelings that might be perceived as being unacceptable to others."

Greenspan called Dr. Molony, who recounted the shock of learning Brian had been arrested. "We were just stunned. We felt if anybody was to be a gambler or to embezzle, he would be the last member of the family to think of." Dr. Molony recalled gambling episodes from Brian's teenaged years – the theft of money while babysitting, Mrs. Molony's discovery of the gambling at the variety store – but said that if they'd had any inkling of his problem they would have acted. They were proud of his success in the bank, and considered him the one in the family who always took control.

Greenspan was bothered by a heavy cold and often had to interrupt himself to blow his nose. Even this seemed part of his performance. He was masterful at manipulating the mood of the court, eliciting laughter on the heels of earnest pleading, slowing the tempo during testimony he considered crucial. Even Judge Rogers seemed to succumb. "On that exhibit," Greenspan said at one point, "I think definitely the last paragraph of page four should not be before Your Honour, at least should not be considered."

"I'll fold it over," said Peter DeJulio, the crown attorney, "as long as Your Honour promises not to peek."

"I might have a compulsion to do so," said Judge Rogers.

"I won't take bets on it," replied DeJulio.

"It's very healthy that you recognize that," said Greenspan.

Chuckles in the courtroom. Taken one way, Rogers' remark indicated skepticism for the whole basis of the defence. But he seemed to be loosening up, and Greenspan could ask only that the court be open to the force of his own deeply felt conviction. There was no evidence to suggest Molony had ever enjoyed a penny from his misdeeds. Look at him – a badly dressed man who drove a jalopy, tipped meagrely, and never even tried on the $10,850 Rolex the casino had given him. His crime had been nonviolent. He had aided with the fraud investigation, saving time, and waived a preliminary hearing and pleaded guilty, saving money. Like a lawyer in a movie, Greenspan opened two manila envelopes and spilled the contents on the table. Enclosed was $2,096 U.S., $185 Canadian, and two casino chips. Molony had found the money in soiled clothes.

Greenspan argued that the casino bore some responsibility. Its agents had whisked Molony to and from Toronto; they'd offered him all manner of enticements; they'd helped facilitate the transfer of funds across the border. Molony, meanwhile, was rehabilitating himself. For nearly two years he'd been active in a support group. He had fulltime work and strong family backing. His incarceration would not deter other compulsive gamblers, Greenspan argued, because they, too, fail to recognize their illness. It began to seem that the greatest injustice would be to deprive Brian Molony of the opportunity to alert others to the perils of compulsive gambling. Here was the chance to blend the punitive, deterrent, and social possibilities of the law. Greenspan suggested one year in prison, three years' probation, and 3,000 hours of community service.

Peter DeJulio was brief in his summation. He had told Greenspan he would ask for a prison term of four to six years – under the Criminal Code, the maximum penalty for theft over $200 was ten – provided Greenspan did indeed call evidence establishing Molony's gross addiction to gambling. If Molony got less than four years, said DeJulio, he would consider recommending an appeal. Greenspan had for several years edited the sentencing section of *Criminal Law Quarterly*. He considered himself an expert on sentencing and had told Molony he thought there was a chance they'd get a year or two. Nothing had happened during the presentence arguments to diminish his optimism.

After the carefully orchestrated, almost leisurely pace of the previous day and a half, Judge Rogers' pronouncement was sudden and swift. "The court recognizes the validity of a disease of impulse control," he told Molony, who stood uneasily before the bench. The magnitude of the crime, however, and the position of trust could not be discounted. Loss of personal freedom remained a very real deterrent. "The sentence of this court is six years in the penitentiary."

Spectators were stunned. Molony wobbled as he was handcuffed and hustled off. In the holding area a student from Greenspan's office was able to speak to him before he was shipped to the Don Jail. She told him she was terribly disappointed and asked if there was anything he wanted passed along to Greenspan. It seemed to Molony somehow important to his own well-being that he cheer up this sad-faced woman.

"Just ask him one thing. Can we get the Rolex back?"

Upstairs, Greenspan stood in the glare of television lights and answered reporters' questions. He blew his nose and rubbed his eyes and lit cigarettes in such a way that his tears went largely unnoticed. They did not go unnoticed by Walt Devlin.

Dr. Molony, surrounded by family and media representatives, was asked his reaction. He didn't catch the reporter's question and had to cup his ear as it was repeated. "I don't agree with the interpretation," he said with a ravaged smile, "but surely you must abide by the law of the land. I believe in the law."

In the twenty-three months between the arrest and the sentencing, Molony had been viewed as many things. A cynical thief, manipulating colleagues to execute his schemes. A naive idealist, believing in the imminence of the impossible. A classic addict, as hooked on gambling as any junkie on heroin. A fascinating personality, in which intellect countermanded the imperatives of emotion. A shortsighted fool, for not having squirrelled money away.

The Don Jail is an ancient fortress of mournful sounds and foul odours, a gruesome place. The three-foot-thick stone walls in the old section of the jail exude despair. Each steel bunk is covered with a thin, soiled mattress. Two bunks per cell, plus a third mattress on the floor, fourteen cells per range, which means more than three dozen men spend twenty-four hours a day in uncomfortable proximity. Most of the inmates Molony was among were very young. Some had spent a year waiting on appeal, waiting for processing, waiting, waiting in an air of frustrated, simmering violence. Many of the guards were themselves intimidated and looked the other way during any dispute.

Waiting to be processed out, Molony had to adapt to a new perception. Fellow prisoners considered him a hero. Not only had he put up numbers that gave him a place in criminal history, he had done it at the expense of that most symbolic repository of establishment values. Guards called him "Big Shooter." Inmates wanted to talk to him. How had he pulled it off? He was questioned about the inside workings of the bank – security systems, cash procedures, the handling of negotiable securities. He gave humorous answers or else said he didn't know much about it, having worked on the credit side. Because of his high profile he had reason to fear; he also had to contend with people who believed he'd put money away. He used his wit deftly and gave every impression of not having grasped the enormity of what he'd done. Ten million dollars. To the others it was the ultimate score, drugs and trips and cars and women; to Molony it seemed no more than a number.

An articling student from Greenspan's office visited him the day after the sentencing and found him bitter and downhearted. But a man who ended up on the same range two days later found him in a different mood, cheerful and optimistic. Playing cards, Molony would look at his watch and say, "Five o'clock. Time to lock the safe and go home." Board games were a popular way of killing time, and he was invited to play Monopoly with members of a motorcycle gang awaiting trial on charges of drug trafficking. Someone had to handle the money while players bought and sold Atlantic City real estate.

"Who's going to be the banker?" said one of the bikers.

"I will," Molony volunteered.

"You will? Like fuck you will."

"As I was saying," Molony said through the laughter, "you'll be the banker."

Six years was difficult to imagine; even a third of it seemed an eternity. But any sentence was better than tortuous uncertainty, and Molony was hopeful his term would be reduced on appeal. Between unpleasant moments – being threatened, strip-searched, assailed by rock music, splashed with a cellmate's urine – Molony found himself thinking of the people who had stood by him, risking careers. He thought of Brenda, her steadfast love and loyalty, and wondered how he could have endured without her support.

On the phone he asked Stu Butts to buy a ring and have Brenda's father present it on her birthday. By Wednesday, her twenty-eighth birthday, she had already used up her two visits. Brian had to wait until Sunday for her response. As always, the visiting room was buzzing with urgent talk and stifled emotion. Brenda's expression was unfathomable – was she restraining joy or bracing herself? Brian took the seat opposite and picked up the receiver.

"Well," he said, behind shatterproof acrylic. "What's your answer?"

"You haven't asked me yet."

"Will you marry me, Bren?"

"Yes. Yes, yes. You owe me a great big hug."

"I love you. As of today, your hug's collecting interest."

11

AFTERMATH

"Trials never end, of course."

– Robert Pirsig, *Zen and the Art of Motorcycle Maintenance*

From the Don Jail, Molony was transferred to Metro East Detention Centre, an overcrowded holding facility in Scarborough, Ontario. Everyone on the penitentiary range was awaiting shipment to a federal institution; the atmosphere was more settled. Molony scribbled questions and ideas about the software company, to keep himself occupied. When a girl from the office came to see him, he used the visit to determine which cheques should be released and contracts executed. One of the principals arranged a special visit to discuss the company's long-term strategy. When Dr. Molony came to offer encouragement, Brian tried to cheer him up. Hopeful his sentence would be reduced on appeal, Molony carried on as if bars and guards were a brief inconvenience.

A month after the sentencing, Eddie Greenspan filed an appeal on the grounds that Judge Rogers had failed to consider the guilty plea as a mitigating factor. Greenspan argued that the six-year sentence was harsh and excessive and asked that it be reduced. The appeal was eventually dismissed by G. Arthur Martin – ironically,

Greenspan's mentor at law school – who said: "The offence itself was as grave a crime of fraud as can well be imagined."

Molony, meanwhile, had been transferred to Joyceville, a medium-security prison set on 1,300 rural acres midway between Toronto and Montreal. Federal prisons in Canada are ranked on a scale of 1 to 7, S1 being minimum security and S7 maximum. Joyceville is rated S4 and, despite the double fencing and guard towers, considered one of the better places to do time. Constructed around an interior courtyard, it's bleak, noisy, and daunting. Each range contains thirty cells and a common room where the men prepare coffee and play cards. The cells are dark and claustrophobic, the doors solid steel with peepholes. Among the 500 inmates are violent offenders serving life terms and burnouts more suited to psychiatric care. The inmate population is older than at many prisons, which makes for a more sedate environment. Still, the population is surprisingly youthful. Tattoos and muscular upper bodies abound; the air is charged with thwarted energy. Here, as Molony oriented himself, the reality of what he was facing hit home.

Molony wrote letters, received encouraging mail from strangers all over North America, and looked forward to seeing Brenda and his family, whose visits were deeply affecting despite the bleak surroundings and oppressive supervision. He was assigned to the accounting department of the prison; his banking skills made him useful, though the staff was wary and insisted he not be allowed near the computer. To tire himself enough to sleep, he played sports fanatically. Adjusting to prison routine, learning the ropes, he was struck by the dearth of reliable information about the available services and programs and the bureaucratic process of transfers and parole. This became the worst part of incarceration – his inability to find out how decisions were made. Most new inmates simply asked long-term inmates, who by definition were not

Depending on your entry date, the advance loan is the only money you'll see for up to five weeks. Budget accordingly"); recreation; arts and crafts; visits and correspondence. Once the research was complete, Molony began spending much of his time in the prison library, writing a script. He also found himself doing something he'd never done before – recording his thoughts and observations in a diary.

April 27. I'm a compulsive gambler who hasn't made a bet in two years. Still suffering withdrawal symptoms. Nightmares, anxiety, claustrophobia.

May 2. Dentist looks like Frankenstein, old, grey-skinned, washed-up guy. His white coat says "Dentist" on the pocket, as if he has to look in the mirror to convince himself. He speaks very deliberately. "I'm here to help you, Brian. Let's see how strong your teeth are." He hauls out these oversize choppers and a giant toothbrush. "Now when you brush, go up and down like this, make sure you cover all the surfaces." It seemed funny, but I guess this is the first time some inmates learn how to brush their teeth.

May 4. Doctor who gave me my mandatory medical said that when there was a killing in the prison, they usually found the guy who'd done it sleeping like a baby.

May 16. Many guys have "FTW" tattoos. FTW used to mean Funds Transferred by Wire. In here it means Fuck the World.

May 20. There's a guy here called The Hammer. A homosexual propositioned him so he killed the guy with a hammer. When he got out another homosexual propositioned him. Killed him, too, so he's back in. So the story goes.

June 12. Guy arrives from Millhaven, about sixty years old. Carries a golf ball, plays with it all the time, uses it as a basketball, baseball, football, volleyball. Hits it with his hand and chases it down like a dog. Too much homebrew, they say.

June 21. Father's Day. One inmate tried to phone home collect with Father's Day greetings. The family wouldn't accept the charge. Pathetic, but how can you blame the family? Some of these guys have been inside fifteen, twenty times. Give a guy one chance, maybe two. But twenty?

June 22. One day after payday. Guys already bumming cigarettes. Drug and gambling debts.

June 29. Inmate named Wright. Girlfriend visits him one day, wife the next. He's always afraid they'll show up on the same day. Very moody guy, either elated or depressed. I said, "Are you Wilbur today, or Orville?" He liked that. "Wilbur," he said. "Orville's the one who gets in trouble."

July 2. Mr. B. is 88 years old. Got ten years for accepting social security in both the U.S. and Canada. U.S. deported him on the understanding he'd go to a nursing home. But no nursing home would take him because of his criminal record, so he ended up here. So the story goes. Smokes and coughs all day. One day somebody tuned in a different show on TV. Mr. B. got up, shuffled over, changed it back to "The 20-Minute Workout."

July 5. Got my own cell. Took an hour of cleaning just to find the sink and the toilet. Nice to look up and not see the top bunk.

July 12. An inmate from 1A stares at the TV for two hours, a zombie. He says, "They're all dead, you know, they're just images." When they put the cuffs on him he says to the guard, "Do you really think this is a good idea?"

July 15. There's a kid here trying to get parole so he can play for his high school basketball team. Good luck. Six years for armed robbery, 18 years old.

July 18. Interesting floor hockey game. On Saturday night I'd say 70 per cent of the population is either drunk or stoned.

July 19. An inmate: "Roses are red, violets are blue, I'm schizophrenic, and so am I."

July 22. Witnessed a bad beating today. Violence is the first resort of a limited mind. One crack equals one fight.

July 26. An inmate got burned out of his cell. They probably thought he was a stool pigeon. Want a guy off your range? Throw paint remover and a match in his cell.

July 27. There's a guy here from Montreal who got three years for robbing a couple. They didn't have any money so they offered him a postdated cheque. He accepted it, giving his real name. So the story goes.

July 29. At 1:45 this morning I was awakened by a three-inch cockroach on my shoulder. Hit him with my shoe 83 times. Not a good night's sleep.

July 30. The search dogs were in, Dobermans. They go into the cells to find drugs. Somebody told me the way they train the dogs is to addict them. One of the dogs crapped in a guy's cell. He says to the guard, "You're going to clean it up, aren't you?" Good luck.

August 6. S. was grabbed and had his head smashed into the concrete. Started convulsing, tried to swallow his tongue. It's called "doing the chicken." All over a card game.

August 8. Strategy for doing time: Make few friends and no enemies.

August 10. Inmate in PC [protective custody] *asks for a haircut. Convict barber goes down and does his hair. In the afternoon the inmate asks for the barber again. His hair isn't short enough. In the meantime the barber has found out the guy is a rapehound. Shaves his head clean. The rapehound had to sit there and take it. The guards would have turned the other way. The barber would have said, "He tried to grab the razor."*

August 16. New guy on the range, K. He hopes to get out soon. He said, "Things are going real well. I'm in a drug rehabilitation program. They're going to continue it on the street." I said, "Have you stopped taking drugs?" He looked at me like I was crazy.

August 17. Way of getting drugs into prison. Fill a dead bird and throw it over the fence. Inmate on yard duty retrieves it.

August 22. Next week I get transferred to Bath.

"I met Brian on the admission range," recalled Andrew C., who was at Joyceville for drug offences. "I was on the range a much shorter time because I was a repeater. Once you've been in the system you proceed fast. Everybody knew who Brian was. You know, 'That's the guy, that's Molony.' Brian never denied it but he was very low key. There was smaller fish than him, walking around like Mafia chiefs. He didn't make anything of what he did. He knew how to behave without changing his character. He saw how to do time.

"When you move into the general population it can get heavy, but he didn't seem scared. The intelligence in jail is a lot lower than his, and he knew how to avoid situations that turn into trouble. If somebody was known as a rat, Brian would treat him like he didn't exist. He didn't get too friendly with anybody. A lot of the inmates thought he had money put away. They'd ask him, 'Where'd you put the bag, Brian?' He'd turn it into a joke. 'I wish,' he'd say, 'I wish.'

"In jail you see guys who are down, down, down. Brian stayed pretty much on the same level. Oh, he had ups and downs, but never too up or too down. I remember one time, these people came up to talk to him. When they were leaving, one of them asked how he got off with such a light sentence. That upset him – it's one of the few times I remember seeing him depressed. He considered his sentence pretty heavy. The thing with the bank, it didn't really go with who he was. I'm not sure he ever saw it as a crime, you know?

"He played tennis, ball hockey, whatever was going. You wouldn't think so looking at him, but he's quick physically. I think that's what he lived off on the inside, sports. We played racquetball, two teams, two guys on each team. Sometimes we'd argue if the ball was in or out. Brian would say, 'It was in.' You couldn't discuss it, he'd made up his mind. He makes this movement with his hand, brushing you aside. End of discussion.

"We played Monopoly and he always had to be the banker. He liked to win, he played hard and usually did win. Everybody gambles in jail – for cigarettes, money, canteen, whatever – but not Brian. He played card games but he never gambled, even with the other guys who were in for gambling. They tried to seduce him – 'Let's play for a pop' – but he wouldn't. Like I said, he makes up his mind and that's it. He started a program for gamblers in the prison and he took it seriously, you could tell. He'd made up his mind he wasn't going to gamble.

"In jail you have these guys going crazy, betrayed by their women. I have my wife, I know it's very difficult. Brenda drove down from Toronto every week. She was always there for Brian, but I don't know if he needs other people that much. He was a banker, right? Well, he's a banker in his personal behaviour, too. He lets you get so close, but not too close. I think Brenda might be the only person he's really close to. Most women would have bailed out. She stuck by him and faced up to what he did. I don't think it hurt their relations because she saw the decent part of him all along.

"Brian's totally reliable, you don't meet many guys like him. If he says he'll do something, it's done. Even after what he did I'd trust him with my money, no question, and there's not many people I'd say that about. Youngest loans manager, eh? He judged people, their ability and their honesty, and usually he was right. He has that talent, you could see it in jail. It doesn't matter that he'll have this in his background. He's the type of guy who'll overcome it. He'll be successful again. As long as he doesn't go back to gambling."

In New Jersey, the investigation by the Division of Gaming Enforcement yielded bountiful evidence of Caesars' suspect dealings with Molony. The DGE filed a complaint charging the company and eleven of its employees with twenty-eight regulatory violations, among them the transferring of cage documents to Toronto for execution, the conducting of cage functions in Toronto, the failure to record details of Colizzi's transactions, and the use of transmittal forms as cash equivalents. The complaint was highly technical and ran to seventy-five pages. The Casino Control Commission liked such complaints to go to hearings; a hearing would generate a neatly documented record and enable the commissioners more easily to grasp the issues. But a hearing was as tedious and protracted as a court action – motions, sworn statements from witnesses, orders, objections to orders – and Thomas O'Brien, the DGE director, wanted to short-circuit that phase. Time, he knew, was on the side of the casino. People change jobs; inertia sets in; new issues arise and supplant old ones.

O'Brien told Caesars' lawyer – Mike Nolan from Pitney, Hardin, Kipp & Szuch in Morristown, New Jersey, who was also representing the casino in the CIBC suit – that the DGE intended to hit Caesars hard. The casino, through Nolan, came back with the idea of a negotiated settlement. What about a fine larger than any that had ever been levied against a casino? O'Brien wanted nothing less than a shutdown. He wanted to tell the industry that the DGE had the clout and the guts to close a casino; that the dubious practices common in Nevada would not be tolerated in New Jersey.

O'Brien and Nolan worked out a settlement whereby the DGE's complaints against three Caesars people – Peter Boynton, the president, and Claire Lodovico and Katherine Campellone, the women who flew to Toronto – were dismissed. The other respondents – Larry Woolf, Michael Neustadter, Jess Lenz, Larry Bertsch, Bill Hessel, and Linc Ebert – were fined sums ranging from $3,000 to $10,000. The casino's certificate of operation was suspended for twenty-four hours, beginning Saturday morning, November 30, 1985. Caesars was ordered to pay employees their normal salaries, benefits, and gratuities.

O'Brien was happy with the deal, believing it showed the DGE's resolve to punish regulatory violations. The five-member Casino Control Commission, which had to approve the settlement, was less enthusiastic. Commissioner E. Kenneth Burdge pointed to the "pattern of conduct in which greed outweighed the requirements of the state and the public interest." Commissioner Carl Zeitz felt that the moral issue underlying the Molony case went unaddressed and that, if it had been addressed, "then the whole construct and concept of casino gambling as a legal industry might be shown to rest on a moral swamp." He also noted that Larry Woolf, who bore final responsibility, had been appointed president of the Caesars operation at Lake Tahoe: "His discipline has been a corporate promotion." Commissioner Valerie Armstrong was disturbed by unanswered questions about Peter Boynton's role, by the casino's "unsatisfactory" explanation of its inability to find out about Molony, and by its failure to investigate Mario Colizzi. Commissioner Joel Jacobson objected to the abandonment of the concept of corporate responsibility: "Mr. Boynton must, in my view, be held accountable." He found it impossible to believe the casino could not determine who approved giving Molony the Rolex watch. And he felt the settlement imposed no sanctions "for the lack of moral judgement about the propriety of casino executives so blinded by the passion for a more lucrative bottom line that they go out of their way to pander to a high roller . . . financing his compulsive gambling habits by robbing a bank."

Despite these reservations the commissioners, by a vote of three to two, accepted the settlement. Molony had thus done something unprecedented. He did what Lee Harvey Oswald did not do by shooting John F. Kennedy, what seven Apollo astronauts did not do by perishing in the *Challenger* shuttle. In a roundabout way, he did what no one had done since the Flamingo opened on the Las Vegas Strip in 1948: he shut a casino. The closure, on Thanksgiving weekend, cost Caesars an estimated $1-million in lost profit. Dr. Robert Custer was invited to speak to the casino employees about compulsive gambling. The occasion is known in Atlantic City as Brian Molony Day.

A pleasant-looking compound of utilitarian one-storey buildings and trailers, Bath Institution overlooks Lake Ontario west of Kingston. If it didn't share grounds with Millhaven, a modern maximum-security prison, it might easily be mistaken for a community college. Molony was transferred to Bath and assigned to work in the kitchen that serves both prisons. Each morning he peeled carrots, onions, and up to half a ton of potatoes, which passed through a peeling machine but were finished by hand. Work began at 5 a.m. and ended at noon, which gave him the rest of the day to himself.

A minimum-security facility, S2 on the Corrections Canada scale, Bath accommodates about 100 inmates. They sleep in cubicles rather than cells, and after thirty days may wear street clothes in the evening. As the information booklet says, the institution "tries to get you as close to the street as possible. To this end, the only fences are decorative." In a strange way that makes them more galling. You're close to freedom but far from free. To return to the street you must win a bureaucratic game of snakes and ladders. Each inmate has a case management officer, a living unit officer, and a parole supervisor – he's part of many caseloads. After a prescribed period of time he may apply for escorted temporary absences, unescorted temporary absences, special escorted temporary absences, limited day parole, day parole, or full parole. Community assessments have to be obtained. Case management teams discuss the applications and make recommendations. The National Parole Board turns out to have a greater say in the true length of your term than the sentencing judge. Bath is not intimidating the way Joyceville is, but even a suite at the Ritz would soon become repellent if you weren't allowed to leave it. The punishment of incarceration is not physical circumstances; it's time. In Bath, as in most institutions, there's plenty to do. There's also nothing to do except wait.

September 9. Police cancelled all inmate passes during the Pope's visit. Apparently they need all available manpower to provide security. An inmate says, "Who the fuck does the Pope think he is?"

September 22. Many inmates working in the kitchen bear a striking resemblance to Anthony Perkins when they have a knife in their hands.

October 2. Played hockey for Bath for the first time. Went to Deseronto. I knew I was in trouble when I looked up at the score clock. It was sponsored by the CIBC.

October 9. Played hockey again. We lost by four goals. I'm not in great shape, but at least I'm not slowed down by drugs. Went to McDonald's afterwards. The bus has CORRECTIONS CANADA on it in huge letters. They park behind the restaurant so nobody can see it. On the way out one of the inmates says, "Look, there's a busload of convicts out there!" Men wrap protective arms around women and children.

October 15. The cook slipped while grinding meat and lost the tip of his finger. An inmate and a guard looked for the fingertip but couldn't find it. After considerable debate, the meat was thrown out.

October 16. The ties worn by Corrections Canada staff are clip-ons. The guards can't be strangled with them.

November 1. Went back to Joyceville to shoot the film. Felt like an outsider even though I've only been out of there 2½ months. The librarian, a minister, assumed I was back because I'd screwed up. "Too bad," he said. "You can have a job with me if you like."

November 4. Sitting in my cell, I can hear the sounds of a card game down the hall, inmates coughing from smoking marijuana, a guy being beaten up. Deprivation of freedom is a very real punishment.

November 7. An inmate got sent to Millhaven for threatening an LU [living unit officer]. *Deep scars on both sides of his nose, somebody tried to bite it off in a fight. R. told me it's painful, as bad as when someone bites off your ear. I'll take his word for it.*

November 15. Who learns from the prison experience? Only the first-timer. Someone who's returning knows what to expect and finds old friends and acquaintances. A sense of belonging.

December 25. Christmas. Inmate walks down the hall. "Ho, ho, fucking ho."

December 28. Allowed to use the barbeque for Brenda's visit. Try finding charcoal in Kingston in the winter. Brenda finally found a 7-Eleven with three bags left. The guy tried to sell her a beach ball and sand bucket.

January 5. Inmates as human inventory. A portion of the inventory is damaged goods. A portion is potentially useful, with refurbishing. A portion is simply waiting on the shelf for productive utilization. I would hope I was once damaged goods but am now ready and waiting for productive utilization.

January 12. Inmate here, an alcoholic, mixes Listerine and Diet Coke. Screams all night, "Come in! Door's open!" In the morning he spits out his apple juice and says, "Yuck. How do you expect people to drink this crap?"

January 23. One time OPP *cops went into Millhaven to play baseball with the cons. The* OPP *complained about the noise, sounded like there was going to be a riot. Next time the* OPP *came back 400 inmates sat through the whole game without making a sound. So the story goes.*

January 31. I've met one guy who strangled his wife, one who shot his wife, one who electrocuted his wife, one who drowned his wife. Great place to improve your interpersonal skills.

February 2. Cell thief was caught and beaten quite badly. Someone suggested that each of his fingers be broken, so inmates at the next prison would know why he'd been shipped there.

February 7. Stu and Patti came to see me. Their house was broken into while they were here. I mentioned it to R. He did break and enters until his own place was broken into. He felt so defiled he never did another B & E. He took up armed robbery instead.

February 11. Turned down for day parole.

March 1. The goalie at Millhaven was killed after a hockey game. His street partner killed him. Heavy betting on the game. It might have been fixed.

March 14. Went on an ETA [escorted temporary absence] *with another guy. Went to a movie, "Witness" with Harrison Ford. There's a tender moment when the female lead needs affection. The theatre is quiet. This guy yells, "Throw her on the floor! Do it!"*

March 15. An inmate says, "My wife hasn't visited me. I should break her nose again. It'd be the fifth time."

April 16. An inmate masturbated on the front window of the car of the woman who teaches life skills.

April 29. Three-day pass. Had lunch with K. He has a Chinese friend who went to Atlantic City and got picked up by the limo at Philadelphia. The limo driver found out he was from Toronto. "I used to drive a guy from Toronto all the time. Brian Molony. Whatever happened to him?" "Brian Molony," said the Chinese guy. "Oh, he's our prime minister now."

May 2. An inmate has crapped his bed three times in two weeks. Turns out his father started sodomizing him when he was four or five years old. No control over his bowels.

May 7. There's a guy here who puts ads in the personal section of "The Globe." You wouldn't recognize him from his description in the ads. He's a scum, yet women drive three hours from Toronto to see him, bringing food for the barbeque. Why?

May 14. I don't think they should segregate white-collar guys and give them special treatment. The white-collar guys are the real screwups. We began with skills and opportunities the other guys never had.

Molony needed an outside job to qualify for day parole. When he returned to Joyceville to shoot the orientation film, he met David Pulver, a reporter on the Kingston *Whig-Standard*. Pulver introduced him to a group of Kingston businessmen who had opened a retail computer store. They had few management skills; after a brief chat it was clear that Molony could help them. They hired him, and he obtained limited day parole to work in Kingston. The store was changing from an independent to a national franchise outlet. Molony found space and arranged financing; he negotiated the franchise agreement and the lease. He worked diligently at the computer store – two days a week, then three, then five, returning each night to Bath. And he began obtaining monthly passes, to return to Toronto and spend the weekend with Brenda.

Even minimum security is deadeningly repetitious, and the most optimistic inmate soon adopts a kind of reverse incentive – the desire to put the experience behind him rather than the eager anticipation of possibilities. That suddenly changed with Brenda's news that she had missed her period, and seen the doctor, and had a wonderful surprise. Brian thought the idea of being a father would have frightened him. Despite his financial straits and the uncertainty of his future, he was as thrilled as Brenda by the prospect of a child. Suddenly his objectives were immediate and concrete. He saved every cent of the $20 a day he earned at the computer store and the $5.90 a day he earned peeling vegetables, and put renewed effort into persuading the Parole Board of his suitability for release.

On a three-day pass, Brian and Brenda were married by the priest from Bath at the Catholic church in Enterprise, Ontario. The wedding and the reception, at an Italian restaurant in Kingston, were family affairs, though Sieg and Sheila came from Milton, Stu and Patti from Toronto, and Doug and Nicole from Sarnia. When Molony signed himself back into the institution on Sunday night, his living unit officer asked how he'd spent the weekend.

"I got married," said Molony. "How was your weekend?"

"I'd read about this guy Molony while I was on the run," recalled Benny S., a lawyer convicted of breach of trust. "The whole scam was reported in the San Francisco paper and he was a hero to me in a sick sort of way. In Bath one day I saw a notice on the bulletin board – 'Gambling problem? Want to do something about it? See Brian Molony.' I introduced myself and said I was interested. It turned out I knew one of his bookies, and I'd come across his friends at card games. We started talking about our gambling experiences and became friends.

"Brian was a good con. He kept to himself, minded his own business. He could always defuse a situation with his humour and his intelligence. He never talked down to anyone, and he became friends with people from lower stations in life in a genuine way. I remember one guy he was friends with was a bank robber. Nobody disliked him.

"He subscribed to all the newspapers and magazines, and he was very active in sports, organizing games, playing hockey, shovelling off the racquetball court so they could play in winter. He definitely had a compulsive side. The sports were like going from heroin to methadone. We'd play gin rummy for fun in the cafeteria, putting the same intensity into it. Gambling has caused me all kinds of problems, yet I sometimes dream of the day when I'll be able to go back to it. I haven't completely admitted to myself I'm licked. I don't think many of us have. Brian was heavily involved in the gambling program, he helped keep it going, but I'm not sure he ever really believed he was a compulsive gambler. He certainly couldn't accept that he was a lousy gambler. He's a bright guy, highly intelligent, but not when it comes to his gambling. These guys weren't sending a plane for him because he was a good gambler.

"In jail you hear a lot of talk about how horny guys are, how they're going to get laid. Brian never made remarks of that kind, before he and Brenda got married or after. He has principles, and he's terribly moral. I don't think he ever believed he was stealing from the bank, just borrowing. That's why he never tipped the dealers or used the money for anything else. Maybe it's why he never enjoyed the benefits they make available to big gamblers. It wasn't his money. He viewed it as a loan.

"When we talked about getting out, he didn't think there'd be a big adjustment. I told him, 'Remember, you'll have a record.' He thought people would be a lot more accepting and understanding than they are. He wanted to become a financial advisor, putting together deals and helping people get funding. How's he going to make it in a business that relies on trust? I told him he should declare bankruptcy, but he said he was going to make settlement offers. He's facing a financial situation that's hopeless, yet he's determined to resolve it. He's a stubborn Irishman. He won't admit defeat.

"Brian's story is exceptional only because of the amount of money involved. In terms of what he put his family and friends through, he caused a lot less suffering than most compulsive gamblers. When I was in action, I wouldn't show up at weddings, dinners, family affairs. One Friday I was at the airport, on the way to Atlantic City, when I found out my wife and kids had been evicted from the house. The mortgage was $18,000 in arrears. I had $50,000 in my pocket. I said, 'Can't you stay at your mother's for the weekend? I'll be back Monday, we'll look after it then.' When I was gambling I didn't care about anyone else. I once extorted money from another lawyer. I once phoned an acquaintance and said, 'My father died, can you send me $350 so I can come back for his funeral?' Tell me, what kind of person would do such a thing?

"Brian never became that kind of animal. Maybe he didn't have to, having access to the bank's money. Unlike most compulsive gamblers, he never ripped off the people close to him. Maybe that's one reason why Brenda was so dedicated while he was in jail. She drove up every week, through snowstorms and everything. There can't be many women that devoted and strong. They'd sit in the visiting room, talking and playing gin for hours and hours. My wife never came to see me, but then Brian didn't hurt Brenda the way I hurt my wife. He kept her sheltered from what was going on. He protected her.

"A compulsive gambler is two people, one hurting the other. You know the way you'll see a stranger and think, 'I don't like that guy.' A compulsive gambler has that attitude toward a part of himself. As a banker, Brian was concerned when a customer was twenty dollars overdrawn. He'd get upset at Brenda if she couldn't get by on so much a month. As a gambler, he'd blow a million dollars in a night. What's that all about? One side hurting the other. At some level the compulsive gambler hates himself, he's unconsciously trying to destroy himself. Brian was a very capable guy. He was from a good family, he had an outstanding career at the bank, he was definitely headed for the top. I wonder what his problem really was."

The one-day shutdown of the casino had ended New Jersey's dispute with Caesars, but the bank's legal ping-pong game was into its third year. In 1984 the CIBC launched a second suit, in United States District Court for the district of New Jersey. The bank sought to recover $4,732,626 U.S. from Boardwalk Regency Corporation (the Atlantic City operation) and $2,120,000 U.S. from Desert Palace Inc. (the Nevada operation), plus interest, costs, and disbursements. As in the Canadian suit, the bank argued that the casino knew or should have known Molony was gambling with funds that didn't belong to him.

The casino maintained it takes no interest in the source of a gambler's money. Peter Boynton, the president, said under oath he did not ask his security director to look into Molony until a month or so before the arrest. "There's a practice in our industry, widely followed," Boynton said, "that with cash customers we do not probe who they are or where their money is coming from." Many people wish to be anonymous, he explained, and would be embarrassed if friends or associates found out they gambled. "Our people are trained not to push for information." According to New Jersey law, when a customer uses cash (rather than so-called credit) the casino is not even obliged to ensure that it has his correct name. Linc Ebert put it succinctly: "I could go in there as Dwight Eisenhower and no one would care less, as long as I'm bringing cash."

Still, the bank could point to many suspicious circumstances. Most people who gamble regularly with large amounts of cash wire it, they don't pull it out of their pockets. An employee in the craps pit who dealt to Molony said, "We'd heard he was a very rich man from Toronto. I've dealt to a lot of people with money. You can see it – their clothes, their jewellery, their manner. Molony did not look like someone with money." It might also be considered unusual that he would leave cash on deposit – sometimes hundreds of thousands of dollars – without asking that it be banked to collect interest. The casino said Molony was treated as any other player. Yet a man who worked on the floor while Molony was a patron said, "Walk in with that kind of cash and I guarantee you, the big boys are on you like stink on shit." The casino claimed to have taken no interest in him until a month before his arrest. Yet Caesars' own security logs record that he was placed under surveillance, and referred to by name, eight months earlier.

John Connors said under oath that, on Peter Boynton's instruction, he did try to establish Molony's identity. He sent someone to the New York Public Library to go through phone books looking for Brian Maloneys in the Toronto area. The phone number of each B. Maloney in the book was compared to numbers Molony had called from his suite, but no match was found. Jess Lenz had the idea Molony was a horse owner in Canada. Connors said under oath he called contacts in the horse world but no one had heard of a Brian Maloney. Larry Woolf believed Molony had made money in the commodities market. Connors said under oath he called a contact in Toronto with knowledge of the commodities market. The contact knew of a wealthy Maloney family in Canada, but none of the men was named Brian. Connors said under oath he checked with Caesars Palace in Las Vegas. They knew who Molony was but could supply no home address. Connors said under oath he checked with the corporate security office. They could tell him only that Molony had played in Las Vegas, that he had apparently won at the Barbary Coast, and that a substantial sum of money had been transferred in his name. Connors said under oath he twice tried to "surveille" Molony in Atlantic City, so his people would get a good look at him in case they had to follow him to his residence. But on both occasions Molony departed unexpectedly. By the time the surveillance people swung into action, said Connors, Molony had left.

People who worked on the floor at Caesars knew Molony as a banker. The pilot of the Learjet told an undercover police officer who passed himself off as ground crew that his passenger worked for a bank and frequently travelled to Atlantic City with large quantities of used bills. Molony had his photo taken at Caesars when he cashed traveller's cheques. He provided Caesars with his birth date. He provided identification to the pilot for customs purposes. He spoke to Beck and Colizzi from his suite at Caesars, so Connors had their Toronto numbers. He always called Brenda from his suite, so Connors had Molony's home number. And on April 19, when Michael Neustadter asked Caesars' Toronto representative to inform Molony that there was a problem with the $920,000 transfer, the representative reported that Molony was already on the way to the airport. How could he have done so if they didn't know how to contact Molony?

None of this was any help to John Connors. As director of corporate security, his job was twofold. He supervised Caesars' surveillance unit, which ensured the integrity of the casino games, and he directed its investigative team, which did checks on key employees. When anyone applied for a sensitive job, Connors' people ran the background search. They contacted local police departments; they used their own informants; they might do any number of things to find out what they needed to know. Connors was in the business of finding out what he needed to know, but Brian Molony stumped him.

Poor John Connors, Rutgers graduate, member of the New Jersey bar, and twenty-five-year FBI man. Imagine his embarrassment, having to break the bad news to the president. Connors had a substantial budget and a staff of twenty-five, yet he was unable to turn up the simple bit of information – who's Brian Molony? – Peter Boynton had asked for. Information Boynton thought it prudent to obtain only after Molony had dropped $5-million cash. Information the Marina in Las Vegas had found it prudent to obtain after he dropped $45,000. Information any first-year journalism student could have obtained in ten minutes on the telephone.

When the bank's lawyers learned that tapes had been made of Molony in action the night before his arrest, they naturally looked forward to viewing them. It would have been fascinating to observe his demeanour, and that of casino personnel. The computer at Caesars could print out a marker every fourteen seconds; it would have been interesting to see whether Molony had requested each of the twenty-four markers he signed that night or whether, anticipating his needs, Caesars had preprinted them. Who knew what the tapes might reveal?

When Bill Kisby, the DGE detective, learned of Molony's arrest from his Metro Toronto Police contact, he went straight to Caesars, found John Connors, and asked for the tapes. Connors said the tapes had been erased. Kisby was furious – the DGE had specifically requested copies. How could they possibly have been erased? Routine, said Connors. The tapes had revealed nothing unusual and been cleared for reuse.

Their exchange took place less than twelve hours after the tapes had been made. Caesars' own procedures manual dictated that tapes be stored for five days before erasure. Casino Control Commission regulations directed that tapes made at the state's mandate be saved for five days. Connors later said under oath that he had the tapes erased "sometime between April 27 and May 1." He explained his decision as follows: "I left the tapes in the hold area and then, after three or four days, the supervisor asked me, 'Should I retain these tapes any longer?' I said, 'I can't think of a single reason why we should retain them.' They contained no information that could ever be of interest to anyone, so I directed that he clear them."

As for the second tape of Molony, the one specifically requested by Larry Woolf, Connors said under oath that he chose not to comply with the request of Caesars' senior vice-president. That tape had never been made. What about the Game Observer's Report, signed by Shelly A. Jones, on which special tape #183 (Mon B) is noted as having been started at 3:41 a.m. and ended at 4:08 a.m.? Connors explained that Shelly A. Jones had been confused. She must have been referring to the regular tape – the one "routinely erased" a few hours after Molony's arrest.

In the course of the DGE investigation, eleven Caesars employees had been forced to give depositions under oath. When the bank's lawyers learned of the existence of these sworn statements, they were naturally interested in reading them. They filed a motion seeking to compel Caesars to produce copies. So began a new game of ping-pong. More motions, orders, and objections bounced back and forth. Questions of procedure, confidentiality, and jurisdiction were raised, objected to, and ruled on.

Finally, in early 1986, legal opposition to production of the depositions seemed to have been exhausted. It looked as if the casino would be forced to hand them over to the bank. At that point, the suit was settled out of court. Rumour in the gaming industry had it that Caesars returned half the roughly $7-million Molony had lost at its tables, but details of the settlement were not revealed. For the bank, the original media deluge had been humiliating enough. The less coverage now, four years later, the better. For the casino, a publicly arbitrated settlement might have established a dangerous precedent. If people read in the newspapers that a casino had regurgitated money it had swallowed up, who could say how many sore losers might call their lawyers?

For all their apparent differences, the bank and the casino also had this in common. Both stood to suffer if the case went to court. Their agreement included a non-disclosure clause. Neither wanted the story of Brian Molony told.

By the time Caesars settled with the bank, Molony had been released on day parole to Toronto. There were those who urged him to move to another city and build a new career. He was determined to resume work in the city and the sphere he knew best. He joined his brother's management company and soon saw a demand for a service he could provide. Many small companies in need of financing did not know how to approach a bank; Molony began advising clients with sound products but no financial expertise how to obtain funding. He visited Brenda, who was on leave from the bank, and looked forward to the birth of their baby – a son, he was certain. He quietly found jobs for people he'd met in prison, talked with other compulsive gamblers and their families, and assumed an active role in the Toronto chapter of a support group. The terms of his parole left him free between 8 a.m. and

7 p.m., and on some weekends, but he had to spend weeknights, along with five dozen other ex-convicts, in a halfway house above a post office in west-end Toronto.

It was four o'clock one morning when the call came from Brenda. He had already made arrangements to sign himself out. By the time he got to the apartment, her water had broken and her contractions were coming every ninety seconds. She insisted on shaving her legs before going to the hospital. He picked up several newspapers but didn't get a chance to finish them. Brenda went into labour before noon. During her extraordinary ordeal he could only stand by, holding her hand, as she had stood by him, and marvel at the creature who strove so mightily for its own emergence. A being of innocence and promise. Unmistakably a Molony. Unmistakably a part of himself.

The baby gave Molony's life a new centre. Like his mother's death, his son's birth put in perspective the myriad complications that awaited him. Release from prison closed one trying chapter of his life but opened another. Within two weeks of his release he received a letter from James Dube of Blake, Cassels & Graydon, acting for the CIBC. The bank wanted to hear his plans for restitution; otherwise it would consider a civil suit.

Since the $10.2-million had been obtained by fraud, the bank could obtain a civil judgement against him even though he'd been criminally prosecuted and even if he declared personal bankruptcy. Molony negotiated with the New York lawyers for Lloyd's of London and eventually made a restitution offer acceptable to the bonding company. He agreed to pay a portion of every dollar he earned for the rest of his life, or until he reached an agreed-on total. The total, no doubt, is considerably less than $10.2-million – the agreement is covered by a non-disclosure clause – but it's considerably more than Lloyd's would have recovered if the bank had antagonized Molony by obtaining a judgement against him.

Having thus averted a civil suit, Molony was left with another thorny financial problem. Since the start of the embezzlement he had not filed tax returns. While in Joyceville, he submitted returns for 1980, 1981, 1982, declaring the fraudulent income and writing off his gambling losses. His 1982 return showed "CIBC employment income" of $12,083.74 and "CIBC other income" of $7,509,000.00. In effect, he asked that the money be considered a non-taxable business loss.

Revenue Canada was preparing a tax-evasion case against Mario Colizzi and wanted Molony to testify against him. As in the criminal proceeding against Colizzi, Molony refused to testify. Revenue Canada decided, two years after he filed the back returns, to contest them. "The question of whether or not you are carrying on a gambling business," a special investigator said in a letter, "is one of fact that can be determined only by an examination of all the evidence and your entire course of conduct. Therefore we require from you full and complete details and documentation of all of your gross winnings and losses . . ."

Right. Recall and document every temperature reading of a fifteen-year fever. Molony sent off an eight-page letter that included a list of all the casinos and racetracks he had ever patronized and a year-by-year breakdown of his estimated gaming wins and losses. He concluded, "I feel my activities indicated a 'business, calling, or vocation' based on the following documentable facts: a) Extensive education garnered through a combination of reading and studying available literature, supplemented by hands-on experience. b) Development of statistical systems which reduced the house advantage both in casino and horse-racing environments.

c) Time requirements were met, as I spent a minimum of 40 hours and as many as 100 hours a week pursuing gambling education and enterprises."

Like the nightmares of being back in action, the aborted deals, and the debts to lawyers, family, and friends, the wrestling match with Revenue Canada threatened to last forever, one more reminder that the ramifications of his gambling compulsion and historic fraud will follow him to the grave.

"I remember Brian thanking me for what I'd done," recalled Walt Devlin. "He said, 'I appreciate the trouble you've gone to. I've got to get you some money.' As if money is what makes everything all right. One of the things you find out when you're gambling is that money doesn't make everything all right. I said, 'Brian, not everybody keeps score the way you do. I don't want money. I want to be your friend.'

"When I talk to him these days about how he's doing, the feeling I get is of impatience. Things aren't happening as fast as he'd like. Not enough action. When a guy self-discovers, he can't understand why the whole world doesn't forgive him right away. I'm OK now, and you'd better know I'm OK, too. I've worked hard to put this behind me and I wish you'd realize that. Can't we just get on with it?

"Maybe things aren't as far along as he'd like, but remember where he was a few years ago. Completely isolated. Caught up in something he couldn't understand and couldn't tell anybody about, something that made him do things Brian Molony wouldn't do. He derailed his career, shamed his family, humiliated himself in public. He had to stand in front of a guy in black robes with the power to put him away for a long, long time. At the age of twenty-seven he was looking into a tunnel and seeing nothing but pitch-black darkness.

"Then he discovered he had a problem, and he went to work on himself. He systematically began to remake his life. Maybe he hasn't bought into the whole recovery process emotionally. That's just the kind of guy he is. He happens to be someone who conducts his life from the ears up. But he understands the importance of the process intellectually, and he's doing what he has to do. Try going without something you've relied on every day of your life for fifteen years. Gamblers Anonymous claims a success rate of less than 5 per cent, and that's a sample of guys who realize they've got a problem and actively seek help.

"I don't think Brian himself has any idea what a terrific success he is. If he fell off the wagon tomorrow, he'd still be a raging success. To see him playing with the little guy, lighting up at the cockeyed smile that kid has. To see him with Brenda and her parents, all of them together in that house. To see how far he's come in a few short years. Sure, it's important what happens from here on. What drives you nuts about this thing is that you're never recovered, you're always recovering. But whatever happens, you can't discount what he's done up to now.

"Not long ago I did some work for a law firm here in New Jersey. They asked me for references and I gave them Brian's name. Know what Brian said when they called his office and asked his opinion of me? 'All in all, I'd rate Mr. Devlin's performance as quite satisfactory.' Brian Patrick Molony. He takes himself so fucking seriously. I'll tell you, I don't like this guy, I love him. Know something? Of all the people I've got involved with, only one ever took the trouble to sit down and write to say he appreciated my efforts. That's Brian."

EPILOGUE

"Let the games begin."

– *A Guide to Casino Games at Caesars*

New Jersey's experiment with casino gambling has been, in economic terms, an extraordinary success. In 1986 eleven Atlantic City casinos had a gross win of $2.3-billion, more than the sixty casinos in Las Vegas. The gaming industry has become New Jersey's biggest employer, ahead of New Jersey Bell and A.T.& T. Atlantic City, though largely in ruins, has surpassed its turn-of-the-century glory days to become the most popular destination resort in the United States. Last year it attracted 30-million visitors, more than Disney World.

The remarkable growth in casino gambling over the past ten years has been accompanied by the parallel recognition and exploitation throughout North American society of gambling as a motivational force. In Canada, legal lotteries did not exist twenty years ago. Now they are widespread and contribute substantially to almost every provincial economy. More than half the states in the United States have lotteries. Television game shows – based on gambling – have moved into prime time and enjoy record audiences. At many racetracks you can bet on races at other tracks. In

New Orleans every hundredth citizen disposing of his trash at the city dump wins a $100 prize. You can scarcely buy a hamburger or a tank of gas without being given a scratch-and-win card. The once-illegal numbers game is state-run, and television stations broadcast winning numbers. Newspapers publish winning lottery numbers. They routinely publish betting lines, point spreads, and detailed injury reports. Betting pervades pro sport, and television commentators talk about spreads and odds almost as much as the game itself, or the heavyweight fight.

Casino gambling, the industry would have you believe, is like any other form of gambling. No one flies you to the racetrack, however, or asks if you'd like dinner. In church-basement bingo no half-naked women bring you bourbon. Sit in on Uncle Fred's poker game and he will not, as you leave, suggest you stay in his penthouse suite. Buy lottery tickets at the corner store and you won't be given a jogging suit, a telephone, or a Rolex watch. Only in the casino are you rewarded for increasing the time you spend gambling and the size of your bets. Only in the casino are you subject to the psychological manipulation made possible by a data bank. Only in the casino is the action continuous. Only in the casino does the house deliberately seek to alter your behaviour. And only in a casino is money treated in such a way that you can walk in with empty pockets and walk out having lost fifty thousand dollars.

Several American states are considering casino gambling. In Canada the Criminal Code has been amended to allow provinces to enter into partnership with gaming interests. British Columbia has introduced slot machines on some ferries, and "Monte Carlo nights" are widespread in Alberta and other provinces. Virgin jurisdictions would do well to study the true nature of casinos, and the hidden social cost of the easy money that can be raised by taxing casino games.

One of the hidden costs is the danger, to themselves and others, posed by compulsive gamblers. Since you can't smell baccarat on someone's breath, or see dice marks on his arm, the phenomenon is all but unnoticed. The public perception of compulsive gambling is as untutored as that of alcoholism in the 1940s, when a hard-drinking man was somebody on his feet and an alcoholic the immoral layabout you tripped over. Robert Custer believes there are between 3-million and 4-million compulsive gamblers in North America; as gambling proliferates, so do their numbers.

There are now twenty-eight treatment programs in the United States (none in Canada), and governments in the U.S. are much more likely than they were ten years ago to allocate funds for treatment and research. The powerful but largely invisible effects of compulsive gambling have yet to be properly weighted in any calculation of the pros and cons of legalized gambling, however, perhaps because the disorder has yet to find a place in the public consciousness.

Brian Molony could have been any assistant manager at any branch of any Canadian bank, a prospect that fostered suspicion and paranoia in the industry. So tight did procedures become at Bay and Richmond after Molony's arrest that the branch came to be known as "Fort Knox." Elsewhere there has been a return to strict, by-the-book procedures. You now have to be in the term-deposit department to sign a term deposit, which is all very well until someone books off sick. The volume of paperwork has increased. At some CIBC branches, two bank employees have to sit in on every credit interview, to prevent the creation of another Roger Oskaner. Assistant managers (now called account managers) have been emasculated. They may have lending authority of $50,000, but they have no real lending power. They can authorize a loan but can't free up the money without further authorization.

Doing your own job efficiently is no longer enough. You're expected to ensure that the people above and below you are doing nothing fishy or irregular. For junior staff this is a positive development. Underlings are now able – indeed, encouraged – to question their superiors. If you think something is amiss, you can go directly to head office. Accountability is the buzzword. If someone you encounter in the bureaucratic structure does something unacceptable, you too bear responsibility. This emphasis on accountability has spilled over to other banks as well; the Molony frauds have been felt through the entire Canadian banking system.

As of summer, 1987, Peter Boynton is still president and chief operating officer of Caesars in Atlantic City.

Larry Woolf is president of Caesars Tahoe in Stateline, Nevada.

Jess Lenz was transferred back to Caesars Palace in Las Vegas, where he's a credit executive.

Michael Neustadter is out of the gaming industry. He works as an account executive for Dean Witter in Atlantic City.

Jim Surgey is still an account executive at Richardson's (now Richardson Greenshields of Canada) in Toronto.

Harry Buckle, retired from the CIBC, lives in Hamilton, Ontario.

Stephen Richardson sued the bank for wrongful dismissal. The bank settled out of court. Richardson is now an assistant branch manager with an insurance company. Leaving the bank, he has told friends, is the best thing that ever happened to him.

Sherry Brydson finally got The Elmwood Club off the ground. It has 12,000 members and has ceased being a cash drain. Brydson believes strongly in karma, and feels it was karma that made her life intersect with Molony's. She still banks at Bay and Richmond.

Alex Osborne never adjusted to Vancouver. The depressed, resource-based economy of British Columbia wasn't an environment he thrived on, even after he was promoted again and became the senior corporate banker in B.C. His wife didn't enjoy the West Coast. People close to him say he was never the same after Molony's arrest. The investigation into the fraud left him feeling that someone in the bank was out to get him. When Ross Brady, a close friend from Commerce Court moved to Vancouver and was killed in an accident, Osborne grew despondent. After erring on his expense account in his own favour, he became convinced he'd be fired and criminally prosecuted. When he began losing weight, he worried that he had cancer. In November, 1986, he was found dead in his garage. He was forty-eight.

Mark Osborne plays for the Toronto Maple Leafs.

Craig Law – The Bulldog – is a staff sergeant with the Intelligence Bureau of the Metro Toronto Police.

Ron Andrews works in the warrants section of the Criminal Investigation Bureau at 55 Division.

Mario Colizzi was tried before Judge H. R. Locke on a charge of possessing stolen goods – the bank's money. Judge Locke concluded his decision: "However skeptical I may be of Mr. Colizzi's total conduct . . . I am left, at the end of all the evidence, with a slight, lingering doubt that the crown has proven guilt to the standard it must achieve. The count is, therefore, dismissed." Charges were then brought against Colizzi by Revenue Canada. He pleaded guilty to evading $83,713.12 in federal taxes and was ordered to pay that amount, plus a fine, within sixty days or serve a year in prison. A few weeks later he showed up at his lawyer's office with a broken elbow and a fractured skull. The man he had fought died of gunshot wounds to the head. As of summer, 1987,

Colizzi was free on bail, awaiting trial on charges of second-degree murder.

No charges were ever brought against Nick Beck. He has not been seen in Toronto in some time. One rumour has it that, while burglarizing a house in an exclusive area of the city, he stumbled on a good deal of money and fled the country. Another rumour has him selling stock in a boiler-room operation in Amsterdam.

Walt Devlin, shaken by the death of his mother and health problems of his own, recently had what compulsive gamblers call "a slip." He found himself back at the racetrack, where he gambled away several thousand dollars before getting himself into a treatment program. He's again involved with many different organizations and individuals, including a young banker from Scranton, Pennsylvania, who defrauded his employer of $1.9-million and lost it in Atlantic City.

Brian Molony lives with his wife, son, and in-laws in a modest house in west-end Toronto. He finds that domesticity has its rewards, but Brenda's parents are not well, there's not much privacy, and the financial pressure is constant. Brenda didn't return to the bank after her maternity leave. Molony makes a point of playing with his son before work and getting home before the boy's bedtime. On Saturday mornings he takes his son to swimming lesson. He often bumps the walls with his elbows when he carries the boy downstairs; he sometimes finds himself studying the race results, or imagining which team he would have bet, or remembering the intensity. "I've been in some very dark valleys," he said. "I've also been on some mountain peaks not many people ever reach. But the peaks aren't worth the valleys. I have better things to do with my time." He believes one of the things that will help keep him clean is the scale of his betting in the year before his arrest. "How can you ever be satisfied with necking once you know what it's like to make love?"

After gaining full parole he struggled in business. He noticed, though, that people told him stories about their own experiences with the bank – the five-day hold, the bounced cheque, the loan inexplicably called at the worst moment. He began thinking about financial institutions and put together a proposed enterprise that now consumes all his energy. He devised the idea of a financial-services store, developed the business plan, sold it to investors, and helped launch what he hopes will prove to be the first two outlets in a national chain.

He's still haunted by the frauds. He dreams the CIBC has agreed to let him return to work, and he starts taking money again. In another dream he's back at his desk, trying to ignore the whispers, determined to make as much money for the bank as he stole. In another dream he's arrested as he's about to enter a casino because he's violating the twenty-five-mile limit of his parole. He dreams he's back at the baccarat table, losing. He dreams he's emerging from prison, to resume life, when the police arrest him. They have deliberately left out one fraud to make him go through it all again. "I don't think I could go through it again. Looking over your shoulder is no way to spend life. I look ahead now."

He attends Mass each week, using the time to reflect on what he's accomplished in the past seven days. His orientation film is still shown to new inmates at Joyceville. He's become something of an expert on compulsive gambling and the casino industry, and has addressed a number of law-enforcement agencies. He remains active in the Toronto chapter of a support group and is considered an excellent moderator, though he rarely tells his own story. He attends faithfully, he says, "to hear stories of people who screw up.

I don't want to forget what that was like. I want to keep it fresh in my mind."

On April 27, 1987, Molony spoke at a party celebrating his fifth anniversary without having made a bet. Because of the Stanley Cup playoffs on TV that night, the turnout wasn't what it might have been. Brenda was among the three dozen people who, in a half-empty church hall, gave him a standing ovation.

APPENDIX

The Frauds

1980				
September	15	$22,300		Nick Beck
	23	16,500		Nick Beck
	26	27,000	U.S.	Nick Beck
October	21	10,000		Nick Beck
	31	20,000		Nick Beck
		50,000	U.S.	Sun Crown Trading
November	19	19,500		Eli Koharski
December	9	35,000		Eli Koharski
	22	48,000	U.S	Sherry Brydson
1981				
January	19	45,000	U.S.	Sherry Brydson
	26	200,000	U.S.	Sherry Brydson
	27	18,000		Eli Koharski
	29	2,500		Nick Beck
	29	1,500	U.S.	Nick Beck
February	25	25,000		Eli Koharski
March	3	30,000		Eli Koharski
	6	177,000	U.S.	Sherry Brydson
	27	30,000		Eli Koharski
April	22	15,000		Eli Koharski
	22	160,000	U.S.	Sherry Brydson
May	12	2,500	U.S.	Sun Crown Trading

	12	30,000		Nick Beck
	14	150,000	U.S.	Sherry Brydson
	21	160,000	U.S.	Sherry Brydson
	26	170,000	U.S.	Sherry Brydson
	26	50,000		Roger Oskaner
	29	50,000		Roger Oskaner
June	2	20,000		Roger Oskaner
	8	15,000	U.S.	Sherry Brydson
	12	50,000		Roger Oskaner
July	16	90,000	U.S.	Sherry Brydson
	21	20,000		Roger Oskaner
	23	150,000	U.S.	Sherry Brydson
		50,000		Roger Oskaner
	31	65,000		Roger Oskaner
August	4	160,000	U.S.	Sherry Brydson
	7	70,000		Roger Oskaner
	10	190,000	U.S.	Sherry Brydson
	31	50,000	U.S.	Sherry Brydson
September	14	150,000	U.S.	Sherry Brydson
	18	100,000		Roger Oskaner
	22	140,000	U.S.	Sherry Brydson
October	16	50,000		Roger Oskaner
	20	10,000		Roger Oskaner
	20	125,000	U.S.	Sherry Brydson
	26	15,000		Roger Oskaner
	29	50,000		Roger Oskaner
	30	45,000		Roger Oskaner
	30	250,000	U.S.	Sherry Brydson
November	17	25,000		Roger Oskaner
	20	75,000		Roger Oskaner
	27	20,000		Roger Oskaner
December	2	70,000	U.S.	Sherry Brydson
	9	60,000		Roger Oskaner
	11	80,000		Eli Koharski
	15	360,000	U.S.	Leo Sherman Investments

	22	25,000		Roger Oskaner
	24	55,000		Roger Oskaner
		45,000		Roger Oskaner

1982

January	6	360,000	U.S.	Leo Sherman Investments
	19	25,000		Roger Oskaner
	21	260,000	U.S.	Leo Sherman Investments
	21	60,000		Roger Oskaner
February	2	100,000	U.S.	Sherry Brydson
	4	20,000		Roger Oskaner
	5	65,000		Roger Oskaner
		60,000		Roger Oskaner
	9	60,000		Roger Oskaner
	11	60,000		Roger Oskaner
	12	60,000		Roger Oskaner
		62,000		Roger Oskaner
	23	60,000		Roger Oskaner
	25	60,000		Roger Oskaner
	26	60,000		Roger Oskaner
		65,000		Roger Oskaner
March	2	65,000		Roger Oskaner
	5	60,000		Roger Oskaner
		70,000		Roger Oskaner
	10	920,000		Kernwood Limited
	14	490,000		Kernwood Limited
		1,800,000		499726 Ontario Ltd.
	25	1,100,000		499726 Ontario Ltd.
	26	300,000		499726 Ontario Ltd.
	29	200,000		Roger Oskaner
		120,000		499726 Ontario Ltd.
	30	70,000		Roger Oskaner
		380,000		Kernwood Limited
	31	200,000		Kernwood Limited
April	1	490,000		499726 Ontario Ltd.

	6	990,000		D.C.L. Customs Brokers
	19	1,120,000		499726 Ontario Ltd.
	26	900,000	U.S.	Elm Street Holdings
		520,000	U.S.	Elm Street Holdings
Total:		$10,395,800	Canadian	
		5,081,000	U.S.	

Some of the fraudulently obtained funds were used to pay down fraudulent loans, leaving the CIBC, at the time of Molony's arrest, with a shortage of approximately $10.2-million. Plus interest.

The Last Night

STARTING SUM **$1,420,000**

TIME	CASH DEPOSITED	GAME	MARKERS TAKEN	ACCOUNT BALANCE
9:34 P.M.		BACCARAT	$120,000	$1,300,00
10:52 P.M.	$620,000		–	$1,920,000
10:56 P.M.		CRAPS	$50,000	$1,870,00
11:14 P.M.		BACCARAT	$100,000	$1,770,000
11:16 P.M.		BACCARAT	$100,000	$1,670,000
11:18 P.M.		BACCARAT	$100,000	$1,570,000
11:20 P.M.		BACCARAT	$100,000	$1,470,000
11:23 P.M.		BACCARAT	$100,000	$1,370,000
11:26 P.M.		CRAPS	$50,000	$1,320,000
11:28 P.M.		CRAPS	$50,000	$1,270,000
11:47 P.M.		BACCARAT	$100,000	$1,170,000
11:50 P.M.		BACCARAT	$100,000	$1,070,000
11:53 P.M.		BACCARAT	$100,000	$970,000
11:54 P.M.		BACCARAT	$100,000	$870,000
12:16 A.M.		BACCARAT	$100,000	$770,000
12:19 A.M.		BACCARAT	$100,000	$670,000
12:39 A.M.		BACCARAT	$100,000	$570,000
12:48 A.M.		BACCARAT	$100,000	$470,000
2:34 A.M.	$500,000		–	$970,000
2:40 A.M.		BACCARAT	$100,000	$870,000
2:42 A.M.		BACCARAT	$100,000	$770,000
2:53 A.M.		BACCARAT	$100,000	$670,000
2:59 A.M.		BACCARAT	$100,000	$570,000
3:04 A.M.		BACCARAT	$100,000	$470,000
3:06 A.M.		BACCARAT	$100,000	$370,000
3:07 A.M.		BACCARAT	$100,000	$270,000
3:55 A.M.	$120,000			$390,000

LEFT IN ACCOUNT $390,000

CASH $27,000

AMOUNT LOST **$1,003,000**

Molony's Gambling Losses

(as per his submission to Revenue Canada)

Taxation Year	Gross Winnings	Gross Losses	Net Gain/Loss
1964 (age ten)	150	100	50
1965	225	200	25
1966	1,400	700	700
1967	2,200	2,400	−200
1968	3,500	3,500	0
1969	7,500	7,800	−300
1970	10,200	12,400	−2,200
1971	18,000	21,000	−3,000
1972	21,000	24,500	−3,500
1973	32,000	34,500	−2,500
1974 (age twenty)	44,000	41,000	3,000
1975	57,000	58,500	−1,500
1976	165,000	173,500	−8,500
1977	330,000	345,000	−15,000
1978	1,100,000	1,120,000	−20,000
1979	2,200,000	2,215,000	−15,000
1980	7,400,000	7,690,000	−290,000
1981	110,000,000	112,470,000	−2,470,000
1982 (to April 26)	450,000,000	457,530,000	−7,530,000

Gary Stephen Ross is the author of two novels and two works of nonfiction. A founding partner of the publishing house Macfarlane Walter & Ross, he lives near White Rock, British Columbia.